Morphological and Biochemical

Correlates of Neural Activity

BY 27 AUTHORS——————————————————————————

R. E. Basford, Ph.D.
Diana S. Beattie, Ph.D.
Harold P. Cohen, Ph.D.
Maynard M. Cohen, M.D., Ph.D.
Shigeyuki Deura, M.D., D.M.S.
Chitta R. Dutta, M.D.
Clement A. Fox, Ph.D.
Ezio Giacobini, M.D.
J. Francis Hartmann, Ph.D.
Helen H. Hess, M.D.
Harold Koenig, M.D., Ph.D.
Edward Lewin, M.D.
Charles N. Loeser, M.D.
Oliver H. Lowry, M.D., Ph.D.
Margaret R. Murray, Ph.D.
Leonard M. Napolitano, Ph.D.
Edith R. Peterson, M.S.
Alfred Pope, M.D.
Floyd Ratliff, Ph.D.
Kenneth A. Siegesmund, Ph.D.
Howard R. Sloan, M.D.
J. C. Smith, Ph.D.
Ray S. Snider, Ph.D.
William L. Stahl, Ph.D.
Donald B. Tower, M.D., Ph.D.
Theodor Wanko, M.D.
Victor J. Wilson, Ph.D.

Morphological and Biochemical Correlates of Neural Activity

Edited by **Maynard M. Cohen, M.D., Ph.D.**

Chairman, Department of Neurology, Presbyterian-St. Luke's Hospital; Professor and Head, Division of Neurology, University of Illinois College of Medicine, Chicago, Illinois

and **Ray S. Snider, Ph.D.**

Director, Center for Brain Research, University of Rochester, Rochester, New York

WITH 141 ILLUSTRATIONS

HOEBER MEDICAL DIVISION

HARPER & ROW, PUBLISHERS

Contents

Contributing Authors

R. E. BASFORD, PH.D.
Associate Professor, University of Pittsburgh School of Medicine, Pittsburgh, Pennsylvania

DIANA S. BEATTIE, PH.D.
Research Associate, University of Pittsburgh School of Medicine, Pittsburgh, Pennsylvania

HAROLD P. COHEN, PH.D.
Associate Professor, Division of Neurology, University of Minnesota Medical School, Minneapolis

MAYNARD M. COHEN, M.D., PH.D.
Chairman, Department of Neurology, Presbyterian-St. Luke's Hospital; Professor and Head, Division of Neurology, University of Illinois College of Medicine, Chicago, Illinois

SHIGEYUKI DEURA, M.D., D.M.S.
Lecturer, Department of Anatomy, Faculty of Medicine, Kyoto University, Kyoto, Japan

CHITTA R. DUTTA, M.D.
Associate Professor of Anatomy, Marquette University School of Medicine, Milwaukee, Wisconsin

CLEMENT A. FOX, PH.D.
Professor of Anatomy, Marquette University School of Medicine, Milwaukee, Wisconsin

EZIO GIACOBINI, M.D.
Associate Professor of Pharmacology, Department of Pharmacology, Karolinska Institute, Stockholm, Sweden

J. FRANCIS HARTMANN, PH.D.
  Professor of Anatomy, University of Minnesota Medical School, Minneapolis

HELEN H. HESS, M.D.
  Research Associate in Neuropathology, Harvard Medical School; Associate Neuropathologist, McLean Hospital, Boston, Massachusetts

HAROLD KOENIG, M.D., PH.D.
  Professor of Neurology and Psychiatry, Northwestern University Medical School; Chief, Neurology Service, Veterans Administration Research Hospital, Chicago, Illinois

EDWARD LEWIN, M.D.
  Assistant Professor of Neurology, University of Colorado School of Medicine; Senior Physician, Veterans Administration Hospital, Denver, Colorado

CHARLES N. LOESER, M.D.
  Associate Professor of Anatomy, Western Reserve University School of Medicine, Cleveland, Ohio; Professor of Neuroanatomy, University of Trujillo School of Medicine, Trujillo, Peru

OLIVER H. LOWRY, M.D., PH.D.
  Professor and Head of the Pharmacology Department, Washington University School of Medicine, St. Louis, Missouri

MARGARET R. MURRAY, PH.D.
  Professor of Anatomy, College of Physicians and Surgeons, Columbia University, New York, New York

LEONARD M. NAPOLITANO, PH.D.
  Assistant Professor, Department of Anatomy, University of Pittsburgh School of Medicine, Pittsburgh, Pennsylvania

EDITH R. PETERSON, M.S.
  Research Associate in Surgery, College of Physicians and Surgeons, Columbia University, New York, New York

ALFRED POPE, M.D.
  Associate Professor of Neuropathology, Harvard Medical School; Neuropathologist, McLean Hospital, Boston, Massachusetts

FLOYD RATLIFF, PH.D.
  Associate Professor, Rockefeller Institute, New York, New York

KENNETH A. SIEGESMUND, PH.D.
  Assistant Professor of Anatomy, Marquette University School of Medicine, Milwaukee, Wisconsin

HOWARD R. SLOAN, M.D.
Fellow in Physiological Chemistry and Assistant Resident, Johns Hopkins University School of Medicine, Baltimore, Maryland

J. C. SMITH, PH.D.
Research Biochemist, Department of Anesthesiology, Montefiore Hospital, New York, New York

RAY S. SNIDER, PH.D.
Director, Center for Brain Research, University of Rochester, Rochester, New York

WILLIAM L. STAHL, PH.D.
United Cerebral Palsy Postdoctoral Fellow, Institute of Psychiatry, Maudsley Hospital, London, England

DONALD B. TOWER, M.D., PH.D.
Acting Chief, Laboratory of Neurochemistry, National Institute of Neurological Diseases and Blindness, National Institutes of Health, Bethesda, Maryland

THEODOR WANKO, M.D.
Ophthalmology Branch, National Institute of Neurological Diseases and Blindness, National Institutes of Health, Bethesda, Maryland

VICTOR J. WILSON, PH.D.
Associate Professor, The Rockefeller Institute, New York, New York

Preface

THIS PUBLICATION IS THE RESULT OF A DESIRE BY THE TWO EDITORS AND all the contributors to foster the increasing emphasis on the interdisciplinary approach to the as yet uncipherable mysteries of the nervous system. These papers should hold considerable interest not only for the specialist, but also for the advanced student in related fields. While attempts are made to exclude clinical data, the modern clinician, with research interests in the nervous system, will find several chapters of special concern to him. It is intended that investigators of morphology, function and/or chemistry of the nervous system be presented with concise, up-to-date information on facets not only pertaining to their own field but to other related disciplines as well.

It is also hoped that some broad perspective may be obtained concerning prominent points of cross over and correlation in the neurologic sciences. The rapid development of new techniques in microchemistry and histochemistry and the application of them to electron microscopic methods, is emphasized in several papers. In addition, the recent phenomenal expansion of micro methods in electrophysiology, with possible cross over into the chemical fields, opens new vistas for the neurological sciences. With this in mind, some papers represent correlations between disciplines; while in others, chemical, physiological, and ultrastructural aspects are dealt with separately.

The editors considered the inclusion of a summarizing chapter in which various aspects of the enclosed papers were bound together into some form of intellectual unity. It soon became apparent that there were still so many gaps, and the implications were so broad from the tenuous facts available that the risk of misguiding the unsuspect-

ing reader in addition to appearing downright foolish a few years
hence made such an attempt unworthy of inclusion in what we consider a worthwhile volume. Accordingly we give the reader the papers
as they were presented at the April 1962 symposium of the American
Academy of Neurology and trust that he will use the material to en-
rich his own meditations in this challenging environment.

MAYNARD M. COHEN
RAY S. SNIDER

CHAPTER 7

Inhibition and Release
of Spinal Motoneurons
by Recurrent Activity

WHEN THE RECURRENT COLLATERALS OF CAT MOTONEURONS BECOME activated, either by antidromic stimulation or as a result of orthodromic excitation of the motoneurons, other motoneurons may be inhibited or facilitated.[1-3] These two conditioning actions, designated recurrent inhibition and recurrent facilitation, have been investigated by means of studies of the behavior of populations of motoneurons and by means of intracellular recording from single units. Both these approaches have provided evidence about the distribution of the two actions within the spinal cord, their possible function, and the manner in which they are carried out. Concerning synaptic mechanisms, it has been demonstrated that in the pathway for recurrent inhibition there is a cholinergic synapse between collaterals and specialized interneurons, termed Renshaw cells.[2] These cells, which respond to single antidromic volleys with a burst of impulses at very high frequency,[4] in turn synapse with motoneurons and inhibit their activity.[2,5] The pathway for recurrent facilitation also contains a cholinergic synapse.[3] A series of experiments concerned with subsequent links in this pathway, and in part described below, has indicated that recurrent facilitation is a disinhibition, which acts by partial release of motoneurons from tonic inhibitory activity.[6-8]

Supported in part by grant B-2619 from the Institute of Neurological Diseases and Blindness, U.S. Public Health Service.

DISTRIBUTION OF RECURRENT ACTIONS

Speculation about the function of recurrent facilitation and inhibition and about the manner in which these actions contribute to the control of movement and posture obviously is closely related to experimental findings on the distribution of the effects among the motoneuron nuclei of the spinal cord. Different investigations which have been performed by studying the effect of antidromic stimulation of de-afferented muscle nerves on the excitability of motoneuron pools, or of single cells, of various muscles have provided considerable information concerning the distribution of recurrent conditioning actions. It has been known since the work of Renshaw[1] that antidromic stimulation of a muscle nerve may result in a mixture of inhibition and facilitation of the monosynaptic reflex recorded in another muscle nerve, and this finding has been confirmed by others.[9-11] Wilson and Talbot[10] have suggested that recurrent inhibition and facilitation exist in various combinations in interactions between motor nuclei, although both effects need not always be present. For each combination of conditioning and testing nerves, the shape of the conditioning curve, of the type shown in Figure 1-1, is determined by the relative magnitude, duration, and latency of the two actions. When the groups of cells used for conditioning and testing are in very close anatomical relation to each other, inhibition is prominent,[1,2,5,12] and this, together with the results of pharmacological investigations, has suggested that the field of facilitatory influence among motor nuclei is wider than is that of inhibitory influence.[10] Early intracellular studies of the distribution of recurrent inhibition by Eccles, Fatt, and Koketsu[2] led these authors to suggest that no meaningful pattern could be detected in this distribution and that the latter was determined solely by proximity in the spinal cord. The results of a similar, but more extensive, recent investigation[12] have emphasized further the importance of proximity of cells as a factor in influencing distribution of inhibition. It is clear that the role of proximity in determining the distribution of the pathways beginning with recurrent collaterals cannot be denied. A considerable amount of evidence makes it equally clear that proximity cannot be the sole determinant of the distribution of inhibition and facilitation and that the organization of the pathways involved is strongly influenced by functional factors. This is shown by the pattern of inhibition and facilitation observed by Wilson, Talbot, and Diecke[11] in experiments utilizing monosynaptic testing. These authors, who studied the distribution of the action which results

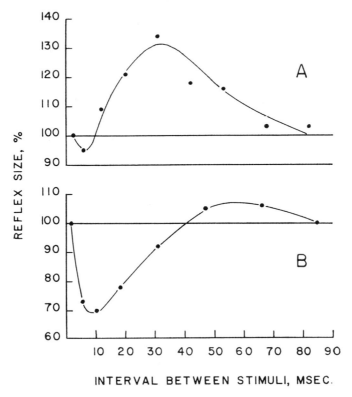

FIG. 1-1.   Recurrent conditioning of monosynaptic reflex as result of antidromic stimulation of muscle nerve. In both *A* and *B* test reflex was evoked by stimulation of central end of cut dorsal roots. In *A*, conditioning of reflex in nerve to tibialis anterior by stimulation of nerve to flexor digitorum longus and tibialis posterior results in facilitation preceded by brief period of inhibition. In *B*, reflex in tibialis anterior nerve is conditioned by stimulation of extensor digitorum longus; result is inhibition, followed by phase of facilitation.

from the algebraic summation of inhibition and facilitation, found that facilitation occurred most often when flexor nuclei were conditioned by antidromic stimulation of extensors. Few consistent actions were obtained when extensors were conditioned by flexors, although quadriceps was facilitated by its antagonist, biceps posterior-semi-tendinosus. When extensors conditioned extensors, or flexors conditioned flexors, inhibition was usually seen. In addition, when pronounced conditioning was present between the muscles of a myotatic unit, the *dominant action* was usually opposite in direction to Ia inhibition or facilitation between the same muscles; in this respect, and in some others, the effect of recurrent conditioning is similar to that of the Ib action evoked by activation of Golgi tendon organs.[13,14] In general, there was an asymmetry in the action of recurrent conditioning which favored flexor nuclei. Such asymmetry in the interactions of extensors and flexors has been observed by others.[14-16] Thus, the distribution of recurrent conditioning described by Wilson, Talbot, and Diecke[11] appears to be meaningful functionally, suggesting that the recurrent connections between motoneurons do not develop in an indiscriminate manner due to proximity alone. In addition, in several cases activation of the collaterals of motoneuron pool may facilitate one nucleus and inhibit another, even though the anatomical relations in the two cases appear to be about the same;[11] exceptions to the proximity hypothesis have also been observed by Eccles *et al.*[12] in their intracellular studies of inhibition, performed in preparations from which facilitation, the more labile phenomenon, was essentially absent. Furthermore, it is known that there are two types of large, α, motoneurons, namely, tonic and phasic motoneurons. Recurrent inhibition is most potent in tonic motoneurons,[12,17,18] and, as pointed out by Eccles *et al.*,[12] this indicates "that some specific factors control the development of recurrent inhibitory pathways in addition to mere proximity." It is worth noting that synergic cell groups frequently are close together in the spinal cord, while there is often considerable distance between the nuclei of antagonists; there may well be a relation between location and function.

In conjunction with the distribution studies, various functions have been proposed for recurrent conditioning. Among them are maintaining a proper balance of excitability between flexors and extensors;[11] limitation of stretch reflexes to their stimulated paths;[5] stabilization of frequency of tonic motoneurons during maintenance of posture;[17] suppression of tonic motoneurons during rapid movement;[11] and a general suppressor action.[2] (For discussion, see Wilson, Talbot, and Diecke[11] and Eccles *et al.*[12]) In agreement with Eccles *et al.*,[12] it can be stated that further work is required to evaluate the relative importance of these functions. However, it is established that recurrent inhibition and facilitation contribute to the control of motoneuron activity, and the findings of Wilson, Talbot, and Diecke[11] suggest that they play a role in organized reflex behavior.

EFFECTS OF RECURRENT CONDITIONING IN SINGLE MOTONEURONS

Discharge of Renshaw cells results in the production of a recurrent inhibitory postsynaptic potential (IPSP) in motoneurons upon which they terminate,[2] and the physiology and pharmacology of this inhibitory synapse are similar to those of all other spinal inhibitory synapses which have been investigated.[19] Inhibition of motoneurons has been studied in experiments utilizing intracellular recording, specifically in experiments in which the presence of an IPSP was used to reveal the presence of inhibition,[12] and also in investigations in which the discharge of single motoneurons was recorded from ventral root filaments. In the latter case, inhibition was revealed by an interruption of, or decrease in, the firing of the cell.[17,20] The results of Granit, Pascoe, and Steg[17] have demonstrated that in conditioning-testing situations in which inhibition would be expected to be present, many phasic motoneurons are unaffected by recurrent inhibition, while few tonic motoneurons escape its action. Subsequent work has confirmed and amplified this finding and has shown that in general tonic cells receive more powerful recurrent inhibition than do phasic ones.[12,18] The effect of the inhibition on cell discharge has been studied in detail by Granit and his collaborators, who have shown that it is an effective factor in the limitation and regulation of discharge, particularly in tonic cells.[20,21]

Recently, we have investigated recurrent facilitation by means of intracellular recording from spinal motoneurons of acute, spinal, unanesthetized cats. For this purpose, motoneuron pools were selected which were known, from the distribution studies, to be facilitated by antidromic stimulation of particular muscle nerves. For test purposes, motoneurons were activated orthodromically by stimulation of the central ends of the cut dorsal roots. Facilitation of a cell was revealed, in most experiments, by changes in the probability of monosynaptic firing of the cell (firing index[22]) or by changes in the latency of polysynaptic discharge. With the use of these criteria, it was found that in some facilitated cells changes in excitability were not accompanied by any visible membrane potential change; in others a small depolarization, the recurrent facilitatory potential (RFP), was observed.[8,23] A typical RFP is shown in Figure 1-2; the largest such potential recorded in a

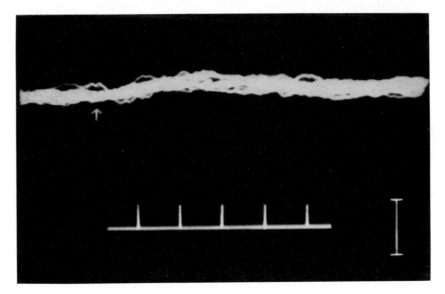

FIG. 1-2. Recurrent facilitatory potential recorded in quadriceps motoneuron with K citrate electrode. This photograph shows approximately fifteen superimposed sweeps. RFP was evoked by stimulus to nerve to biceps posterior-semitendinosus; stimulus was delivered at time shown by arrow. Voltage calibration, 10 mv. Time, 10 milliseconds.

series of experiments had an amplitude of 3 mv. It was also observed that recurrent facilitation is widespread among the individual cells of facilitated nuclei;[23,24] 62 per cent of the deep peroneal cells studied were facilitated by antidromic stimulation of gastrocnemius-soleus, and 83 per cent of quadriceps cells were facilitated by antidromic stimulation of biceps posterior-semitendinosus.[24] Within the two nuclei studied, particularly in quadriceps, both tonic and phasic cells were encountered (these two types of cells were distinguished on the basis of duration of their positive after-potential, tonic cells having a longer after-hyperpolarization than phasic cells[18,25]); in these nuclei, recurrent facilitation was just as likely to be present in phasic as in tonic cells.[24] In this regard, the distribution of facilitation is different from that of inhibition, the latter, as described above, being found more frequently among tonic than among phasic cells. Many of the flexor cells studied in our experiments fired repetitively in response to a single strong dorsal root shock, in a manner similar to that described by Perl.[26] Present indications are that facilitation is found more frequently among repetitive than among nonrepetitive flexor cells.[24]

The change in excitability brought about by recurrent facilitation can have a significant effect on the firing probability of the cell, whether the cell is activated by intracellular[8] or orthodromic[24] stimulation. Changes from a firing index of 20 or 30 to a firing index of 70 or 80 have been observed frequently. Such an increase in firing probability under experimental conditions suggests that recurrent facilitation should be able to influence strongly the frequency of discharge of motoneurons under conditions of normal function.

RECURRENT FACILITATION: A RELEASE PHENOMENON

Facilitation can be produced in one of two general ways: addition of excitatory action or removal of inhibition. Early results suggested that the latter mechanism, similar to the release observed in the eye of *Limulus* by Hartline and Ratliff[27] and termed by them disinhibition, might be involved in recurrent facilitation. Strong initial support for the hypothesis that recurrent facilitation was in fact due to partial release from inhibition, i.e., to disinhibition, was provided by the results of pharmacological experiments. In these experiments, use was made of the fact that tetanus toxin specifically blocks inhibitory synapses in cat spinal cord.[19] (Recent findings also demonstrate that the toxin blocks at least one kind of inhibition in cat cerebral cortex.[28]) Therefore, tetanus toxin, while not blocking an ordinary facilitatory pathway, should block, at least partially, a disinhibitory system (which must contain inhibitory synapses). In experiments in which tetanus toxin was injected directly into the spinal cord, recurrent facilitation was indeed abolished or reduced, while orthodromic polysynaptic facilitation was not.[6]

More recently, it has been possible to test the disinhibition hypothesis directly by means of studies on single motoneurons. As mentioned above, a small depolarization (RFP) is frequently found in facilitated motoneurons; this RFP could be produced either by a

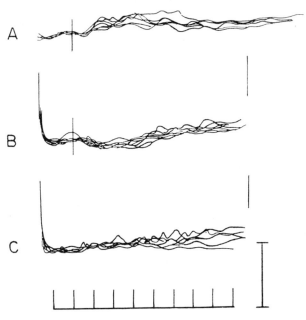

FIG. 1-3. Superimposed tracings showing effect of hyperpolarizing current pulses on RFP evoked in quadriceps motoneuron by antidromic stimulation of nerve to biceps posterior-semitendinosus. Conditioning stimulus delivered at artifact. A, RFP alone. B, RFP accompanied by hyperpolarizing pulse 2.26×10^{-8} A in amplitude and 105 milliseconds in duration. C, hyperpolarizing pulse alone. This control shows that with current pulse on but conditioning off base line is quite flat. Time, 10 milliseconds. Voltage calibration, 10 mv. Vertical lines are part of bridge transient used for aligning potentials for tracing. (From Wilson and Burgess.[8])

typical excitatory process such as the one which produces excitatory synaptic potentials (EPSP) or by a decrease in background inhibitory activity. These two possibilities can be distinguished by changing the level of potential of the cell. An EPSP would be decreased by depolarization and not changed significantly by hyperpolarization.[19] On the contrary, decreasing the membrane potential would increase a depolarization due to decrease in background inhibition: according to present concepts,[19] depolarizing the cell would move the membrane potential further from inhibitory equilibrium, thus increasing the hyperpolarizing effect of background inhibition on the resting potential and as a consequence increasing the RFP. According to the same concepts, hyperpolarization of the cell would decrease the RFP.

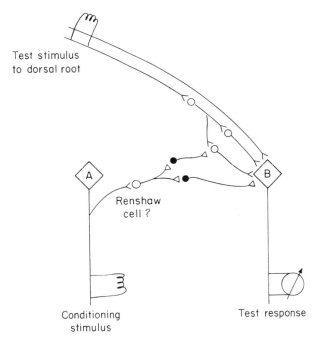

Test stimulus
to dorsal root

A

Renshaw
cell ?

B

Conditioning
stimulus

Test response

FIG. 1-4. Probable pathway for recurrent facilitation. *A* and *B*, motoneurons. Black dots, tonic interneurons. Forks denote excitatory endings, triangles inhibitory endings. Further description in text. (From Wilson and Burgess.[8])

In fact, if the cell is hyperpolarized sufficiently to shift the membrane potential to the other side of inhibitory equilibrium, background inhibition will actually depolarize the cell, and disinhibition will result in hyperpolarization: the RFP will be reversed. In experiments in which use of a bridge circuit made it possible to pass current through the cell with the same microelectrode that was used for recording, we have obtained such a reversal of the RFP in several cells, of both deep peroneal and quadriceps.[7,8] A typical result is shown in Figure 1-3. In other cells in which it was not possible to pass enough current to reverse the RFP, the latter was consistently decreased by hyper-polarizing pulses or increased by depolarizing pulses. Disinhibition appears to be the only explanation of such results, and on the basis of this evidence and of the results of the pharmacological investigations, it can be concluded that recurrent facilitation is due to reduction of inhibition and is a release phenomenon.

A probable pathway for such a release phenomenon is shown in Figure 1-4. Some motoneurons (*B*) are inhibited tonically by inter-neurons which fire spontaneously (shown in black). Impulses in collaterals of other motoneurons (*A*) excite interneurons which are presumably Renshaw cells and which act to interrupt the firing of some of the tonic inhibitory interneurons, releasing motoneurons *B* and rendering them more excitable. It is of interest that interneurons which fire spontaneously and could be inhibiting motoneurons, and which are inhibited by antidromic stimulation of ventral roots or muscle nerves, have been observed by several investigators.[24,29–31] The duration of the silent period resulting from antidromic stimulation is compatible with the duration of recurrent facilitation.

We have seen above that recurrent facilitation is widespread among the cells of facilitated nuclei and can exert a significant effect on their firing probability. Furthermore, recurrent inhibition and facilitation display a pattern of organization which suggests that they play a role in spinal reflex activity. It therefore appears that in the case of recurrent facilitation we are dealing with a release phenomenon, brought about not by a pathological condition but rather by physiological activity and playing a role in the regulation of activity of spinal motoneurons.

REFERENCES

1. RENSHAW, B. Influence of discharge of motoneurons upon excitation of neighboring motoneurons. *J. Neurophysiol.* 4:167, 1941.

2. ECCLES, J. C., FATT, P., and KOKETSU, K. Cholinergic and inhibitory synapses in a pathway from motor-axon collaterals to motoneurones. *J. Physiol.* 126:524, 1954.

3. WILSON, V. J. Recurrent facilitation of spinal reflexes. *J. Gen. Physiol.* 42:703, 1959.

4. RENSHAW, B. Central effects of centripetal impulses in axons of spinal ventral roots. *J. Neurophysiol.* 9:191, 1946.

5. Brooks, V. B., and Wilson, V. J. Recurrent inhibition in the cat's spinal cord. *J. Physiol. 146*:380, 1959.

6. Wilson, V. J., Diecke, F. P. J., and Talbot, W. H. Action of tetanus toxin on conditioning of spinal motoneurons. *J. Neurophysiol. 23*:659, 1960.

7. Wilson, V. J., and Burgess, P. R. Changes in the membrane during recurrent disinhibition of spinal motoneurons. *Nature 191*:918, 1961.

8. Wilson, V. J., and Burgess, P. R. Disinhibition in the cat spinal cord. *J. Neurophysiol. 25*:392, 1962.

9. Lloyd, D. P. C. After-currents, after-potentials, excitability and ventral root electrotonus in spinal motoneurons. *J. Gen. Physiol. 35*:289, 1951.

10. Wilson, V. J., and Talbot, W. H. Recurrent conditioning in the cat spinal cord: Differential effect of meprobamate on recurrent facilitation and inhibition. *J. Gen. Physiol. 43*:495, 1960.

11. Wilson, V. J., Talbot, W. H., and Diecke, F. P. J. Distribution of recurrent facilitation and inhibition in cat spinal cord. *J. Neurophysiol. 23*:144, 1960.

12. Eccles, J. C., Eccles, R. M., Iggo, A., and Ito, M. Distribution of recurrent inhibition among motoneurones. *J. Physiol. 159*:479, 1961.

13. Laporte, Y., and Lloyd, D. P. C. Nature and significance of the reflex connections established by large afferent fibers of muscular origin. *Am. J. Physiol. 169*:609, 1952.

14. Eccles, J. C., Eccles, R. M., and Lundberg, A. Synaptic actions in montoneurones caused by impulses in Golgi tendon organ afferents. *J. Physiol. 138*:227, 1957.

15. Sherrington, C. S. On innervation of antagonistic muscles: Ninth note: Successive spinal induction. *Proc. Roy. Soc. London, S.B. 77*:478, 1906.

16. Granit, R. Reflexes to stretch and contraction of antagonists around ankle joint. *J. Neurophysiol. 15*:269, 1952.

17. Granit, R., Pascoe, J. E., and Steg, G. Behaviour of tonic α and γ motoneurones during stimulation of recurrent collaterals. *J. Physiol. 138*:381, 1957.

18. Kuno, M. Excitability following antidromic activation in spinal motoneurones supplying red muscles. *J. Physiol. 149*:374, 1959.

19. Eccles, J. C. *The Physiology of Nerve Cells*. Baltimore, Johns Hopkins, 1957.

20. Granit, R., and Rutledge, L. T. Surplus excitation in reflex action of motoneurones as measured by recurrent inhibition. *J. Physiol. 154*:288, 1960.

21. Granit, R., Haase, J., and Rutledge, L. T. Recurrent inhibition in relation to frequency of firing and limitation of discharge rate of extensor motoneurones. *J. Physiol. 154*:308, 1960.

22. Lloyd, D. P. C., and McIntyre, A. K. Monosynaptic reflex responses of individual motoneurons. *J. Gen. Physiol. 38*:771, 1955.

23. Wilson, V. J., and Burgess, P. R. Intracellular study of recurrent facilitation. *Science 134*:337, 1961.

24. Wilson, V. J., and Burgess, P. R. Effects of antidromic conditioning on some motoneurons and interneurons. *J. Neurophysiol. 25*:636, 1962.

25. Eccles, J. C., Eccles, R. M., and Lundberg, A. The action potentials of the alpha motoneurones supplying fast and slow muscles. *J. Physiol. 142*:275, 1958.

26. Perl, E. R. Discharge of flexor motoneurons to graded cutaneous and muscle nerve volleys. *The Physiologist 3*:124, 1960.

27. Hartline, H. K., and Ratliff, F. Inhibition in the eye of *Limulus.* *J. Gen. Physiol. 40*:357, 1957.

28. Brooks, V. B., and Asanuma, H. Action of tetanus toxin in cerebral cortex. *Science 137*:674, 1962.

29. Frank, K., and Fuortes, M. G. F. Unitary activity of spinal interneurones of cats. *J. Physiol. 131*:424, 1956.

30. Hunt, C. C., and Kuno, M. Background discharge and evoked responses of spinal interneurones. *J. Physiol. 147*:364, 1959.

31. Koizumi, K., Ushiyama, J., and Brooks, C. McC. A study of reticular formation action on spinal interneurons and motoneurons. *Jap. J. Physiol. 9*:282, 1959.

DISCUSSION

FLOYD RATLIFF

The enormous anatomical and functional complexity of the nervous system poses formidable problems for those who would study it. And yet the problems are not insurmountable. For example, we have just seen, in Dr. Wilson's experiments, how the careful analytical study of the behavior of a single cell can yield information about the nature and extent of the activity of many other cells which are—directly or indirectly—exerting excitatory and inhibitory influences upon it. By observing only the membrane potential of a particular cell, he was able to show that an apparent excitatory effect in that cell was actually a release from inhibition exerted on it by some of its neighbors. An understanding of the properties of just one cell can thus lead to a better understanding of the functional organization of a whole system of interconnected and interacting cells.

Of course, the exact nature of all the functional and anatomical interconnections in the spinal cord is not yet known. On the basis of what we do know, how can we conceive of any functionally significant order coming out of the apparent chaos of profuse interconnections that exists here and elsewhere in the nervous system? I should like to suggest that more or less random interconnections may, simply because they do branch and gradually thin out, give rise to functionally significant organizations of interacting elements. One need only assume that the branches thin out in such a way that any influences exerted over them will, on the average, diminish with distance.

For example, in the lateral eye of the horseshoe crab, *Limulus*, the approximately 1,000 photoreceptors, from which optic nerve fibers arise, are interconnected with a fine feltwork of profusely branching fibers over which the receptors exert inhibitory influences on one another. And here the magnitudes of the inhibitory influences exerted by any element on its neighbors do, in fact, diminish with distance. As a consequence of this one simple principle, important functional properties can arise. Suppose, for example, that two neighboring receptors are inhibiting one another. If additional receptors are illuminated in the vicinity of this interacting pair, too far from one of the receptors to inhibit it directly but near enough to the second to inhibit it, the frequency of the discharge of the first one increases as it is partially released from the inhibition exerted on it by the other. Thus, in this retina disinhibition simulates facilitation in much the same way as described by Dr. Wilson for motoneurons of the spinal cord. Perhaps this same principle—that the inhibition diminishes with distance—may account, in part, for the phenomenon he has observed.

In the same way, inhibitory influences that diminish with distance may serve to accentuate differences in the responses of neighboring groups of neurons. In the retina, contrast effects may be expected to be greatest at or near the boundary between a dimly illuminated region and a brightly illuminated region. A unit within the dimly illuminated region, but near this boundary, will be inhibited not only by dimly illuminated neighbors but also by brightly illuminated ones. The total inhibition exerted on such a unit will be greater, therefore, than that exerted on other dimly illuminated elements that are farther from the boundary; consequently its frequency of response will be less than theirs. Similarly a unit within but near the boundary of the equally brightly illuminated fields will have a higher frequency of discharge than other equally illuminated units that are located well within the bright field but are subject to stronger inhibition since all their immediate neighbors are also brightly illuminated. Thus the differences in activity of elements on either side of the boundary will be exaggerated, and the discontinuity in this pattern of illumination will be accentuated in the pattern of neural response.

It is clear that inhibitory interaction among neighboring elements is a fundamental neural mechanism common to many neural systems, and its principal functional properties appear to be much the same wherever it is found.* Basic principles derived from observations on a particular species and in a particular part of the nervous system are likely to be useful in interpreting activity in diverse parts of the nervous system and in a wide variety of species. I am confident that Dr. Wilson's work on inhibitory phenomena in the spinal cord will have general value in the analysis of the complex interactions that characterize the action of all nervous centers.

---

* Cf. *Nervous Inhibition,* ed. by Florey, E., New York, Pergamon Press, 1961, and *Sensory Communication,* ed. by Rosenblith, W., Cambridge, Mass., MIT Press, 1961.

Metabolic Relations between Glia and Neurons Studied in Single Cells

THE GLIAL ELEMENTS OUTNUMBER NEURONS IN THE CENTRAL NERVOUS system perhaps as much as tenfold (Table 2-1). Though generally smaller than the neurons, these cells must constitute a large proportion of the actively metabolizing tissue and undoubtedly have an important and special metabolic function. In spite of this, 116 years after Rudolf Virchow[1] described neuroglia, our information about its function is conspicuously lacking. Is this because the low electrical activity and the difficulty of recording it have discouraged electrophysiologists and the difficulty of obtaining pure samples of these cells has frightened the biochemists?

Some comparative quantitative data concerning the number, volume, metabolic relations, and electrical activity of glia and neurons are summarized in Table 2-1. Since some of these results have been obtained by means of varying techniques (for examples, see Table 2-1, "Respiration") in different preparations (cell cultures, neoplastic tissue, homogenates of brain tissue, etc.), it is sometimes difficult to estimate the relative contribution of the neuronal and the nonneuronal components to the total activity. The data reported for the relative volume (Table 2-1) of each of the components are also

The results here reported are based on investigations made by the author at the Department of Physiology, Karolinska Institute, Stockholm, Sweden, and at the Department of Pharmacology, University of Florida, Gainesville, Florida.

15

TABLE 2-1. Comparison of General Biological Characteristics of Glial Cells and Neurons

	GLIA		NEURON	
NUMBER	$7.6–5.8 \times 10^{-7}$/g	←	$0–2.3 \times 10^{-7}$/g	(corpus callosum > cerebral cortex > cerebellar cortex) Nurnberger, 1958,[89] Pope, 1952[91]
VOLUME (absolute)	7,000–2,500 μ^3	→	50,000 μ^3	(Deiters' cell, oligodendroglia, rat) Giacobini, 1961[28]
VOLUME (relative)	(dendrites + vessels) 8% (fibers + vessels) 35% (glial tissue) 30%	← ← → →	2% 5% 30% 60%	(gray cortex, man) (30,000 neurons/mm³) Shariff, 1953[100] (dendrites 25%, cortex) Pope, 1955[92,93] (dendrites) Hortsmann and Meves, 1959[78]
MASS	0.20 pg/μ^3	↔	0.21 pg/μ^3	(Deiters' cell, oligodendroglia, rabbit) Hydén, 1959[79]
RNA	123 pg	→	1,545 pg	(Deiters' cell, oligodendroglia, rabbit) Hydén and Pigon, 1960[30]
RNA COMPOSITION	high cytosine	↔	high guanine	(Deiters' cell, oligodendroglia, rabbit) Egyhazi and Hydén, 1961[69]

TABLE 2-1. (*Continued.*)

	GLIA	NEURON	
RESPIRATION	0.19(astroc.)–1.4(olig.)	→ 1.9 (cortex)	(glial cultures) Abood et al., 1952[64] (glial neoplasms) Heller and Elliott, 1955, 1957[70,75]
	(nonneuronal) 30%	→ 70%	(cerebral cortex) Nurnberger and Gordon, 1957[88]
		→	(glial neoplasms) Brierly and McIlwain, 1956[67]
	(nonneuronal) 34% (5.7×10^{-6} μl. O_2/hr/cell)	→ 66–71%	(cortex and corpus callosum) Elliott and Heller, 1957[70] (63×10^{-6} μl. O_2/hr/cell)
	(nonneuronal) 23% (12.5×10^{-6} μl. O_2/hr/cell)	→ 67%	(cortex) Korey and Orchen, 1959[85] (136×10^{-6} μl. O_2/hr/neuron)
		→ 90%	(area 9 cortex) Allen, 1957[65]
ACETYLCHOLINE TURNOVER	(only nonspecif. ChE) 9	→ 3	(μl. $CO_2 \times 10^{-4}$/hr/spinal ganglion cell) Giacobini, 1956[5] (no ACh synthesis in glia) Hebb, 1961[21]
ELECTRICAL ACTIVITY	40 mv	→ 40–70 mv	(resting potential) (glial cultures, astrocytes) Tasaki and Chang, 1958,[101] Hild and Tasaki, 1962[76]
	4–5 sec.	← 1 msec.	(impulse activity) Tasaki and Chang, 1958[101]
MECHANICAL CONTRACTION	7–16 min.	← none	(cell cultures) Chang and Hild, 1959[68]
TEMPERATURE, CO_2, NH_4	← opposite effects →		(fish retina) Svaetichin et al., 1960[32]

difficult to interpret, since fibers (dendrites, axons) and vessels are included with the glial cells.

The introduction of quantitative methods for the study of enzyme activities of single units of the nervous system in the last 10 years[2-8] has made it possible to study separately the metabolism of glia and nerve cells in very discrete areas. The single cell preparation can be obtained directly by dissection of either fresh tissue[5,9] or freeze-dried samples.[2,3,8] In either case the chemical analysis can be performed at the cellular as well as at the subcellular level.[8,10]

The present author became interested in the metabolic relations between glia and neurons in the course of investigation of the localization of cholinesterases in the nervous system.[9,11] Two types of neuroglial cell preparations easily accessible to micromanipulation were selected: first, the oligodendrocytes which encapsulate the nerve cell bodies in spinal and sympathetic ganglia and those which surround the large neurons of the lateral vestibular nucleus of Deiters; and second, the protoplasmic astrocytes of the spinal cord (Fig. 2-1). Two different enzymes were studied in these cells: the cholinesterases (ChE) and carbonic anhydrase (CA).

CHOLINESTERASE ACTIVITY IN GLIAL TISSUE

The question whether the cholinesterases are present in the glial and vascular tissue is of primary importance for the study of the localization of these enzymes in nervous tissue. The presence of such enzymes in nonnervous tissue of the brain, cord, and ganglia, which is intermingled with the nervous elements, may be a serious source of error when estimating the ChE activity of these structures *in toto*.

Koelle,[12] using a histochemical method, reported nonspecific ChE in the glial cells of the spinal and sympathetic ganglia and in the Schwann cells of myelinated nerves. He also suggested that nonspecific ChE is present both in the fibrous astrocytes and in the vascular endothelium of the spinal cord of the cat. The findings of Koelle on the vascular tissue were later confirmed by the biochemical investigation of Thompson and Thickner,[13] who showed that the arteries dissected from the human brain contain active ChE which is predominantly nonspecific ChE.

Hebb *et al.*,[14] found nonspecific ChE in the glial cells and septa of rabbit optic nerve.

In 1955, Koelle[15] confirmed his earlier findings in cat tissue in the central nervous system of the rat, where he was able to show heavy staining of glial cells and capillaries. Further support of these results has come from studies on the ChE content of a variety of brain tumors.

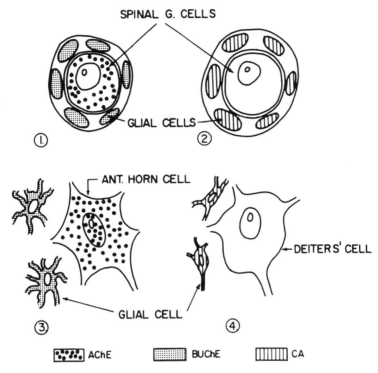

FIG. 2-1. Schematic representation of enzymatic relationships between glial and nerve cells.

Youngstrom, Woodhall, and Graves[16] were the first to measure ChE activity in pathological nervous tissue. They found considerably more activity in tumors of the astrocytic series than in neuromas, meningiomas, or medulloblastomas. In 1953, Bülbring, Philpot, and Bosanquet[17] found the highest values of nonspecific ChE in tumors of the astrocytic series and in ependymomas. Cavanagh, Thompson, and Webster[18] studied the ChE activity of twenty-one cerebral tumors.

These authors found very high levels of activity in astrocytic tumors as compared with normal brain. Meningiomas and juvenile medullo-blastomas showed only low activity.

Further support of the extranervous localization of nonspecific ChE came from degeneration experiments of Sawyer[19] and of Cavanagh, Thompson, and Webster,[18] who demonstrated that non-specific ChE was practically unaffected after complete disintegration of the nerve fibers. From these experiments it was concluded that this enzyme is wholly a sheath component, probably situated in the Schwann cells.

Finally, mention should be made of the investigation by Lumsden[20] of the alterations of ChE in certain types of plaques in multiple sclerosis. His results suggest that nonspecific ChE has a dual source, from oligodendrocytes and from microglial histiocytes.

The results obtained by the present author with the Cartesian diver technique are schematically given in Figure 2-1, and the activity values are reported in Table 2-2. In three different preparations it was found that neither oligodendrocytes nor astrocytes showed any specific ChE activity (AChE) while nonspecific ChE was found in higher levels in the glia than in nerve cells (spinal ganglion cells, sympathetic ganglion cells). The activity ratio (N/G in Table 2-2) was 0.7 in the spinal ganglion cells and 0.3 in the sympathetic ganglion cells. No nonspecific ChE activity was found in the anterior horn cells, whereas the astrocytes from the same region exhibited a very high nonspecific ChE activity (Table 2-2).

These results, together with those of Hebb,[21] who found that certain fractions (obtained by low-speed centrifugation of brain homogenates in which glia are concentrated) have an extremely low specific synthetic activity for acetylcholine, cast doubt whether glial cells can be implicated in the chemical transmission mechanism. Even the report[22] that inhibition of nonspecific ChE influences be-havior, brain waves, and evoked response amplitude in the cat seems to add little evidence against this doubt because of difficulty in selectively inhibiting nonspecific ChE (i.e., leaving unaltered the specific ChE) with the type of inhibitors used by these authors.

In other words, the significance of the high concentration of non-specific ChE in glial cells (both astrocytes and oligodendrocytes) summarized in Table 2-2 seems difficult to interpret functionally.

TABLE 2-2. Enzyme Activity in Individual Glial and Nerve Cells

Cell type	Metabolic pathway	Enzyme	Activity			Author	Year
			N	G	N/G		
Deiters' cell	Cell respiration	Cytochrome oxidase	4.2	11.5	0.4	Hydén, Pigon* (30)	1960
		Succinoxidase	2.2	4.5	0.5	Hydén, Pigon* (30)	1960
	ATP hydrolysis	ATPase	1	1.7	0.6	Cummins, Hydén§ (34)	1962
Oligodendrocyte	CO₂ hydration	Carboanhydrase	6.4	385	0.02	Giacobini‡ (28) (29)	1961
Anterior horn cell	ACh metabolism	AChE	10-50	0		Giacobini* (11)	1959
Astrocyte		Nonspecif. ChE	0	4.1		Giacobini* (11)	1959
	Glycolysis	Hexokinase	7.2	2.2	3.3	Lowry† (8)	1957
		Phosphogluco isomerase	49	24	2	Lowry† (8)	1957
Spinal ganglion cell		Lactic DH	50	28	1.8	Lowry† (8)	1957
Oligodendrocyte	Oxidative shunt	G 6-P DH	2.1	4.8	0.5	Lowry† (8)	1957
		6-PG DH	1.3	2.2	0.6	Lowry† (8)	1957
		Isocitric DH	4.5	6.2	0.7	Lowry† (8)	1957
	Citric acid cycle	Malic DH	231	90	2.6	Lowry† (8)	1957
		Succinic DH	0.3	0.5	0.6	Hydén, Løvtrup, and Pigon* (33)	1958

TABLE 2-2. (*Continued.*)

					Source	
Spinal ganglion cell	Glutamate oxid. Amino acid metabolism	Glutamic DH	2.5	1.6	1.6	Lowry† (8)	1957
		Glutamic-aspartic transaminase	35	6.5	5.4	Lowry† (8)	1957
	ACh metabolism	AChE	2–20	0		Giacobini* (11)	1959
Oligodendrocyte		Nonspecif. ChE	5	7	0.7	Giacobini* (11)	1959
		Cytochrome oxidase	0.9	1.6	0.6	Hydén, Løvtrup, and Pigon* (33)	1958
	Cell respiration	Succinoxidase	0.7	5.1	0.14	Hydén, Løvtrup, and Pigon* (33)	1958
Sympathetic ganglion cell	ACh metabolism	AChE	2–30	0		Giacobini* (6)	1957
Oligodendrocyte		Nonspecif. ChE	3	9	0.3	Giacobini* (6)	1957

Numbers in parentheses in the Source column refer to references.
* Microliters of CO_2 or O_2 per hour per cell or equivalent volume $\times 10^{-4}$.
† Moles of substrate converted per kilogram of lipid-free dry weight per hour per cell or equivalent volume.
‡ Moles of enzyme $\times 10^{-20}$/cell or equivalent volume.
§ Micromicromoles of ATP hydrolyzed per hour per intact cell or in homogenized preparation (per cell membrane $= 0.14\ \mu\mu M$ of ATP).

CARBONIC ANHYDRASE ACTIVITY IN GLIAL TISSUE

The presence of CA in the nervous system and the difficulty of precisely localizing it in nerve tissue are the major obstacles to interpretation of the varying hypotheses proposed to explain the function of this enzyme.

Studies in which the inhibition of CA altered the formation and electrolyte composition of the cerebrospinal fluid implicate this enzyme in its production. It has been reported[23] that there is a potential difference of 5 to 30 mv between cerebrospinal and extracellular fluid of several mammals, cerebrospinal fluid being negative with respect to extracellular fluid. Since chloride moves into cerebrospinal fluid against both chemical and electrical potential gradients, it must be actively transported into cerebrospinal fluid. The inhibitors of CA are known to modify the composition of the cerebrospinal fluid as well as to inhibit its rate of formation in laboratory animals and in man.[24-26] There is a strong possibility that a transport mechanism exists, and the idea that the enzyme CA is implicated in this mechanism is attractive.

The development of a sensitive micromethod based on a modification of the Cartesian diver technique of Linderstrøm-Lang[27] allowing determination of CA in single tissue elements[28,29] offered the possibility of investigating this problem and also the functional relation between glia and neurons.

Samples of single nerve cells and of the glial cells surrounding them (oligodendrocytes) were isolated under the microscope from fresh, unstained preparations of the lateral vestibular nucleus of Deiters, according to the technique previously described.[9]

Equivalent volumes of nerve and glial cells were dissected out[28,29] and their CA activity measured separately by CO_2 evolution at 25°C. from $NaHCO_3$ (final concentration, 1×10^{-4} M) in the presence of 0.1 M sodium phosphate buffer at pH 7.5. The uncatalyzed reaction and the activity curves of different known concentrations of semipurified CA preparations were determined for each experiment and compared with the curve obtained from the isolated cell preparation, as shown in Figure 2-2.

Control experiments done with either the semipurified samples of

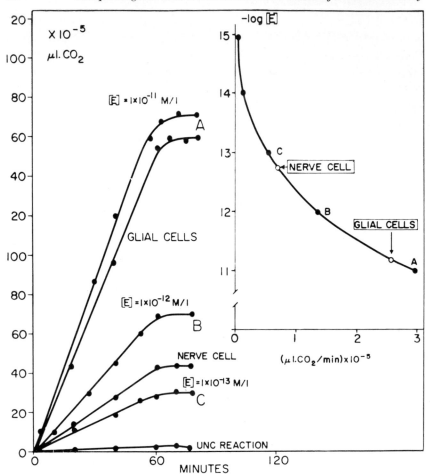

FIG. 2-2. Activity curves (*A, B,* and *C* at left) for three different concentrations of semipurified CA preparation and curve for uncatalyzed (UNC) reaction. These are compared (insert) with activity of single nerve cell and equivalent volume of glial cells.

CA or the cell preparations in the presence of acetazolamide (6×10^{-7} M) showed a complete inhibition of enzyme activity.

The enzyme activity of a cell preparation which was found to be equivalent to that observed in a diver filled with the semipurified CA solution (see Fig. 2-2) varied between 38 and 360×10^{-13} M (mean, 99×10^{-13} M) in the glial cells, while in the corresponding nerve cells the activity was only 0.45 to 5×10^{-13} M (mean, $1.95 \times$

10^{-13} M); the ratio between the glial and the nerve cell activity varied in a single preparation between 28 and 85 (sixteen experiments). Volumes varying between 18 and $50 \times 10^3 \mu^3$ of oligodendroglia (representing 7 to 20 glial cells) therefore exhibited concentrations of CA (moles per unit volume) up to 120 times greater than a single nerve cell of equivalent volume.

The activity of CA in a single intact red cell preparation was estimated as 2×10^{-20} M, in a single nerve cell as 3×10^{-20} M, in a glial cell as 18×10^{-20} M, and in a single cell of the choroid plexus as 300×10^{-20} M.

On the basis of the activity of CA per unit volume, it may be calculated that the red cell has 670 times, the choroid cell 250 times, and the glial cell 120 times higher activity than the nerve cell of the nucleus of Deiters.

Since the mass per unit volume of fresh glial cells in this nucleus has been found to be the same as that of the corresponding nerve cells (about 0.20 $\mu\mu$g. per cubic micron[30]),* it is appropriate to make a direct comparison of equivalent volumes of glial and nerve cells.

The demonstration of high localization of CA in the glial elements of the central nervous system indicates these cells to be the site of action of CO_2 hydration process. Figure 2-3 shows schematically the localization of CA in nervous tissue and a representation of a possible two-step mechanism for the transport of chloride (and eventually sodium). This can be summarized as follows:

1. CO_2, which has recently been recognized[31] as the immediate product of the decarboxylation reactions in the brain, can rapidly diffuse inside the neuron and from it into the adjacent glial cells, where it is rapidly hydrated to carbonic acid (HCO_3^- at body pH) in the presence of CA.

2. A selective exchange of chloride from the adjacent capillary into the cell and from here to the interstitial space and CSF can then take place.

In this way the high intracellular HCO_3^- rapidly made available from CO_2 and H_2O in the presence of CA may be linked with active transport of chloride into the interstitial space and CSF.

It can finally be pointed out that in the structure studied (the nucleus of Deiters in the rat) the anatomical interrelation of the glial

* (1 $\mu\mu$g = 1 pg = 1 picogram = 10^{-12}g)

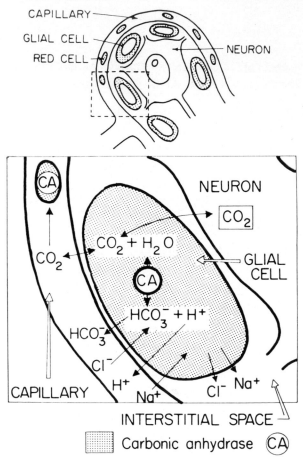

FIG. 2-3. *Top,* cellular localization of carbonic anhydrase in central nervous system. *Bottom,* proposed mechanism for transport of chloride and sodium (see text).

cells to the neuron and to the capillaries[29] gives further support to a strategic position (Fig. 2-3, *upper part*) of the glia in the postulated secretion mechanism.

Of particular interest in view of the results of the present work is the finding of Svaetichin *et al.*[32] that a lowering or lack of CO_2 promptly produced a decrease of the glial membrane potential, whereas an increase of O_2 and/or a decrease in CO_2 increased the glial membrane potential. The amplitude of the S-potential of the neurons was inversely related to the height of the glial membrane potential (Table 2-1).

ENZYME CONCENTRATIONS IN INDIVIDUAL NERVE AND GLIAL CELLS

The data available from single cell studies of enzyme activity of glial and nerve cells obtained by different authors are given in Table 2-2. In the four glia-neuron preparations listed in this table the activity of enzymes representing various metabolic pathways was studied with different methods. The neuron/glia (N/G) activity ratio is reported together with the activity of the two types of cells separately (N and G).

In Deiters' nucleus the four enzymes studied (Table 2-2) show higher concentrations in the glia than in nerve cells. The difference is especially striking for CA. On the basis of the data obtained in the same nucleus, Hydén *et al.*[30,33,34] hypothesized (Table 2-5) that glial cells supply energy-rich compounds to the neuron. The investigations of Lowry *et al.*[3,4,7] in spinal ganglion cells and oligodendrocytes using fluorometric methods (Table 2-2), demonstrate the contrast between the enzyme activity of the cell bodies and the glial cells. In comparison with the cell bodies, the oligodendrocytes are very low in hexokinase, phosphoglucoisomerase, lactic and malic dehydrogenase, glutamic dehydrogenase, glutamic aspartic transaminase, and relatively rich in glucose 6-phosphate and 6-phosphogluconate dehydrogenase, isocitric dehydrogenase, and succinic dehydrogenase. Cytochrome oxidase and succinoxidase are both present in higher levels in the glia than in the nerve cells.[33]

The results also indicate that some of the steps of a certain metabolic pathway (e.g., citric acid cycle) can be most effectively performed in the glia, and others in the nerve cell.

As reported previously, no AChE is present in any glial cell obtained by the four different preparations.[11]

METABOLIC ACTIVITY OF DIFFERENT TYPES OF GLIA

From the limited data available from the literature and those reported in this paper, it is possible to establish some differences

TABLE 2-3. Comparison of General Metabolic Properties of Astroglia and Oligodendroglia

ASTROGLIA		OLIGODENDROGLIA	
low	—— RNA —→	high	Koenig, 1958, 1959, 1962[80,82,84]
low	—— Protein turnover —→	high	Koenig, 1958, 1959, 1962[80,82,84]
low	—— Respiration —→	high	Koenig, 1958, 1959, 1962[80,82,84]
0.19		1.4	(tumoral tissue, μl. O_2/hr/mg) Heller and Elliott, 1955[75]
			(tumoral tissue) Victor and Wolff, 1937[102]
			(tumoral tissue) Elliott and Heller, 1957[70]
low	—— Oxidative enzymes activity —→	high	Robins and Smith, 1953[97] Lowry et al., 1954[4] Pope et al., 1956[95] Friede, 1961[73]
0.18	—— Anaerobic glycolysis —→	.63	(tumoral tissue, μl/hr/mg) Heller and Elliott, 1955[75]
10% (astrocytic tumors)	—— cytochrome oxidase activity —→	70%	(total cortex activity) Allen, 1957[65]
high	—— succinic DH activity —→	low	(oligodendrogliomas) Mossakowski, 1962[87]
4, 1	—— nonspecific AChE —→	9–7	(μl. $CO_2 \times 10^{-4}$/hr) Giacobini, 1959[11]
less frequent and slow	—— Rhythmical pulsation —→	fast and more frequent	

and peculiarities in metabolism as well as in physiological properties between two major groups of glial cells. These are summarized in Table 2-3. It can be seen that the oligodendroglial cell is more active than the astrocyte in terms of RNA content, protein turnover, respiration, glycolysis, and activity of oxidative and other enzymes. The data still do not allow a clear distinction on a functional basis but do

TABLE 2-4. Metabolic Changes in the Glia in Pathological Conditions

LOCAL BRAIN INJURY	increase of oxidative enzyme activity in astrocytes, Rubinstein, Klatzo, and Miquel, 1962.[98]
	cold $\longrightarrow$ generalized increase of tetrazolium reduction activity, Rubinstein, Klatzo, and Miquel, 1962.[98]
	spinal fluid pumping $\longrightarrow$ active incorporation of RNA, DNA, and protein labeled precursors, Koenig, 1958, 1962;[80,81,84] Altman, 1962.[66]
AHLHEIMER'S DISEASE	high acid phosphatase activity, Friede and Magee, 1962.[74]
	high oxidative enzyme activity, Friede and Magee, 1962.[74]
GLIAL TUMORS	low oxidative metabolism, Heller and Elliott, 1955.[75]
	low cytochrome oxidase activity, Pope *et al.*, 1956[95]; Pope *et al.*, 1957.[96]
	low cytochrome oxidase activity (10% in astrocytomas and 70% in oligodendrogliomas of total cortex activity), Allen, 1957.[65]
	low succinic DH activity, Ogawa and Zimmerman, 1959[90]; Friede, 1959.[71,72]
	relat. high succinic DH activity (astrocytomas > oligodendrogliomas), Mossakowski, 1962.[87]
	low respiratory rate, Brierly and McIlwain, 1956.[67]
	relat. high respiratory rate (astrocytomas .19; oligodendrogliomas 1.4), Heller and Elliott, 1955.[75]
	high calcification (oligodendrogliomas 70%, astrocytoma 27%), Schiffer, Sibour and Vesco, 1961.[99]
	high β-glucuronidase and β-galactosidase activity, Lehrer and Hirsch, 1961.[86]
	anaerobic glycolysis (astrocytomas .18; oligodendrogliomas .63; cortex 2), Heller and Elliott, 1955.[75]
GLIAL PROLIFERATION, WALLERIAN DEGENERATION	high β-glycosidase activity, Hollinger and Rossiter, 1952[77]; McCaman and Robins, 1959[35]; Robins, Fisher, Lowe, 1961.[36]

suggest a very distinct type of metabolism in the two types of glial cells.

METABOLIC CHANGES IN PATHOLOGICAL CONDITIONS

A summary of some metabolic changes in four different pathological conditions is reported in Table 2-4. Some of these results have been obtained with histochemical staining techniques and are therefore of little quantitative value. The results reported under glial proliferation have been obtained with quantitative microchemical methods.[35,36]

GENERAL CONCLUSIONS: A THEORY OF FUNCTIONAL DIFFERENTIATION OF THE GLIA

On the basis of data obtained at the cellular level and other biochemical, morphological, and electrophysiological data reviewed,[37-63] a tentative diagram of functional relations between the glia and the neuron is presented in Table 2-5.

TABLE 2-5. Diagrammatic Representation of Biological Properties (Left) and Suggested Functions (Right) of the Neuroglia (See Text)

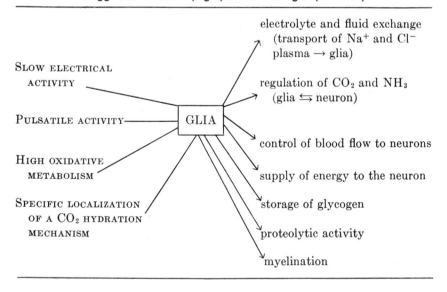

Some metabolic, electrical, and mechanical properties peculiar to the glial tissue are listed on the left side of the figure, while the suggested mechanism is located at the right side.

It is emphasized, on the basis of the data showing definite differences between astroglia and oligodendroglia (Table 2-3) that such

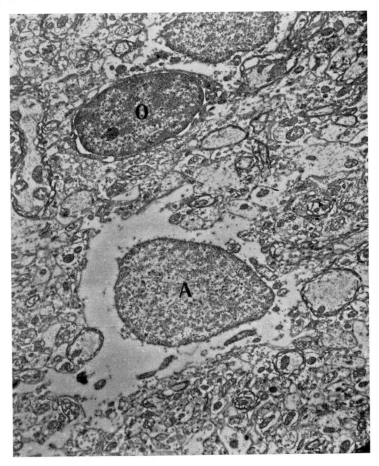

FIG. 2-4. Nuclear and cytoplasmic characteristics of typical oligodendroglial (*O*) and astroglial (*A*) cells of cerebral cortex of rat. ×11,000. (From Hartmann.[48])

a diagram reflects only the general properties of the neuroglia. The data which we possess today do not yet allow any precise demonstration of the distinct function of the different types of glial cells. However, they do point strongly toward a high differentiation of activity.

SUMMARY

Quantitative enzyme analyses in single cells make it possible to investigate metabolic and functional relations between the glia and the neuron. Some results obtained utilizing a micromodification of the Cartesian diver technique to study fine localization of ChE and CA in single cell preparations of glia and neurons have been presented.

Only nonspecific ChE was found in astrocytes and oligodendrocytes. CA was specifically localized in the glial components of the nucleus of Deiters. This selective localization supports the implication of the glial cell in a mechanism for the active transport of chloride from the capillaries to the interstitial fluid. These results are compared and discussed in the light of investigations by others on single cell preparations.

The general biological differences between glial cells and neurons in both normal and pathological conditions are reviewed, and differentiated function is proposed for the various types of glial cells.

REFERENCES

1. Virchow, R. Ueber das granulirte Ansehen der Wandungen der Gehirnventrikel. *Allg. Ztg. Psych.* 3:244, 1846.

2. Lowry, O. H. Quantitative histochemistry of the brain: Histological sampling. *J. Histochem.* 1:420, 1953.

3. Lowry, O. H., Roberts, N. R., Leiner, K. Y., Wu, M. L., and Farr, A. L. Quantitative histochemistry of brain: I. Chemical methods. *J. Biol. Chem.* 207:1, 1954.

4. Lowry, O. H., Roberts, N. R., Leiner, K. Y., Wu, M. L., Farr, A. L., and Albers, R. W. Quantitative histochemistry of brain: III. Ammon's horn. *J. Biol. Chem.* 207:39, 1954.

5. Giacobini, E., and Zajicek, J. Quantitative determination of acetylcholinesterase activity in individual nerve cells. *Nature* 177:185, 1956.

6. Giacobini, E. Quantitative determination of cholinesterase in individual sympathetic cells. *J. Neurochem.* 1:234, 1957.

7. Lowry, O. H., Roberts, N. R., and Kapphahn, I. F. Fluorometric measurement of pyridine nucleotides. *J. Biol. Chem.* 224:1047, 1957.

8. Lowry, O. H. "Enzyme Concentrations in Individual Nerve Cell Bodies," in *Metabolism of the Nervous System,* ed. by Richter, D. New York, Pergamon Press, 1957, p. 323.

9. GIACOBINI, E. Histochemical demonstration of ACHE activity in isolated nerve cells. *Acta physiol. scandinav. 36*:276, 1956.

10. GIACOBINI, E. Determination of cholinesterase in the cellular components of neurones. *Acta physiol. scandinav. 45*:311, 1959.

11. GIACOBINI, E. Distribution and localization of cholinesterases in nerve cells. *Acta physiol. scandinav. 45*(Suppl. 156):1, 1959.

12. KOELLE, G. B. Elimination of enzymatic diffusion artifacts in the histochemical localization of cholinesterases and a survey of their cellular distributions. *J. Pharmacol. & Exper. Therap. 103*:153, 1951.

13. THOMPSON, R. H. S., and THICKNER, A. Cholinesterase activity of arteries. *J. Physiol. 121*:623, 1953.

14. HEBB, C. O., SILVER, A., SWAN, A. A. B., and WAELSH, E. G. A histochemical study of cholinesterases of rabbit retina and optic nerve. *Quart. J. Exper. Physiol. 38*:185, 1953.

15. KOELLE, G. B. Cholinesterases of the central nervous system. *J. Neuropath. & Exper. Neurol. 14*:23, 1955.

16. YONGSTROM, K. A., WOODHALL, V., and GRAVES, R. W. Acetylcholine esterase content of brain tumors. *Proc. Soc. Exper. Biol. & Med. 48*:555, 1941.

17. BÜLBRING, E., PHILPOT, F. J., and BOSANQUET, F. D. Amine oxidase, pressor amines, and cholinesterase in brain tumours. *Lancet 1*:865, 1953.

18. CAVANAGH, J. B., THOMPSON, R. H. S., and WEBSTER, G. R. Localization of pseudo-cholinesterase activity in nervous tissue. *Quart. J. Exper. Physiol. 39*:185, 1954.

19. SAWYER, C. H. Cholinesterases in degenerating and regenerating peripheral nerves. *Am. J. Physiol. 146*:246, 1946.

20. LUMSDEN, C. E. "The Problem of Correlation of Quantitative Methods and Tissue Morphology in the Central Nervous System (The Distribution of Cholinesterase)," in *Metabolism of the Nervous System*, ed. by Richter, D. New York, Pergamon Press, 1957, p. 91.

21. HEBB, C. Cholinergic neurons in vertebrates. *Nature 192*:527, 1961.

22. DESMEDT, J. E., and LAGRUTTA, G. Effect of selective inhibition of pseudo-cholinesterase on the spontaneous and evoked activity of the cat's cerebral cortex. *J. Physiol. 136*:20, 1957.

23. TSCHIRGI, R. D., and TAYLOR, J. L. A steady bioelectric potential between the blood and the cerebrospinal fluid (CSF). *Fed. Proc. 13*:154, 1954.

24. MAREN, T. H., and FISCHER, F. J. Abolition of the plasma-cerebrospinal fluid chloride gradient by acetazolamide: Role of carbonic anhydrase in CSF secretion. *Fed. Proc. 18*:419, 1959.

25. TSCHIRGI, R. D., FROST, R. W., and TAYLOR, J. L. Inhibition of cerebrospinal fluid formation by a carbonic anhydrase inhibitor, 2-acetylamino-1, 3, 4-thiadiazole-5-sulfonamide (diamox). *Proc. Soc. Exper. Biol. & Med. 87*:101, 1954.

26. Maren, T. H., and Robinson, B. Pharmacology of acetazolamide as related to cerebrospinal fluid and the treatment of hydrocephalus. *Bull. Johns Hopkins Hosp. 106*:1, 1960.

27. Linderstrøm-Lang, K. Principle of the Cartesian diver applied to gasometric technique. *Nature 140*:108, 1937.

28. Giacobini, E. Localization of carbonic anhydrase in the nervous system. *Science 134*:1524, 1961.

29. Giacobini, E. A cytochemical study of the localization of carbonic anhydrase in the nervous system. *J. Neurochem. 9*:169, 1962.

30. Hydén, H., and Pigon, A. A cytophysiological study of the functional relationship between oligodendroglial cells and nerve cells of Deiters' nucleus. *J. Neurochem. 6*:57, 1960.

31. Palmer, R. F. A method for the identification of the immediate product of decarboxylation reactions. *Biochem. J. 78*:839, 1961.

32. Laufer, M., Svaetichin, G., Mitarai, G., Fatehchand, R., Vallecalle, E., and Villegas, J. "The Visual System," in *Neurophysiology and Psychophysics Symposium* (August 1960). Berlin, Springer, 1961, p. 457.

33. Hydén, H., Løvtrup, S., Pigon, A. Cytochrome oxidase and succinoxidase activities in spinal ganglion cells and glial capsule cells. *J. Neurochem. 2*:304, 1958.

34. Cummins, J., and Hydén, H. ATP levels and ATPases in neurons, glia and neuronal membranes of the vestibular nucleus. *Biochem. et biophys. acta 60*:271, 1962.

35. McCaman, R. E., and Robins, E. Quantitative biochemical studies of Wallerian degeneration of the peripheral and central nervous systems: II. Twelve enzymes. *J. Neurochem. 5*:32, 1959.

36. Robins, E., Fisher, K., and Lowe, I. P. Quantitative histochemical studies of the morphogenesis of the cerebellum: II. Two β-glycosidases. *J. Neurochem. 8*:96, 1961.

37. Ramón y Cajal, S. Contribución al conocimiento de la neuroglia del cerebro humano. *Trab. Lab. invest. Biol., Univ. Madrid 11*:255, 1913.

38. Ramón y Cajal, S. *Degeneration and Regeneration of the Nervous System.* London, Milford, 1928.

39. Lumsden, C. E., and Pomerat, C. M. Normal oligodendrocytes in tissue culture: A preliminary report on the pulsatile glial cells in tissue cultures from the corpus callosum of the normal adult rat brain. *Exper. Cell Res. 2*:103, 1951.

40. Pomerat, C. M. Pulsatile activity of cells from the human brain in tissue culture. *J. Nerv. & Ment. Dis. 114*:430, 1951.

41. Pomerat, C. M. Dynamic neurogliology. *Texas Rep. Biol. & Med. 10*:885, 1952.

42. Hild, W. Das Morphologische, Kinetische und Endokrinologische Verhalten von Hypothalamischem und Neurohypophysärem Gewebe in vitro. *Ztschr. Zellforsch. 40*:257, 1954.

43. Glees, P. *Neuroglia: Morphology and Function.* Philadelphia, Davis, 1955.

44. Maynard, E. A., and Pease, D. C. Electron microscopy of the cerebral cortex of the rat. *Anat. Rec. 121*:440, 1955.

45. Pomerat, C. M. Dynamic neuropathology. *J. Neuropath. & Exper. Neurol. 14*:28, 1955.

46. Luse, S. A. Electron microscopy of glial cells. *Anat. Rec. 124*:329, 1956.

47. Luse, S. A. Formation of myelin in the central nervous system of mice and rats, as studied with the electron microscope. *J. Biophys. & Biochem. Cytol. 2*:777, 1956.

48. Farquhar, M. G., and Hartmann, J. F. Neuroglial structure and relationships as revealed by electron microscopy. *J. Neuropath. & Exper. Neurol. 16*:18, 1957.

49. Maynard, E. A., Schultz, R. L., and Pease, D. C. Electron microscopy of the vascular bed of rat cerebral cortex. *Am. J. Anat. 100*:409, 1957.

50. Schultz, R. L., Maynard, E. A., and Pease, D. C. Electron microscopy of neurons and neuroglia of cerebral cortex and corpus callosum. *Am. J. Anat. 100*:369, 1957.

51. Windle, W. F. (ed.). *Biology of Neuroglia.* Springfield, Ill., Charles C Thomas, 1958.

52. Hild, W., Chang, J. J., and Tasaki, I. Electrical responses of astrocytic glia from the mammalian central nervous system cultivated in vitro. *Experientia 14*:220, 1958.

53. Pomerat, C. M. "Functional Concepts Based on Tissue Culture Studies of Neuroglia Cells," in *Biology of Neuroglia,* ed. by Windle, W. F. Springfield, Ill., Charles C Thomas, 1958.

54. Tschirgi, R. D. "Blood Brain Barrier," in *Biology of Neuroglia,* ed. by Windle, W. F. Springfield, Ill., Charles C Thomas, 1958, p. 130.

55. Cammermeyer, J. Is the perivascular oligodendrocyte another element controlling the blood supply to neurons? *Angiology 11*:508, 1960.

56. Sjöstrand, F. S. The visual system: Neurophysiol. & Psychophysics, Symposium, August 1960. *Berlin*, Springer-Verlag, 1961, p. 13.

57. Sjöstrand, F. S. "Electron Microscopy of Myelin and of Nerve Cells and Tissue," in *Modern Scientific Aspects of Neurology.* Baltimore, Williams & Wilkins, 1960, p. 189.

58. Cammermeyer, J. Distribution of oligodendrocytes in cerebral gray and white matter of several mammals. *Am. J. Anat. 107*:107, 1960.

59. Tschirgi, R. D. "Chemical Environment of the Central Nervous System," in *Handbook of Physiology,* ed. by Field, J. 1960, vol. 3, sec. 1, p. 1865. Washington, D.C., American Physiological Society.

60. Galambos, R. A glia-neural theory of brain function. *Proc. Nat. Acad. Sc. 47*:129, 1961.

61. Robins, E., and Lowe, I. P. Quantitative histochemical studies of the morphogenesis of the cerebellum: I. Total lipid and four enzymes. *J. Neurochem.* 8:81, 1961.

62. Giacobini, E. "Use of Microgasometric Techniques in Pharmacological Studies," in *Biochemical Pharmacology,* ed. by Lowry, O. H., New York, Pergamon Press 9:155, 1962.

63. DeRobertis, E. and Gerschenfeld, M. M. Submicroscopic morphology and function of glial cells. *Internat. Rev. Neurobiol.* 3:1, 1961.

64. Abood, L. G., Gerard, R. W., Banks, J., and Tschirgi, R. D. Substrate and enzyme distribution in cells and cell fractions of the nervous system. *Am. J. Physiol.* 168:728, 1952.

65. Allen, N. Cytochrome oxidase in human brain tumours. *J. Neurochem.* 2:37, 1957.

66. Altman, J. Autoradiographic study of degenerative and regenerative proliferation of neuroglia cell with tritiated thymidine. *Exper. Neurol.* 5:302, 1962.

67. Brierly, J. B., and McIlwain, H. Metabolic properties of cerebral tissues modified by neoplasia and by freezing. *J. Neurochem.* 1:109, 1956.

68. Chang, J. J., and Hild, W. Contractile responses to electrical stimulation of glial cells from the mammalian central nervous system cultivated in vitro. *J. Cell. & Comp. Physiol.* 53:139, 1959.

69. Egyhazi, E., and Hydén, H. Experimentally induced changes in the base composition of the ribonucleic acids of isolated nerve cells and their oligodendroglial cells. *J. Biophys. & Biochem. Cytol.* 10:403, 1961.

70. Elliott, K. A. C., and Heller, I. H. "Metabolism of Neurons and Glia," in *Metabolism of the Nervous System,* ed. by Richter, D. New York, Pergamon Press, 1957, p. 286.

71. Friede, R. L. Histochemischer Nachweis von Succinodehydrogenase in Biopsien von mensohlichem Hirngewebe. *Arch. path. Anat.* 332:216, 1959.

72. Friede, R. L. Histochemical investigations on succinic dehydrogenase in the central nervous system: I. The postnatal development of rat brain. *J. Neurochem.* 4:101, 1959.

73. Friede, R. L. A histochemical study of DPN-diaphorase in human white matter with some notes on myelination. *J. Neurochem.* 8:17, 1961.

74. Friede, R. L., and Magee, K. Alzheimer's disease: Presentation of a case with pathologic and enzymatic histochemical observations. *Neurology* 12:213, 1962.

75. Heller, I. H., and Elliott, K. A. C. Metabolism of normal brain and human gliomas in relation to cell type and density. *Canad. J. Biochem. & Physiol.* 33:395, 1955.

76. Hild, W., and Tasaki, I. Morphological and physiological properties of neurons and glial cells in tissue culture. *J. Neurophysiol.* 25:277, 1962.

77. Hollinger, D. M., and Rossiter, R. J. Chemical studies of peripheral nerve during Wallerian degeneration: β-glucuronidase. *Biochem. J.* 52:659, 1952.

78. HORSTMANN, E., and MEVES, H. Die Feinstruktur des Molekularen Rinden Graues und Ihre physiologische Bedeutung. *Ztschr. Zellforsch.* 49:569, 1959.

79. HYDÉN, H. Quantitative assay compounds in isolated fresh nerve cells and glial cells from control and stimulated animals. *Nature 184*:433, 1959.

80. KOENIG, H. An autoradiographic study of nucleic acid and protein turnover in the mammalian neuraxis. *J. Biophys. & Biochem. Cytol. 4*:785, 1958.

81. KOENIG, H. Incorporation of adenine-8-C-¹⁴ and orotic-6-C-¹⁴ acid into nucleic acids of the feline neuraxis. *Proc. Soc. Exper. Biol. & Med.* 97:255, 1958.

82. KOENIG, H. A radioisotopic study of nucleic acid and protein turnover in white matter of the mammalian neural axis. IV. *Prog. Neurobiol.*, ed. by S. Korey, New York, Hoeber, 1959.

83. KOENIG, H. Autoradiographic studies of deoxyribonucleic acid (DNA) turnover in the feline neuraxis. *J. Histochem.* 8:337, 1960.

84. KOENIG, H., BUNGE, M., and BUNGE, R. P. Nucleic acid and protein metabolism in white matter: Observations during experimental demyelination and remyelination; A histochemical and autoradiographic study of spinal cord of the adult rat. *A.M.A. Arch. Neurol.* 6:177, 1962.

85. KOREY, S. R., and ORCHEN, M. Relative respiration of neuronal and glial cells. *J. Neurochem.* 3:277, 1959.

86. LEHRER, G. M., and HIRSCH, H. E. Quoted by Robins, E., Fisher, K., and Lowe, I. P. Quantitative histochemical studies of the morphogenesis of the cerebellum: II. Two β-glycosidases. *J. Neurochem.* 8:96, 1961.

87. MOSSAKOWSKI, M. J. The activity of succinic dehydrogenase in glial tumors. *J. Neuropath. & Exper. Neurol.* 21:137, 1962.

88. NURNBERGER, J. I., and GORDON, M. W. "Cell Density of Neurotissue: Direct Counting Method and Possible Applications as a Biologic Referent," in *Progress in Neurobiology.* II. *The Ultrastructure and Cellular Chemistry of Neural Tissue*, ed. by Waelsch, H. New York, Hoeber-Harper, 1957, p. 100.

89. NURNBERGER, J. I. "Direct Enumeration of Cells of the Brain," in *Biology of Neuroglia*, ed. by Windle, W. F. Springfield, Ill., Charles C Thomas, 1958, p. 193.

90. OGAWA, K., and ZIMMERMAN, H. M. Activity of succinic dehydrogenase in the experimental ependymoma of C3H mice. *J. Histochem.* 1:342, 1959.

91. POPE, A. Quantitative distribution of dipeptidase and acetylcholine esterase in architectonic layers of rat cerebral cortex. *J. Neurophysiol.* 15:115, 1952.

92. POPE, A. Application of quantitative histochemical methods to the study of the nervous system. *J. Neuropath & Exper. Neurol.* 14:39, 1955.

93. POPE, A. "The Relationship of Neurochemistry to the Microscopic Anatomy of the Nervous System," in *Biochemistry of the Developing Nervous System*, ed. by Waelsch, H. New York, Academic Press, 1955, p. 341.

94. POPE, A., and HESS, H. H. "Cytochemistry of Neurone and Neuroglia," in *Metabolism of the Nervous System,* ed. by Richter, D. New York, Pergamon Press, 1957, p. 72.

95. POPE, A., HESS, H. H., WARE, J. R., and THOMSON, R. H. Intralaminar distribution of cytochrome oxidase and DPN in rat cerebral cortex. *J. Neurophysiol.* 19:259, 1956.

96. POPE, A., HESS, H. H., and ALLEN, J. N. "Quantitative Histochemistry of Proteolytic and Oxidative Enzymes in Human Cerebral Cortex and Brain Tumors," in *Progress in Neurobiology.* II. *Ultrastructure and Cellular Chemistry of Neural Tissue,* ed. by Waelsch, H. New York, Harper-Hoeber, 1957, pp. 182–191.

97. ROBINS, E., and SMITH, D. E. A quantitative histochemical study of eight enzymes of the cerebellar cortex and subadjacent white matter in the monkey. *Res. Publ. A. Nerv. & Ment. Dis.* 32:305, 1953.

98. RUBINSTEIN, L. J. KLATZO, I., and MIQUEL, J. Histochemical observations on oxidative enzyme activity of glial cells in a local brain injury. *J. Neuropath. & Exper. Neurol.* 21:116, 1962.

99. SCHIFFER, D., SIBOUR, F., and VESCO, C. Les calcifications dans les tumeurs cérébrales. *World Neurology* 2:1069, 1961.

100. SHARIFF, G. H. Cell counts in the primate cerebral cortex. *J. Comp. Neurol.* 98:381, 1953.

101. TASAKI, I., and CHANG, J. J. Electric response of glia cells in cat brain. *Science* 128:1209, 1958.

102. VICTOR, J., and WOLFF, A. Metabolism of brain tumors. *Res. Publ. A. Nerv. & Ment. Dis.* 16:44, 1937.

CHAPTER 2

RNA Metabolism in the Nervous System: Some RNA-dependent Functions of Neurons and Glia

SOME 20 YEARS HAVE PASSED SINCE CASPERSSON AND BRACHET INDE-pendently demonstrated the presence of RNA in the basophilic substance of cytoplasm ("ergastoplasm") and in nucleoli of diverse cell types. Their insightful proposal that RNA is concerned with protein synthesis has been amply confirmed. In this communication some results of histochemical studies will be briefly presented and an attempt made to correlate RNA of neuronal and nonneuronal elements with ongoing cell functions.

NEURONS

Somatochrome neurons are a classic example of RNA-rich cells. At the other extreme stand the karyochrome neurons with their scant cytoplasm, e.g., cerebellar granule cells. Both types of neurons display active incorporation of RNA precursors.[7] As elsewhere, nuclear RNA turns over more rapidly than cytoplasmic RNA. Radioactive adenine is lost slowly from cytoplasmic RNA; appreciable radio-

Supported by grant B-1456, Cl-C3, from the U.S. Public Health Service; contract AT(11-1)-89 from the Atomic Energy Commission; and grant 304 from the National Multiple Sclerosis Society.

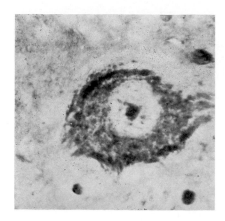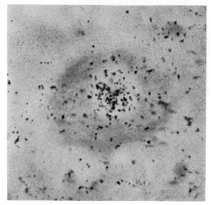

FIG. 3-1. Spinal motoneuron from cat given adenine-8-C¹⁴ by subarachnoidal injection 4 hours before sacrifice. Note concentration of silver grains over nucleus. A, thionin stain. B, radioautograph. ×670.

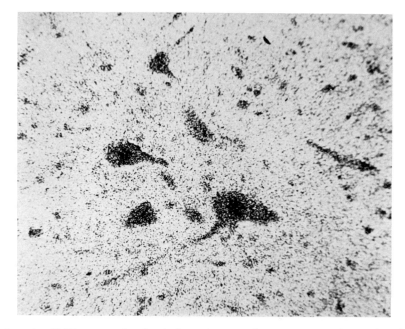

FIG. 3-2. Radioautograph of spinal gray matter from cat given glycine-2-H³ by subarachnoid injection 4 hours before sacrifice. Note blackening over neurons, glia, and neuropil. ×230.

activity is still present 50 days after administration (Fig. 3-1). Neurons do not incorporate precursors into DNA in adult animals.

This metabolically active RNA pool in neurons implies the presence of vigorous protein biosynthesis. Studies of amino acid uptake demonstrate this rather dramatically (Fig. 3-2).[7] Let us now consider some of the probable functions of protein synthesis in neurons.

Peripheral Flow of Axoplasm

Weiss and Hiscoe,[34] from studies of the morphological consequences of peripheral nerve compression, inferred that axoplasm migrates peripherally in normal adult neurons. They proposed a process of perpetual neuronal growth in which the perikaryon elaborates axoplasmic material that is transported distally to replace catabolized axoplasm. In studies performed several years ago, an apparent peripheral movement of axoplasm labeled with glycine-C^{14} and methionine-S^{35} was detected.[8] These amino acids were injected intrathecally to attain maximum incorporation into neuronal protein while suppressing uptake into Schwann cells of peripheral nerve. Ulnar or sciatic nerves were sectioned into centimeter lengths at several stages following injection, and the radioactivity of the crude protein fraction was determined (Fig. 3-3). Apparent flow rates of 2 to 11 mm per day were obtained. In control experiments, labeled protein accumulated proximal to a compressing clip and failed to pass beyond the clip.

Other workers, including Samuels *et al.*,[32] Waelsch and Lajtha,[33] Ochs and Burger,[26] and Friede,[3] have presented experimental data which give support to the concept of the distal movement of axoplasm. This would entail the daily elaboration of axoplasm several times greater in volume than that of the neuronal soma itself. A substantial quantity of protein would have to be synthesized for this purpose.

Respiratory Enzymes in Neurons

Neurons have a relatively high oxygen consumption, their principal, if not exclusive, energy substrate in vivo being glucose. Neurons contain ample quantities of respiratory enzymes, as has been shown by many workers[27,29,31,35] (Koenig and Barron, unpublished data). Thus, neurons and their dendritic processes are rich in DPNH and TPNH reductases; cytochrome oxidase; and succinic, malic, and lactic dehydrogenases (Fig. 3-4). Numerous other enzymes also are present in neurons. Curiously, glutamic and α-glycerophosphate

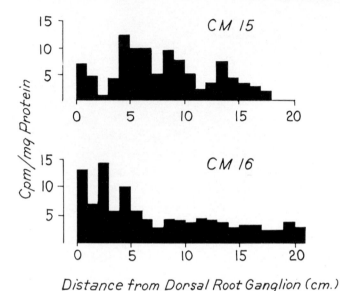

Distance from Dorsal Root Ganglion (cm.)

FIG. 3-3. Methionine-S[35] was injected into cisterna magna of cat 14 days (*CM 16*) and 28 days (*CM 15*) before sacrifice. Ulnar nerve was removed and cut into centimeter segments distal to C-8 and T-1 ganglia. Tissue samples were homogenized, extracted in cold dilute acid and lipid solvents, and resulting crude protein powder was plated for radioactivity measurements. Results are presented graphically. Apparent distal migration of several peaks of radioactive protein is evident, fastest moving at 7 mm. a day, slowest at about 3 mm. a day.

dehydrogenases appear to be lacking in nerve cells in formalin-fixed frozen section[17] (Fig. 3-12—Koenig and Barron, unpublished data).

Although there is no direct evidence at this time, it seems likely that neuronal enzymes turn over; i.e., they are consumed in normal usage and are replaced by the formation of new enzyme molecules. Turnover of total body cytochrome-C has been demonstrated recently in the rat.[24] The disposal of senescent, and the formation of new, enzyme-bearing organelles such as mitochondria and lysosomes prob-

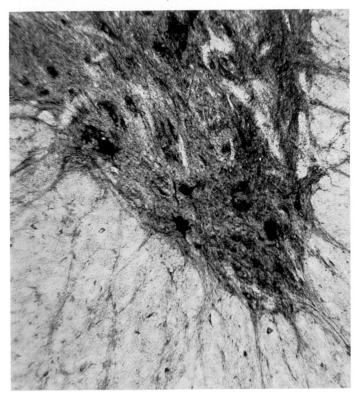

FIG. 3-4. Ventral gray column from cat spinal cord stained with nitro B tetra-zolium for TPN diaphorase. Formazan deposits are heavily concentrated in neurons, neuropil, and oligodendroglia. ×120.

ably are involved in enzyme turnover. Neuronal RNA would be expected to play a central role in the production of enzymes and organelles.

Some Effects of a Nucleic Acid Antimetabolite

Certain pyrimidine analogues inhibit the biosynthesis of RNA in the nervous system. These have been useful tools for studying the metabolic pathways and roles of RNA in the neural axis. Of these, 5-fluoroorotic acid (FO) has been most extensively investigated in our laboratory. This orotic acid analogue is converted to acid-soluble nucleotides and is incorporated into neuronal (and glial) RNA as 5-fluorouridylic acid.[14] Administered intrathecally, FO produces quite striking structural, functional, and metabolic alterations in neurons.[9,11,14] RNA concentration falls by 30 to 50 per cent in 7 to 10 days. The earliest change is a reduction in nucleolar RNA, followed by loss of cytoplasmic RNA. Neuronal recovery is signaled by a sharp increase in nucleolar RNA. A regeneration of cytoplasmic RNA occurs subsequently. The utilization of exogenous orotic acid is impaired by FO, but the mechanism is as yet unclear.[14]

These observations suggest that the synthesis of cytoplasmic RNA is in some way dependent upon nuclear (or nucleolar) function. Of particular relevance to our theme here is the dependence of protein synthesis on RNA. As cytoplasmic RNA diminishes, so protein synthesis declines, judging from the reduced uptake of labeled amino acids into neuronal protein. It is significant that physiological disturbances parallel the impairment in RNA and protein synthesis.[14] A loss of respiratory enzymes seems to occur in neurons and in neuropil after FO administration which may be caused by the disturbance in protein synthesis (Koenig and Barron, unpublished data).

GLIA

Glia make up about 90 per cent of the total cell population of the neural axis. Our interest in glia was aroused by the observation that white matter contains a substantial quantity of RNA which is metabolically active. Indeed, RNA in white matter incorporates labeled precursors as actively as RNA in gray matter.[7,10] Autoradiographic studies have shown that oligodendrocytes and Schwann cells are particularly active in this respect (Fig. 3-5). Astrocytes show relatively slight uptake of RNA precursors. Nonneuronal cells seem to turn over slowly; except for astrocytes, they incorporate DNA precursors.[7,10] DNA labeling is greatly enhanced in lesions accompanied by glial proliferation[12,20] (Koenig, unpublished data).

Glia do not appear to be particularly rich in RNA in formalin-fixed tissues stained by the ordinary Nissl methods. A modified method, therefore, was developed which involves the preliminary removal of chromophilic DNA by DNAse and oxidative deamination of basic proteins with nitrous acid to enhance the basophilia of RNA.[13] With this method, it was easy to demonstrate that oligodendrocytes possess substantial quantities of nucleolar, nucleoplasmic, and cytoplasmic RNA. Indeed, it can be computed from published data, as well as from our own, that the concentration of RNA in oligodendroglial cytoplasm exceeds that in large neurons by a factor of five or ten. Astrocytes, however, contain scant cytoplasmic RNA (Figs. 3-6 to 3-8). Schwann cells and satellite cells in sensory ganglia also

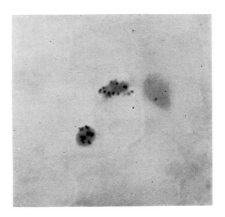

FIG. 3-5. Radioautograph of spinal white matter of cat given cytidine-H[3] by intracisternal injection 4 hours earlier. Note heavy blackening over the chromophilic nuclei of oligodendroglia and virtual absence of silver grains over large astrocytic nucleus. Chromalum-gallocyanin stain. ×700.

possess appreciable nuclear and cytoplasmic RNA (Figs. 3-9 and 3-10).

Oligodendrocytes display vigorous incorporation of labeled amino acids into protein (Figs. 3-2 and 3-18). Astrocytes are considerably less active in this regard, as would be anticipated from their sparse RNA content.

Respiratory Enzymes in Glia

Oligodendrocytes have a rather high oxygen consumption, but astrocytes apparently do not.[5,22] Other workers have noted the presence of oxidative enzymes in glia, Schwann cells, and perineuronal satellite cells.[3,4,27,29,35] Dr. K. D. Barron and I have studied a num-

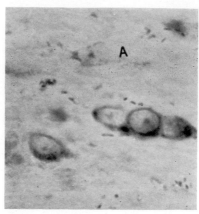

FIG. 3-6.   Cerebellar white matter of cat, stained for RNA. Nucleoli and peri-karya of oligodendroglia are well stained. Perikaryon of astrocyte (A) is barely stained. ×1,000.

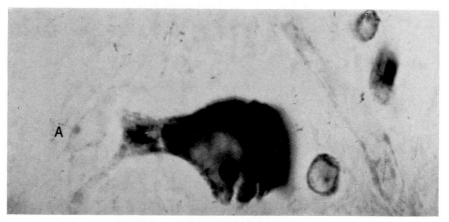

FIG. 3-7.   Spinal gray matter of cat, stained for RNA. Large satellite astrocyte (A) is nearly unstained, while oligodendroglia are strongly stained. ×1,000.

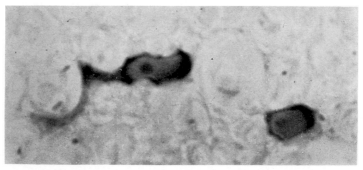

FIG. 3-8.   Oligodendroglia in spinal white matter of monkey, stained for RNA. One cell has conspicuous process which partly embraces large medullated axon. ×2,100.

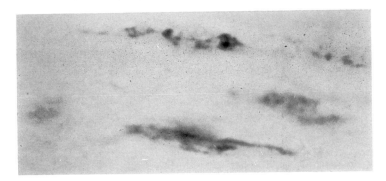

FIG. 3-9. Schwann cells in spinal nerve root of monkey, stained for RNA. ×2,100.

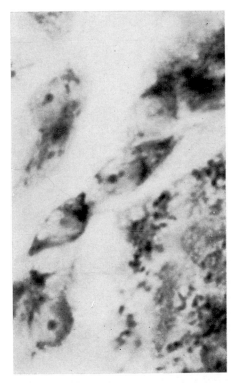

FIG. 3-10. Perineuronal satellite cells in dorsal root ganglion of cat, stained for RNA. ×2,100.

ber of oxidative enzymes in frozen sections of tissues fixed in cold calcium-formalin. We find that those enzymes which are present in neurons, namely DPN and TPN diaphorases, malic and lactic dehydrogenases, occur in oligodendrocytes, but seem to be essentially

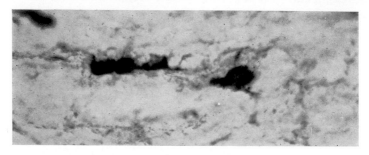

FIG. 3-11. Oligodendroglia in spinal white matter of cat, stained for DPN diaphorase. ×700.

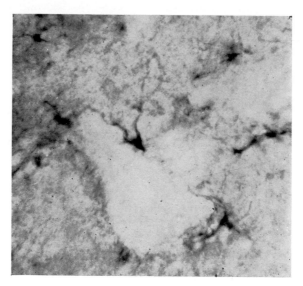

FIG. 3-12. Spinal gray matter of cat, stained for glutamic dehydrogenase. There are almost no formazan deposits in neuron, while perineuronal astrocytic processes are well stained. ×700.

absent from astrocytes[17,19] (Fig. 3-11). Astrocytes, however, give a moderately strong reaction for glutamic and α-glycerophosphate dehydrogenases (and also 5′-nucleotidase), whereas neurons and oligodendrocytes react weakly or not at all for these enzymes (Fig. 3-12).

The latter enzymes are particularly conspicuous in neuropil and surrounding blood vessels, where astrocytic cytoplasm is most abundant.[17,19] The presence of glutamic dehydrogenase in pericapillary astrocytic cytoplasm may serve to protect the brain from hematogenous ammonia by catalyzing the reaction of ammonia with α-ketoglutarate to form glutamate.

Oligodendrocytes thus resemble neurons in that they possess considerable RNA, display active incorporation of RNA and protein precursors, have a high QO_2, are rich in DPN and TPN diaphorases and malic and lactic dehydrogenases, and are deficient in glycerophosphate and glutamic dehydrogenases. Schwann and satellite cells seem to share some of these attributes. It has long been thought that oligodendrocytes and Schwann cells serve a "trophic" function in maintaining the structural and functional integrity of white matter and peripheral nerve. This trophic role may consist, in part, in the provision of respiratory, and other, enzymes to the conducting pathways which are remote from the enzyme-forming systems in neuronal perikarya.

Glia and Myelin Biosynthesis

The precursor cells of adult Schwann cells and oligodendroglia are responsible for the formation of myelin. This apparently is accomplished through the spiral wrapping of plasma membranes derived from these cells. These cells are well suited for this purpose. They possess considerably more cytoplasmic RNA, and display more active uptake of RNA and protein precursors, than their adult progeny[10] (Fig. 3-13). They also are richer in oxidative enzymes[3,27,35] (Barron and Koenig, unpublished data). It seems reasonable to suppose that RNA in these cells is concerned with the synthesis of plasma membrane and respiratory enzymes.

Reactive Gliosis

Reactive gliosis is seen in a wide assortment of experimental and spontaneous neural lesions. We have examined the glial reactions in several experimental lesions: cerebral injury after freezing; secondary degeneration of central myelin following cord transection; and the demyelination lesion produced by cerebrospinal fluid barbatage[17,19,20] (Koenig and Barron, in preparation). We also have had the opportunity to correlate enzymorphology and histochemistry of reacting glia in three cases of multiple sclerosis, one of diffuse sclerosis of Schilder, and one of amyotrophic lateral sclerosis[17,19] (Barron and Koenig, unpublished data). Oligodendroglia, rather than astrocytes, appear to be the glia which react by proliferation and

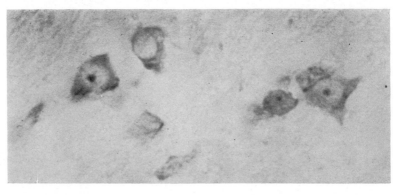

FIG. 3-13. Immature oligodendroglia in myelinating spinal white matter from 15-day-old-rat, stained for RNA. Voluminous perikarya contain much RNA. ×1,000.

enlargement. Oligodendroglia initially show uptake of DNA precursors in the lesion produced by cerebrospinal fluid barbotage,[20] ischemia,[12] and freezing injury (Koenig, unpublished data). Reacting oligodendroglia acquire increased complements of nucleolar and cytoplasmic RNA; show more intense reactions for respiratory enzymes already present; and give reactions for α-glycerophosphate and glutamic dehydrogenases, and for 5'-nucleotidase, enzymes normally found in astrocytes[17,19] (Koenig and Barron, unpublished data) (Figs. 3-14 to 3-16). Oligodendrocytes (and Schwann cells also) in the earlier stages of reaction closely resemble less mature forms in their morphological and metabolic characteristics. Like their counterpart in peripheral nerve, these reacting oligodendrocytes can re-form myelin in the adult neural axis.[1] In more chronic lesions, reacting glia elaborate "astroglial" scar tissue and concomitantly show a diminution

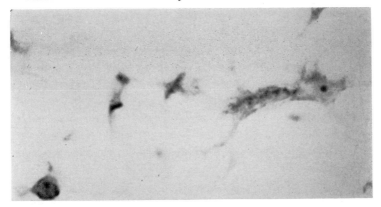

FIG. 3-14. Reacting glia in 14-day cerebrospinal fluid-exchange lesion stained for RNA. ×1,400.

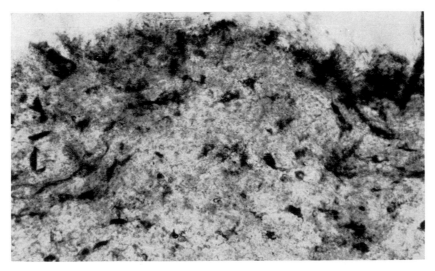

FIG. 3-15. Reacting glia in 9-day cerebrospinal fluid-exchange lesion stained for DPN diaphorase. ×200.

in RNA and oxidative enzymes. Schwann cells in transected nerve trunks show a similar increase in nucleolar and cytoplasmic RNA[25] and in oxidative enzymes[3] (Barron, personal communication). RNA in these cells probably is concerned with the synthesis of the proteins necessary for cell growth, the production of enzymes, the (re-) formation of myelin, and cicatrization. Hydén and Pigon[6] have

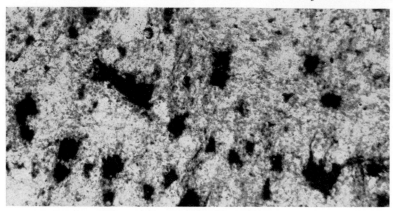

FIG. 3-16.   Reacting glia in cerebral white matter near margin of focus of demyelination from case of multiple sclerosis, stained for lactic dehydrogenase. ×200.

suggested that perineuronal glia supply respiratory enzymes to nerve cells.

Effects of a Nucleic Acid Antimetabolite

FO affects oligodendroglia and Schwann cells in much the same manner as its affects neurons. It inhibits the incorporation of exogenous orotic acid into RNA, brings about a depletion of RNA, and interferes with protein biosynthesis.[14] A spongy degeneration in white matter ensues.[11] This may be caused by the loss of respiratory enzymes that seems to occur in affected white matter (Koenig and Barron, unpublished data).

PHAGOCYTOSIS IN THE NEURAL AXIS

Neural phagocytes appear to derive from pial and perivascular cells; some may be derived from the blood stream.[21,23] These probably do not differ fundamentally from phagocytes in other organs. Their primary attribute appears to be the possession of numerous large cytoplasmic inclusions, lysosomes,[2] which are rich in acid phosphatase and other acid hydrolases. Lysosomes also contain acidic glycolipid

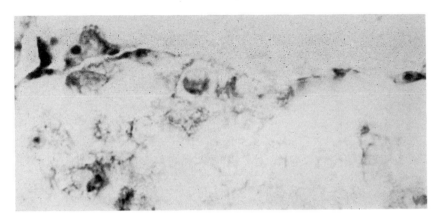

FIG. 3-17. Spinal cord of cat 3 days after cerebrospinal fluid-exchange. Hyperplasia, hypertrophy, and increased RNA content are evident in young phagocytes developing in pia mater. ×1,400.

FIG. 3-18. Radioautograph of cat spinal white matter containing zone of softening. Glycine-2-H³ injected subarachnoidally 4 hours before sacrifice. Note heavy blackening over gitter cells and over normal interfascicular oligodendroglia. ×120.

complexed with protein[15] and an autofluorescent substance.[16] As pial and adventitial elements undergo transformation to phagocytes, they display nucleolar hypertrophy, a net accumulation of cytoplasmic RNA, and increased uptake of RNA and protein precursors[20] (Figs. 3-17 and 3-18). These cells also show an increased content of DPN and TPN diaphorase and lactic and malic dehydrogenases (Barron and Koenig, unpublished data). Rubinstein and Smith[30] emphasize the TPN-linked enzymes in phagocytes. It seems likely that RNA in these cells participates in the biosynthesis of lysosomal constituents and respiratory enzymes.

SUMMARY

Active RNA and protein synthesis are attributes of nearly all cells in the neuraxis, although astrocytes are relatively sluggish in this regard. In neurons, these activities probably are concerned with the continuous formation of axoplasmic constituents and with the replacement of oxidative and other enzymes consumed in normal usage. In oligodendrocytes and Schwann cells, RNA is implicated in the formation of myelin, the synthesis of respiratory and other enzymes required for the maintenance of conducting tissues, and the biosynthetic activities which accompany reactive gliosis. In phagocytic cells, RNA may be involved in the synthesis of respiratory enzymes and in the formation of lysosomal constituents.

REFERENCES

1. BUNGE, M. B., BUNGE, R. P., and RIS, H. Ultrastructural study of remyelination in an experimental lesion in adult cat spinal cord. *J. Biophys. & Biochem. Cytol.* 10:67, 1961.

2. DUVE, C. DE. "Lysosomes: A New Group of Cytoplasmic Particles," in *Subcellular Particles,* ed. by Hayashi, T. New York, Ronald Press, 1959, p. 128.

3. FRIEDE, R. L. Transport of oxidative enzymes in nerve fibers: A histochemical investigation of the regenerative cycle in neurons. *Exper. Neurol.* 1:441, 1959.

4. FRIEDE, R. L. A histochemical study of DPN-diaphorase in human white matter with some notes on myelination. *J. Neurochem.* 8:17, 1961.

5. HELLER, I. J., and ELLIOTT, K. A. C. Metabolism of normal brain and human gliomas in relation to cell type and density. *Canad. J. Biochem. & Physiol. 33*:395, 1955.

6. HYDÉN, H., and PIGON, A. A cytophysiological study of the functional relationship between oligodendroglial cells and nerve cells of Deiters' nucleus. *J. Neurochem. 6*:57, 1960.

7. KOENIG, H. An autoradiographic study of nucleic acid and protein turnover in the mammalian neuraxis. *J. Biophys. & Biochem. Cytol. 4*:785, 1958.

8. KOENIG, H. Synthesis and peripheral flow of axoplasm. *Trans. Am. Neurol. Assn.*, 162, 1958.

9. KOENIG, H. Production of injury to feline central nervous system with nucleic acid antimetabolite. *Science 127*:1238, 1958.

10. KOENIG, H. "A Radioisotopic Study of Nucleic Acid and Protein Turnover in White Matter of the Mammalian Neural Axis," in *Progress in Neurobiology. IV. Biology of Myelin*, ed. by Korey, S. New York, Hoeber-Harper, 1959, p. 241.

11. KOENIG, H. Experimental myelopathy produced with a pyrimidine analogue. *AMA Arch. Neurol. 2*:463, 1960.

12. KOENIG, H. Autoradiographic studies of deoxyribonucleic acid (DNA) turnover in the feline neuraxis. *J. Histochem. & Cytochem. 8*:337, 1960.

13. KOENIG, H. Nucleic acid histochemistry of glia. *J. Histochem. & Cytochem. 9*:619, 1961.

14. KOENIG, H. "Some Effects of Nucleic Acid Antimetabolites on the Central Nervous System of the Cat." in *Response of the Nervous System to Ionizing Radiation*, ed. by Haley, T., and Snider, R. New York, Academic Press, 1962, p. 109.

15. KOENIG, H. Histological distribution of brain gangliosides: Lysosomes as glycolipoprotein granules. *Nature 195*:782, 1962.

16. KOENIG, H. The autofluorescence of lysosomes: Its value for the identification of lysosomal constituents. *J. Histochem. & Cytochem.* In press.

17. KOENIG, H., and BARRON, K. D. Morphologic and enzymic alterations of reacting glia in an experimental demyelinating lesion. *Anat. Rec. 142*:249, 1962.

18. KOENIG, H., and BARRON, K. D. Glycolipoprotein granules as lysosomes. *J. Histochem. & Cytochem. 10*:648, 1962.

19. KOENIG, H., and BARRON, K. D. Morphological and enzymic alterations in reacting glia. *Acta neurol. scandinav. 38* (Suppl. 1):72, 1962.

20. KOENIG, H., BUNGE, M. B. and BUNGE, R. P. Nucleic acid and protein metabolism in white matter: Observations during experimental demyelination and remyelination: A histochemical and autoradiographic study of spinal cord of the adult cat. *AMA Arch. Neurol. 6*:177, 1962.

21. KONIGSMARK, B. W., and SIDMAN, R. L. Origin of gitter cells in the mouse brain. *J. Neuropath. & Exper. Neurol.* In press.

22. KOREY, S. R., and ORCHEN, M. Relative respiration of neuronal and glial cells. *J. Neurochem.* 3:277, 1959.

23. KOSUNEN, T. U., and WAKSMAN, B. H. Radio-autographic studies of experimental allergic encephalomyelitis (EAE) in rats. *J. Neuropath. & Exper. Neurol.* In press.

24. McCONNELL, K. P., and DALLAM, R. D. Time-distribution examination of the *in vivo* incorporation of selenium into cytochrome-C of the rat and its turnover. *Nature* 193:746, 1962.

25. NOBACK, C. R. Metachromasia in the nervous system. *J. Neuropath. & Exper. Neurol.* 13:161, 1954.

26. OCHS, S., and BURGER, E. Movement of substance proximodistally in nerve axons as studied with spinal cord injections of radioactive phosphorus. *Am. J. Physiol.* 194:499, 1958.

27. POTANOS, J. N., WOLF, A., and COWEN, D. Cytochemical localization of oxidative enzymes in human nerve cells and neuroglia. *J. Neuropath. & Exper. Neurol.* 18:627, 1959.

28. ROBINS, E., and LOWE, I. P. Quantitative histochemical studies of the morphogenesis of the cerebellum: I. Total lipid and four enzymes. *J. Neurochem.* 8:81, 1961.

29. ROMANUL, F. C. A., and COHEN, R. B. A histochemical study of dehydrogenases in the central and peripheral nervous systems. *J. Neuropath. & Exper. Neurol.* 19:135, 1960.

30. RUBINSTEIN, L. J., and SMITH, B. Histochemistry: Triphosphopyridine nucleotide (TPN) diaphorase and TPN dependent dehydrogenase activity of reactive macrophages in tissue necrosis. *Nature* 193:895, 1962.

31. SAMORAJSKI, T. Application of diphosphopyridine nucleotide diaphorase methods in a study of dorsal ganglia and spinal cord. *J. Neurochem.* 5:349, 1960.

32. SAMUELS, A. J., BOYARSKY, L. L., GERARD, R. W., LIBET, R., and BRUST, M. Distribution, exchange and migration of phosphate compounds in the nervous system. *Am. J. Physiol.* 164:1, 1951.

33. WAELSCH, H., and LAJTHA, A. "Protein Metabolism of the Nervous System," in *Neurochemistry of Nucleotides and Amino Acids*, ed. by Brady, R. O., and Tower, D. B. New York, Wiley, 1960, p. 205.

34. WEISS, P., and HISCOE, H. B. Experiments on the mechanism of nerve growth. *J. Exper. Zool.* 107:315, 1946.

35. WOLFRAM, F., and ROSE, A. S. Histochemical demonstration of dehydrogenases in neuroglia. *Exper. Cell Res.* 17:526, 1959.

36. YONEZAWA, T., BORNSTEIN, M. B., and MURRAY, M. R. A histochemical study of oxidative enzymes in cultures of central nerve tissue. *J. Neuropath. & Exper. Neurol.* 20:280, 1961.

CHAPTER 4

MAYNARD M. COHEN and
J. FRANCIS HARTMANN

Biochemical and Ultrastructural Correlates of Cerebral Cortex Slices Metabolizing in Vitro

THE ULTIMATE INTENT OF NEUROLOGICAL RESEARCH IS THE DELINEATION of normal and pathological states of the nervous system in the living animal. Since this is often impossible with currently available chemical technology, in vitro techniques have been substituted and attempts then made to translate the findings into the living state. However, measurements of those biochemical phenomena which can be analyzed both in vivo and in vitro often have been inconsistent, making the translation difficult. Alterations in tissue structure follow in vitro incubation and conceivably could be related to such inconsistencies. The ultrastructure of many elements associated with specific biochemical functions may be assessed through the use of the electron microscope. Those elements so associated include mitochondria, which are concerned with oxidative phenomena and the coupling of oxidation to phosphorylation; the microsomes, related to protein synthesis and nucleic acid formation; the membranes and myelin, concerned with phospholipid metabolism; and the fluid compartments and membranes, related to ion and water exchange.

The requirements for maintenance of optimal phosphorylative

Supported by grants B-3364, H-5013, NB00782, and MH00388 from the National Institutes of Health, U.S. Public Health Service.

mechanisms in vitro are among the most stringent. In this investigation we have attempted to correlate ultrastructural alterations with the measurement of phosphorylative ability. Those biochemical parameters found most useful were the concentrations of phosphocreatine and adenosine triphosphate, and the incorporation of radioactive phosphorus into ATP and phosphoethanolamine. Incorporation of inorganic phosphate into lipid and nucleic acid phosphorus was also investigated but did not augment the information obtained.

MATERIALS AND METHODS

Chemical Studies

Saline Solutions

The basic solution employed contained the following concentrations: NaCl, 128 mM; KCl, 6.3 mM; $CaCl_2$, 2.7 mM; $MgSO_4$, 1.28 mM. The buffer utilized was trihydroxymethylaminomethane (Tris) 50 mM, and the pH of the solution was 7.4 unless otherwise indicated. The concentration of glucose, glutamic acid, or aspartic acid when utilized was 10 mM.

Tissues

Cortical slices were prepared from the brains of young mature rabbits weighing between 1 and 1½ kg. using a long razor blade and a recessed plate as a guide as described by McIlwain.[1] Three slices weighing up to 300 mg. each and measuring approximately 0.35 mm. in thickness were obtained from each cerebral hemisphere. The slices were trimmed with a scalpel, weighed, floated into the rapid-transfer holder of Heald and McIlwain,[2] and placed in a saline solution maintained at 37°C. within 20 minutes of sacrifice of the animal. Histological sections of brain were prepared to exclude the possibility of encephalitis or other cerebral diseases.

Clinical Studies

All slices were incubated in oxygenated saline for 5 minutes to allow reconstitution of labile phosphates. At the end of this period of equilibration each tissue slice was transferred in the holder into an appropriate fresh saline solution containing 0.2 ml. of a solution with 0.4 to 0.5 μc. of radioactive phosphorus. Three slices from one hemisphere were individually incubated in the presence of oxygen to serve as control for three slices from the second hemisphere incubated under the experimental conditions. Stirring was generally achieved by means of a stream of oxygen[2] except when anoxia was being studied; under these circumstances a stream of nitrogen was substituted.

In experiments testing residual damage the tissues were transferred into fresh media containing radioactive phosphorus after varying periods, as indicated in the text, and incubated further in the presence of oxygen for 15 minutes. At the conclusion of the incubation the tissues were washed twice for 10 seconds in oxygenated saline at 37°C. The tissue was then rapidly transferred to 5 ml. of ice-cold 5% perchloric acid (w/v) and homogenized in the cold.

Separation and quantitation of the acid-soluble phosphates were carried out by modifying the method of Lin and Cohen,[3] using small Dowex columns allowing processing extracts from 100 to 300 mg. of tissue. Separation of ribonucleic acid and lipid phosphate and all radioactivity analyses were carried out as described by Cohen.[4]

Radioactivity Units

Specific activity is defined as counts per minute per micromole of phosphorus in the compound studied. Relative specific activity (R.S.A.) is defined as the specific activity of the phosphate determined divided by the specific activity of the tissue inorganic phophorus or, in the case of ethanolamine phosphate, by its precursor, ATP phosphorus.

Radiophosphate was utilized in the form of sodium phosphate containing approximately 0.025 mg. of orthophosphate as a carrier and was obtained from the Radiochemical Division of Abbott Laboratories.

Calculations

The concentration and specific activities of the constituents studied varied somewhat between cortical slices at different levels as well as between different animals. To facilitate comparisons and offset these variations, the mean value was calculated of all control experiments (i.e., glucose as substrate, Tris buffer at pH 7.4, K^+ concentration of 6.3 mM, and adequate oxygenation). Experimental values were then corrected to reflect differences from this mean. In this manner comparisons could be made among all experiments despite variation among slices or individual animals.

Electron Microscopic Studies

All tissues for electron microscopic examination were fixed in buffered osmium tetroxide after incubation under conditions identical with those observed during the chemical experiments, and embedded in Epon. Sections were cut from each slice of brain thus prepared, and 30 to 150 representative electron micrographs were made. Throughout the morphological analysis of the tissue the different slices were identified only by numbers which gave no clue to the previous chemical treatment of the particular slice. Qualitative estimation of how the micrographs from each slice compared with those of normal rabbit cerebral cortex was made.

Each accompanying electron micrograph is considered to be representative of the ultrastructural features exhibited by the various photographs from a given slice.

RESULTS

Figure 4-1 is from a slice used as a control. It is to be stressed that this does not represent normal tissue ideally fixed but rather represents the ultrastructural appearance of tissue that was incubated under conditions considered optimal for chemical studies of brain and is used for comparison with tissues incubated under experimental conditions. The structural features to which particular attention was directed include the mitochondria in both neuronal and neuroglial processes; the cross-sectional area of astrocyte processes relative to normal; and the degree of disruption, if any, of the limiting membranes of such processes. In this slice, although some astrocyte processes

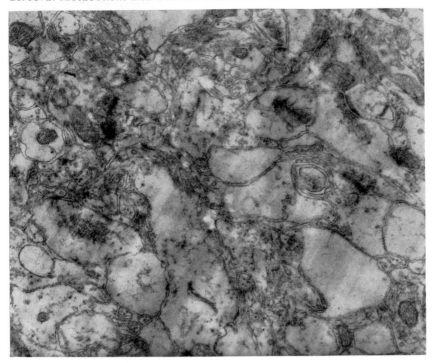

FIG. 4-1. Section from control slice, i.e., one incubated under conditions normally considered optimal for biochemical studies. Mitochondria and astrocyte processes compare favorably with tissue from normal rabbits. ×22,000.

appear swollen, their membranes are intact, and the mitochondria present in the field are normal in appearance.

Influence of Substrate

Role of Added Substrate

Adequate substrate is essential for metabolism of cerebral tissue both in vitro and in vivo. Glucose appears to be the sole substrate available to the brain from the general circulation, and no other material has been found which is superior to glucose or its products in the maintenance of in vitro metabolism of cerebral cortex.

Figure 4-2 is an electron micrograph of a slice of cerebral cortex incubated 30 minutes in saline solution in the absence of any added substrate. Even allowing for the fact that it represents a higher magnification than Figure 4-1, this micrograph shows swelling of

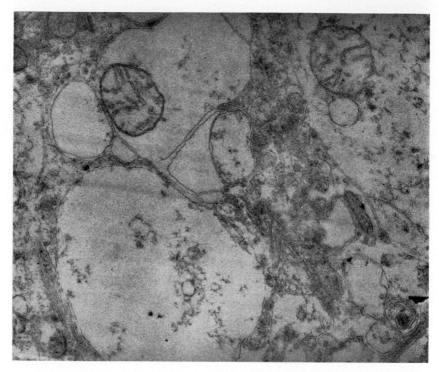

FIG. 4-2.   Section from slice incubated in presence of inadequate substrate. Large optically empty spaces are profiles of astrocyte processes, some of whose limiting membranes are ruptured. Severe swelling of mitochondria is also seen. ×21,000.

astrocyte processes and their contained mitochondria. There appears to be a rupture of the membrane bounding the swollen astrocyte process at the top of the figure. The vertically oriented, denser band of neuropil in the figure suggests that the astrocyte swelling has taken place at the expense of compression of neuronal or microglial processes.

Table 4-1 demonstrates the known need for an adequate substrate to maintain phosphorylation. When the cortical slice is incubated in

TABLE 4-1. Concentrations and Relative Specific Activities of Phosphates in Rabbit Cerebral Cortex Metabolizing in Vitro*

Substrate	K† concentration (mM)	Buffer	pH	Phosphocreatine	Inorganic phosphate	ATP	ATP/Pi	PEA/ATP
Glucose	6.3	Tris	7.4	1.60	2.09	0.80	0.97	0.09
None (1 hr.)	6.3	Tris	7.4	0.23†	8.00†	0.27†	0.81†	
None (1 hr.) then glucose (1 hr.)	6.3	Tris	7.4	1.22†	3.43	0.62†	1.30	0.05
Glutamate	6.3	Tris	7.4	0.37†	3.67†	0.50†	0.74†	0.02†
Aspartate	6.3	Tris	7.4	0.09†	8.40†	0.18†	0.80†	0.005†
Glucose (post anoxia)‡	6.3	Tris	7.4	0.55†	4.87†	0.30†	0.91	0.05†
Glucose	100	Tris	7.4	0.81†	2.80†	0.79	1.17	0.09
Glucose	6.3	NaHCO$_3$	8.9	1.07†	1.62†	0.36†	0.64†	0.08
Glucose	6.3	Glycylglycine	7.4	1.31†	2.16	0.72	0.66	0.03†
Glucose	6.3	Glycylglycine	6.4	0.65†	1.71	0.61†	0.37†	0.008†

* Incubation in rapid-transfer holders of Heald and McIlwain in media as described under "Materials and Methods."

† Difference from normal significant: <P = 0.01.

‡ Forty minutes of anoxia followed by incubation with P^{32} for 15 minutes in presence of oxygen.

the absence of exogenous substrate, concentrations of phosphocreatine and ATP are not maintained, and there is a concomitant rise in inorganic phosphate. The decrease in the R.S.A. of ATP indicates a deficiency in the capacity to incorporate phosphorus into ATP.

If the tissues are allowed to metabolize for 1 hour in the absence of substrate and then transferred to media containing adequate concentration of glucose, the residual damage can be measured (Table 4-1). Phosphocreatine and ATP cannot be resynthesized to concentrations comparable to those observed with glucose as substrate, and there is a compensatory rise in inorganic phosphate. The significance of the increased R.S.A. of ATP is difficult to assess; however, there is damage to phosphorylating ability as evidenced by the decreased R.S.A. of phosphoethanolamine.

The adverse effects of substrate lack on phosphorylating mechanisms may be correlated with the mitochondrial swelling. Rupture of the membranes may then be related to the subsequent swelling of the processes on a purely mechanical basis or, conversely, inadequate energy in the form of high-energy phosphate may result in failure of preservation of membranes with resultant swelling due to changes in fluid and ionic relation.

Influence of Glutamic and Aspartic Acids

Glutamic acid is unique among the amino acids in being able to support oxygen consumption of cerebral preparations in vitro at rates comparable to those obtained with glucose as substrate.

Despite the ability of glutamic acid to support oxygen consumption of cerebral slices in vitro, this substrate is inadequate in itself to maintain oxidative phosphorylation beyond levels supported by endogenous metabolism.[5] This is also evidenced in Table 4-1 by the lowered concentrations of phosphocreatine and ATP, the increased concentrations of inorganic phosphate, and the decreased incorporation of labeled phosphate into ATP and phosphoethanolamine.

Although the formation and maintenance of high-energy phosphates seems impaired, Figure 4-3 indicates the ultrastructure to be maintained better than in the absence of any exogenous substrate. At a magnification comparable to that of the previous micrograph, it shows ultrastructure that in terms of its state of apparent preservation is intermediate between Figures 4-1 and 4-2. That is to say, there is moderate swelling of mitochondria and of astrocyte processes as compared with the control slice, but structural integrity is better than that shown in Figure 4-2. Figure 4-4 is a micrograph of cortical

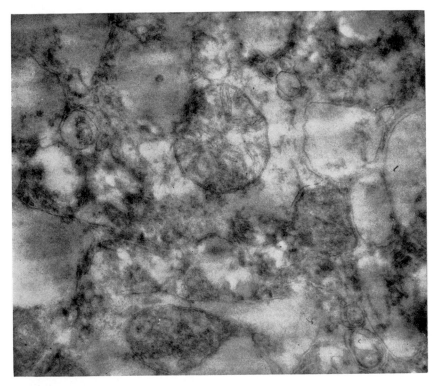

FIG. 4-3. Section from slice incubated with glutamate as substrate. Some mitochondrial swelling and some swelling of astrocyte processes is evident as compared with Figure 4-1, but preservation of structure is better than that shown in Figure 4-2. ×26,750.

tissue incubated with aspartic acid as substrate. Taken at a lower magnification than the previous micrograph, it shows more severe tissue damage. Swelling of astrocyte processes is greater, and there is more rupture of their limiting membranes, so that the section presents a somewhat lacy appearance. Some mitochondria are swollen, while others have approximately normal dimensions.

The more severe structural damage is reflected chemically in the inhibition of phosphorylation. ATP and phosphocreatine concentrations as well as the R.S.A. of ATP are below values obtained with endogenous substrate alone.

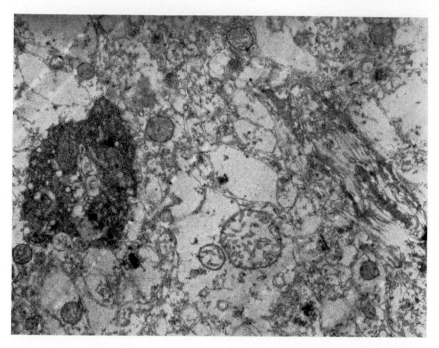

FIG. 4-4. Section from slice incubated in presence of aspartate. Rupture of most of limiting membranes of astrocyte processes gives this field a typically lacy appearance. ×17,750

Anoxia

The most noxious condition to which cerebral tissue can be exposed in vivo is anoxia. Table 4-1 indicates the severe damage to phosphorylating mechanism that results from 40 minutes of oxygen deprivation. When the cortical slices were returned to adequately oxygenated media at the end of the period, phosphocreatine and ATP could be resynthesized to slightly over one-third of the concentration obtained with adequate oxygenation. There is an accompanying diminution in labeling of phosphoethanolamine from ATP.

The electron microscopic findings were consistent with the degree of damage to chemical mechanisms. Figure 4-5 shows accentuation of the changes noted in the previous micrograph. Rupture of astrocyte membranes is more widespread, and the greatly swollen mitochondrion

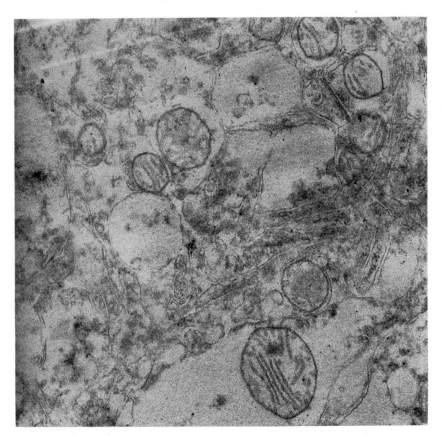

FIG. 4-5. Section from slice incubated under conditions of anoxia. Mitochondrial swelling is severe, and some of these organelles have fewer cristae than normal. As in Figure 4-4, most astrocyte limiting membranes have ruptured. ×28,200.

in the lower right part of the figure is typical of the mitochondrial alteration seen throughout this particular slice.

Influence of Potassium Ion Concentration

When cerebral cortex preparations respire in vitro, the oxygen consumption approximates half that calculated from in vivo studies.

By increasing potassium ion concentrations or by the application of electrical pulses in vitro, the oxygen consumption of cortex slices may be increased to match in vivo values. Phosphorylation does not keep pace with the increased oxygen consumption, as demonstrated in Table 4-1. Phosphocreatine concentration markedly decreases while

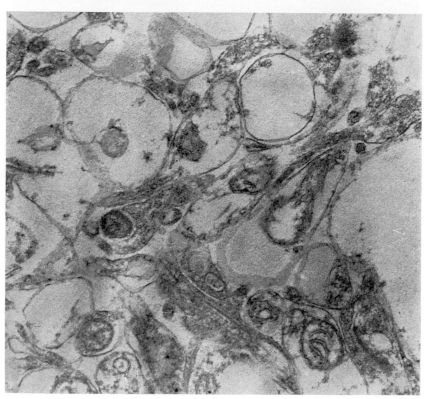

FIG. 4-6. Section from slice incubated in 100 mM potassium, showing severe damage and type of membrane alteration not encountered in other experiments. Near top of figure especially, astrocyte membranes are broad and pale, as if undergoing a sort of lysis. ×33,200.

that of inorganic phosphate rises. That phosphorylation does not appear seriously impaired is evidenced by maintenance of the R.S.A. of ATP and phosphoethanolamine.

There appeared to be a disproportion between the mild alteration in phosphorylating mechanisms and the more severe ultrastructural damage. Figure 4-6 shows still greater mitochondrial and astrocyte

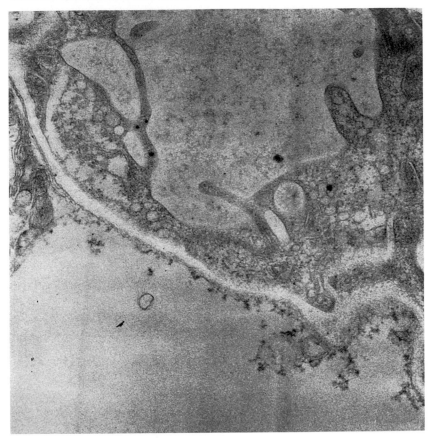

FIG. 4-7. Section through part of capillary from slice incubated with 100 mM potassium. Capillary lumen at top, swollen and optically empty astrocyte process at lower part of figure. Capillary basement membrane, normally of about same density as endothelium, here appears as negative image traversing field from upper left to lower right. ×26,750.

swelling, with a type of membrane alteration not seen in other brain slices. The membranes of the astrocyte processes show a thickening and a diminution of electron density that suggest the possibility that some sort of lytic process is going on. In all sections taken from this slice of cortex, the capillary basement membranes also show a significant loss of electron density, but without clear evidence of swelling (Fig. 4-7).

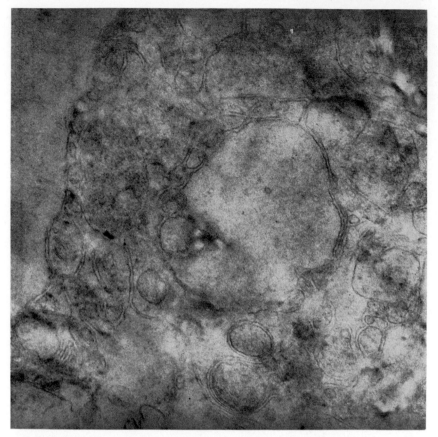

FIG. 4-8.   Section from slice incubated with bicarbonate buffer, pH 8.4. Although over-all background density has here lowered contrast and therefore apparent sharpness of image, structural preservation of elements of neuropil compares favorably with that of control slice. ×38,000.

Influence of pH and Incubation Buffer

The effect of varying buffers and pH is also demonstrated in Table 4-1. Tris at pH 7.4 permits maintenance of higher concentration of phosphocreatine and a greater degree of labeling of ATP and phosphoethanolamine than does glycylglycine. When glycylglycine is employed with an acid pH of 6.4, there is even greater derangement of phosphorylative ability. With a bicarbonate buffer at an alkaline pH, there is also decreased ability to resynthesize phosphocreatine and maintain ATP concentrations.

Figure 4-8 shows the electron microscopic appearance of a cortical slice incubated in a bicarbonate buffer at pH 8.4. The field shown is

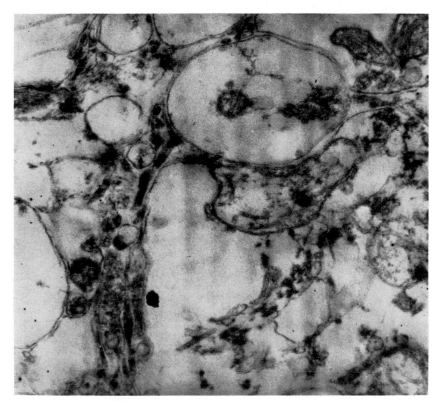

FIG. 4-9. Section from slice incubated with glycylglycine buffer, pH 6.4. Swelling of astrocyte processes is pronounced as compared with Figure 4-8, and there has been considerable rupture of astrocyte membranes. ×33,000.

dominated by a centrally placed swollen astrocyte process. Other tissue components in this figure compare favorably in appearance with the control slice.

An electron micrograph of a cortical slice incubated in glycylglycine at pH 6.4 (Fig. 4-9) shows tissue damage comparable to that seen in Figure 4-2 (absence of added substrate). Astrocyte swelling is more pronounced than in Figure 4-8, and rupture of astrocyte membranes is evident in places.

A micrograph prepared from a cortical slice incubated in glycylglycine at pH 7.4 contained a nerve cell which exhibited structural abnormality. There was considerable clumping of nucleoplasm, although the double nuclear membrane was reasonably well preserved. The profiles of the endoplasmic reticulum were very much swollen but retained their complement of RNP particles. The markedly swollen mitochondria in this nerve cell contrast sharply with normal appearing mitochondria in the adjacent neuropil. Throughout this slice, the neuropil appeared very well preserved, except for some increase in width of the intercellular space.

The most severe structural damage in experiments varying buffers and pH thus occurred at pH 6.4 with a glycylglycine buffer, consistent with the most extensive damage to phosphorylating mechanism. Although a moderate interference with phosphorylative ability is related to incubation in media buffered to pH 8.9 with bicarbonate, the ultrastructural changes were mild.

Discussion

Since the energy supplied through the medium of energy-rich phosphates is considered a requisite for maintenance of structural integrity, it would be anticipated that interference with phosphorylative processes would be associated with structural damage. It might also be expected that damage to mitochondria, which are concerned with these oxidative phosphorylations, might further impair phosphorylative ability. In general, wherever phosphorylative capacity was damaged the accompanying tissue damage could be correlated with the degree of metabolic deficiency. This was particularly true of experiments in the absence of added substrate or with the addition of aspartate with anoxia and with excessive acidity. Observations in those circumstances where the parallelism between labeling of high-energy phosphate and ultrastructure was not so precise may be of interest.

When glutamate was present as the sole added oxidizable substrate, phosphorylation was markedly inhibited. However, ultrastructural changes were mild. It has already been noted that oxygen consumption proceeds briskly despite the lack of phosphorylation. The preservation of ultrastructure conceivably may indicate that glutamic acid oxidation is related to sufficient energy formation not related to formation of ATP or phosphocreatine to maintain structure. However, there is as yet no evidence to substantiate this possibility.

Conversely, severe ultrastructural changes accompanied the mild inhibition of phosphorylation associated with increased concentrations of potassium ions. This suggests that high-energy phosphates are not available or could not be effectively employed in the maintenance of structural integrity.

SUMMARY

1. Slices of rabbit cerebral cortex were incubated under varying experimental conditions, and ultrastructural and chemical analyses of this material were carried out.

2. In the absence of exogenous substrate, severe ultrastructural damage occurred. This involved principally swelling of astrocyte processes and mitochondria, with rupture of plasma membranes.

3. With glutamate as substrate, ultrastructure was preserved nearly as well as when glucose was used as substrate. Aspartate was not as effective in maintaining ultrastructure during incubation.

4. Of the various conditions investigated, anoxia was accompanied by the most severe ultrastructural damage.

5. Optimal preservation of tissue structure was found when Tris buffer was employed at pH 7.4. Use of glycylglycine at pH 7.4 and 6.4, as well as bicarbonate at pH 8.4, was accompanied by more extensive ultrastructural damage in each case.

6. In general, an impairment of phosphorylative capacity was present in all cases in which ultrastructural damage was encountered.

7. Exceptions to the above were found in the case of glutamate, where structure seemed well preserved but phosphorylation was depressed, and in the case of increased concentration of potassium ions, where the converse was observed.

8. Any chemical study in which substrate is withheld during active metabolism prior to initiation of experimental conditions bears scrutiny

on the basis of evidence here presented that both metabolism and ultrastructure suffer during this interval.

REFERENCES

1. McIlwain, H. Metabolic response *in vitro* to electrical stimulation of sections of mammalian brain. *Biochem. J.* 49:382, 1951.

2. Heald, P. J., and McIlwain, H. Techniques in tissue metabolism: 4. Apparatus for maintaining and rapidly transferring tissue sections. *Biochem. J.* 63:231, 1956.

3. Lin, S., and Cohen, H. P. Effects of scorbutus and pentobarbital on the in vivo levels of "energy rich" phosphates and their turnover in guinea pig cerebral tissue. *Arch. Biochem.* 88:256, 1960.

4. Cohen, M. M. Effects of anoxia on the chemistry and morphology of cerebral cortex slices *in vitro*. *J. Neurochem.* 9:337, 1962.

5. Cohen, M. M. Cohen, H. P., and Chain, E. B. Effect of glutamic acids on phosphorylative activity in cerebral tissue *in vitro*. *Acta neurol. Scandinav.* 38 (Suppl. 1):12, 1962.

THEODOR WANKO and_____
DONALD B. TOWER

CHAPTER

5

Combined Morphological and Biochemical Studies of Incubated Slices of Cerebral Cortex

CORRELATIONS BETWEEN THE BIOCHEMICAL BEHAVIOR OF SLICES OF cerebral cortex incubated in vitro and their morphological characteristics as seen by electron microscopy are under investigation in our laboratory. Initially the study has been concerned with fluid spaces and electrolyte metabolism because of various problems posed by fluid distribution in incubated brain slices and the possibility that some aspects of fluid shifts therein would be discernible in electron micrographs. Our interest was stimulated by the observation[1] of a significantly smaller nonchloride and nonsucrose fluid space in slices of cerebral cortex incubated in the presence of 10 mM of NH_4Cl compared with control slices incubated in its absence. These experiments have been repeated, and electron micrographs of slices fixed after incubation have been examined to determine whether such changes measured chemically could be visualized morphologically. Representative findings are discussed here, together with general comments on the morphological features of incubated cerebral cortex slices examined in this manner.

MATERIALS AND METHODS

Normal adult cat brains excised after crush decapitation were used throughout. Slices of cerebral cortex were cut without moistening in a humid chamber at a thickness of 0.45 to 0.5 mm. with a Stadie-Riggs type of microtome. Initial weight of slices ranged from 50 to 150 mg., the smaller being used for electron microscopy and the larger for chemical analyses. Care was taken to obtain as nearly identical slices from homologous cortical areas for each set of control and ammonia-treated samples. Most chemical analyses were carried out on pairs of slices, consisting of a pial, or "first," slice and subpial, or "second," slice, in order to include the entire thickness of cortex in each sample. Since second slices are subject to more distortion during slicing, only pial, or first, slices, having a single cut surface, were used for electron microscopy in order to minimize this source of artifact. Special experiments comparing fluid spaces (chloride and sucrose) of first versus second slices indicated that the chemically demonstrable changes associated with the presence of 10 mM of NH_4Cl in the incubation medium were similar in both.

After weighing, the slices were placed in Warburg vessels containing a bicarbonate-saline(with 3 mM K^+)-glucose medium, gassed with 95% O_2 and 5% CO_2, and equilibrated at 37°C. for 5 minutes. The side-bulb contents of the vessels were then tipped in; initial, or zero-time, samples were removed and processed at this point; and the remaining samples were incubated at 37°C. for 1 hour. Vessel side bulbs contained bicarbonate-saline-glucose medium with sufficient extra K^+ to bring the final vessel K^+ concentration to 27 mM, and where NH_4Cl was to be added, sufficient NH_4Cl dissolved in the same medium to bring the final vessel NH_4^+ concentration to 10 mM. Where sucrose spaces were to be determined, 29 mM of sucrose (1%) was present in the incubation media. Details of the methods of preparation, incubation, and analyses of slices for the electrolytes and fluid spaces have been reported elsewhere.[2] The time interval from sacrifice of the animal to the start of incubation averaged 40 ($\pm$5) minutes.

Slices to be fixed for electron microscopy were incubated in specially modified Warburg vessels described by McKhann and Tower.[3] The principal modification is a large port on the side of the vessel sealable with a removable rubber and aluminum cap assembly. Fixation was carried out directly in the vessel and the side port opened to permit floatation of the fixed slices out into rinsing and dehydrating solutions without any direct handling of the specimens. In this way, handling artifacts of the friable slices at this stage were minimized.

Fixation was accomplished by addition to the vessel contents of an equal volume of the same bicarbonate-saline(with 27 mM K$^+$)-glucose medium (pH 7.4) containing 2% osmium tetroxide, to yield a final osmium concentration on mixing of 1%. Fixation time was 30 minutes at room temperature, after which the fixed slices were floated out of the vessels, rinsed, and rapidly dehydrated in increasing concentrations of ethanol. The specimens, divided into small blocks, were then embedded in either one of the following embedding media: (1) a 9:1 mixture of butyl and methyl methacrylate with 0.075% uranyl nitrate introduced as a filler[4] and with 0.25% of the initiator, benzoylperoxide, added prior to prepolymerization; or (2) Araldite epoxy resin, as supplied by the New York Society for Electron Microscopy. Sections were cut with either an LKB or a Servall-Porter-Blum ultramicrotome, transferred to collodion carbon-filmed grids, and examined with an RCA EMU-3C electron microscope. Observations were recorded at magnifications from 3,000 to 8,000 and photographically enlarged three to five times. (For reproduction purposes the original illustrations are reduced 20%.)

Three series of control slices and slices incubated with 10 mM of NH$_4$Cl have been run, the first embedded in methacrylate and the latter two in both methacrylate and epoxy resins. In each case, the samples were identified only by a code number, so that the microscopist was unaware which were controls and which were ammonia-treated. No significant differences attributable to the type of embedding resin employed were apparent. Additional control sections of cat cerebral cortex fixed *in situ* with the same fixative, and of freshly cut unincubated slices similarly fixed, have been examined for comparison with the incubated slice specimens.

RESULTS AND DISCUSSION

The various effects on oxidative, glycolytic, and amino acid metabolism and on electrolyte distribution observed in cerebral cortex when incubated with 10 mM of NH$_4$Cl have been considered in detail elsewhere[1,5,6] and will not be discussed here. The situation with respect to fluid spaces and distribution in control and ammonia-treated slices is summarized in Table 5-1. The significance of the changes of

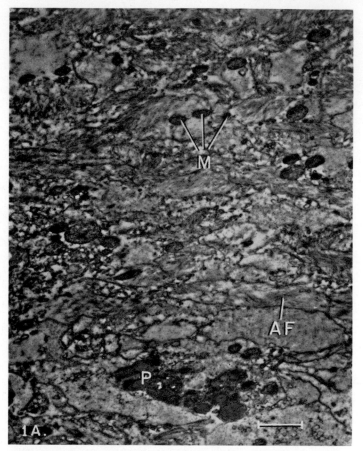

FIG. 5-1. Over-all views of fields of cell processes. Sections fixed in 1% (final concentration) osmium tetroxide and embedded in methacrylate, as detailed in the text. Calibration bars represent 1 μ. *A,* control slice. Note relatively uniform density with absence of pale, empty spaces. Astrocyte filaments (*AF*) are prominent. Pigment granules (*P*) and well-preserved mitochondria (*M*) are numerous. ×11,000.

fluid distribution between the initial slices (immersed briefly in incubation medium but not incubated) and those incubated for 1 hour is not at present clear. Presumably, the redistributions of fluid reflect restoration of optimal in vitro energy production, as indicated by expulsion of excess Na$^+$, reconcentration of lost K$^+$, and restoration of free amino acid levels (glutamic acid and glutamine) demonstrable

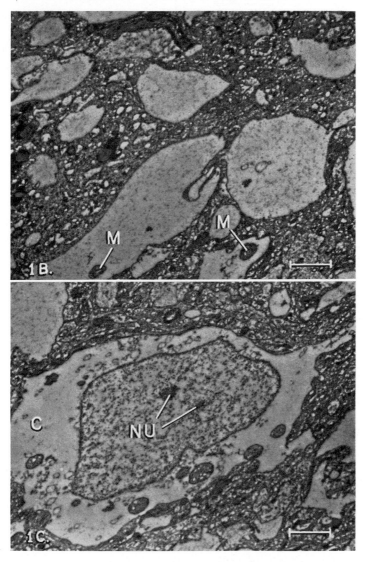

FIG. 5-1 (*Continued*). *B*, ammonia-treated slice. Note lack of uniformity of field, prominence of pale, empty or swollen processes and apparent increased compactness of other elements between these processes. Compared with *A*, mitochondria (*M*) appear less well preserved. ×10,000. *C*, similar view to *B*, showing a glial cell nucleus (astrocyte) with two nucleoli (*NU*) and pale, swollen perikaryal cytoplasm (*C*). ×10,000.

in cat cerebral cortex slices under these same conditions.[2] Such changes are attributable to disturbances of normal metabolic relations within slice cells concomitant with hypoxic conditions during brain excision and slice preparation, and their reversal on institution of optimal in vitro incubation conditions. Whatever the basis for fluid shifts in slices under the foregoing circumstances may be, it is obvious from the data in Table 5-1 that the presence of 10 mM of NH_4Cl in the incubation medium significantly alters the fluid distribution from that found in control slices after incubation for 1 hour. The nonchloride and nonsucrose space of neurons is smaller, and the total chloride and sucrose space is larger, in the presence of 10 mM of NH_4Cl.

Electron micrographs of osmium-fixed slices, which had been incubated under identical conditions, are illustrated in the accompanying figures. These figures are a representative selection of the large total number available and have been chosen as reasonably representative of the total examined. It is important to note that both the control and ammonia-treated slices exhibit many morphological characteristics in common and that differences between the two sets of samples are often a matter of degree rather than absolute. Nevertheless, the differences were so consistent, reproducible, and characteristic that they are considered to be valid and significant.

Figure 5-1 illustrates under low-power magnification typical over-all views of fields consisting primarily of cell processes in control (A) and ammonia-treated (B and C) slice sections. The control slice section exhibits a fairly uniform over-all density with few empty spaces and with prominent astrocyte filaments. Pigment granules and well-preserved mitochondria are readily discerned and occupy, together with the filamentous material, the whole of the intracellular compartment. In contrast the sections of an ammonia-treated slice are less uniform, with numerous large empty spaces and a suggestion of greater compactness of the cell processes adjoining such spaces, compared with analogous elements in the control section. No astrocyte filaments are visible, and the mitochondria seem less well preserved. The identity of the empty spaces may be deduced from Figure 5-1C, showing an astrocyte nucleus and its perikaryal cytoplasm, which is similar in appearance to the empty processes seen elsewhere in these sections. The evidence permitting the identification of these cells as astrocytes is discussed in connection with succeeding figures. The presence of two nucleoli, visible in the cell nucleus shown in Figure 5-1C, and the absence of any prominent endoplasmic reticulum in the cytoplasm indicate that this is a glial cell.

Figure 5-2 illustrates capillaries surrounded by glial processes in a control slice section (A) and in a section from an ammonia-treated slice (B). The capillaries are identifiable by the prominent basement membrane enclosing the lumina and the mural pericytes. The control section shows some of the large, pale or empty processes characteristic of the ammonia-treated slice sections and emphasizes the observation mentioned earlier—that the differences between the two types of samples are a matter of degree. From a comparison of Figure 5-2A and B, it may be appreciated that the elements surrounding the capillary in the latter (ammonia-treated) are less compact and seem to be more swollen. For example, the small vesicular profiles in the control section exhibit in general smaller lumina. The identity of the cell of origin for the pale, pericapillary glial processes is indicated in Figure 5-2B by clearly distinguishable fragments of astrocyte filaments persisting in the vicinity of the capillary basement membrane.

Details at higher magnification of astrocyte perikarya are shown from a control slice section in Figure 5-3A and from a section of an ammonia-treated slice in Figure 5-3B. In the former, typical cytoplasmic filaments are abundant around the cell nucleus and in peripheral processes. None are distinguishable in the swollen astrocyte (B), and it may be surmised that in the course of swelling the filaments fragment into the scattered fine granular debris visible in the pale cytoplasm and processes.

For contrast, Figure 5-4 illustrates a typical oligodendroglial nucleus and cytoplasm and part of a microglial cell seen in the same ammonia-treated slice sections from which Figure 5-3B was obtained. The denser nucleoplasm and less extensive cytoplasm filled with mitochondria and endoplasmic reticulum are clearly consistent with the identification of the cell illustrated as oligodendroglial.

From these typical and representative sections we conclude, in agreement with earlier reports by Farquhar and Hartmann,[9] De Robertis and associates,[10] and others, that the pale swollen glia in these preparations are undoubtedly astrocytes. Luse[11] has disagreed and favors identification of these cells as oligodendroglia. On the

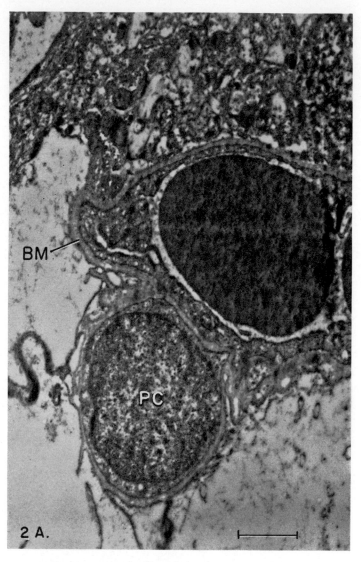

FIG. 5-2. Capillaries and surrounding glial processes. Fixation and embedding conditions and calibrations same as for Figure 5-1. *A*, control slice. Capillary with prominent basement membrane (*BM*) and pericyte (*PC*) in a field of glial processes. Note presence of some pale, swollen processes in one-half of field and denser, uniform glial elements elsewhere. ×15,000.

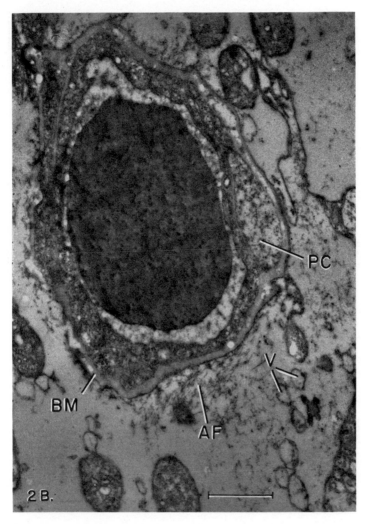

FIG. 5-2 (*Continued*). *B*, ammonia-treated slice. Capillary with basement membrane (*BM*) and pericyte (*PC*) in field of pale, swollen glial processes. Compare sizes of vesicular profiles (*V*) within these processes with those in control section. Note remnants of astrocyte filaments (*AF*) in glial process adjacent to portion of capillary basement membrane. ×17,000.

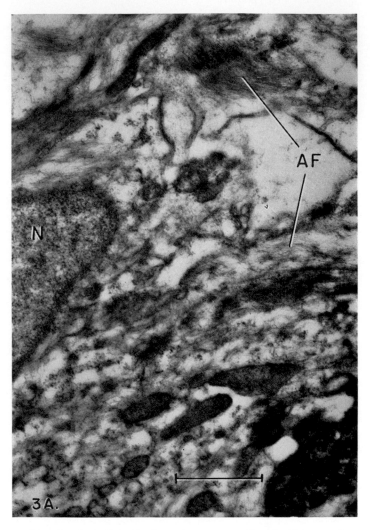

FIG. 5-3. Details of astrocyte perikarya. Fixation and embedding conditions and calibrations same as for Figure 5-1. A, control slice. Cell nucleus (*N*) and prominent cytoplasmic filaments (*AF*) are illustrated. Well-preserved mitochondria are present. ×22,000.

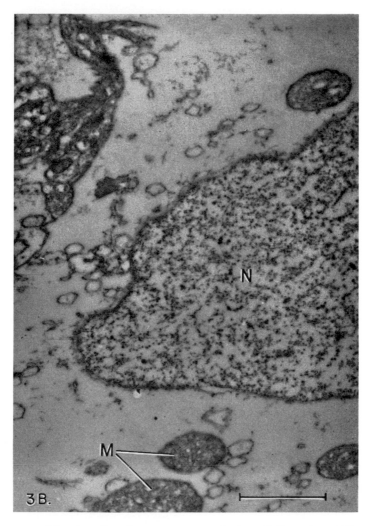

FIG. 5-3. (*Continued*). *B,* ammonia-treated slice. Cell nucleus (*N*) is surrounded by pale, swollen cytoplasm with poorly preserved mitochondria (*M*) and no identifiable filaments. ×22,000.

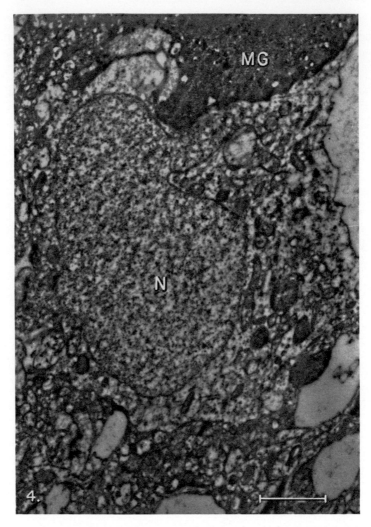

FIG. 5-4. Ammonia-treated slice. View from same section as Figure 5-3*B*, showing nucleus (*N*) and perikaryal cytoplasm of oligodendroglial cell. Note denser appearance of cytoplasm with presence of mitochondria and endoplasmic reticulum. Dark cell (*MG*) at margin of field is typically appearing microglial cell. ×17,000.

basis of criteria originally detailed by Farquhar and Hartmann[9] and of the morphological characteristics of these cells illustrated in the present study, we are unable to support the conclusions reached by Luse.[11] Furthermore, recent unpublished studies by Pomerat[12] on tissue cultures of cerebral glia also indicate that the glial cell which exhibits swelling analogous to that discussed here is the astrocyte.

Figure 5-5A and *B* illustrates at high magnification morphological details of neuronal cytoplasm in sections from control and ammonia-treated slices, respectively. Again, there is some similarity in general characteristics between the two, but the differences are still evident and typical. The control section exhibits a dense and quite regularly ordered endoplasmic reticulum interrupted in some places by swollen endoplasmic reticulum lumina. On the other hand, the section from an ammonia-treated slice shows a less regularly organized endoplasmic reticulum with a greater number of swollen lumina, so that when many such fields are scanned, the neurons present a Swiss-cheese appearance. These changes are not regarded as autolytic because they occur within well-defined intracytoplasmic membranes. Other cytoplasmic elements, such as mitochondria, pigment granules, and nuclei, appear relatively normal in sections from both types of samples.

The identification of these intracytoplasmic spaces as swollen lumina of endoplasmic reticulum is based on fields such as that illustrated in Figure 5-6, where the luminal membranes still encrusted with ribosomal granules are clearly distinguishable. This characteristic of incubated slices raises an interesting question about the nature of the luminal fluid and the finely granular elements discernible therein. Is this fluid extracellular and hence measurable as part of the chloride and sucrose spaces, or is it intracellular fluid abnormally loculated? Several investigators have concluded that the lumina of the endoplasmic reticulum communicate, at least intermittently, with fluid external to the cytoplasmic membrane,[13,14] so that according to their view the luminal fluid would be extracellular. Recent studies by Birks[15] suggest that swelling of endoplasmic reticulum lumina may indeed represent excess uptake of extracellular fluid into these spaces, but our own studies do not permit a decision for or against this possibility at present.

The last two figures illustrate two other general features of the morphology of incubated slice sections, namely, synaptic vesicles

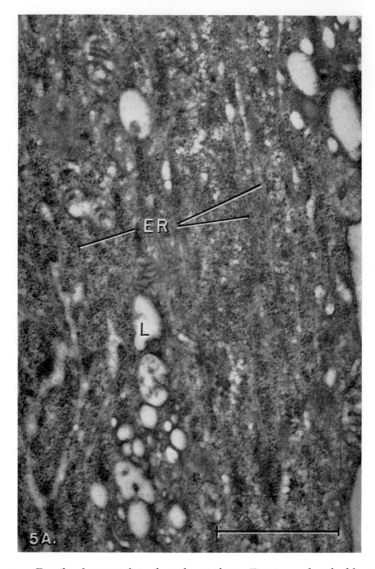

FIG. 5-5. Details of neuronal perikaryal cytoplasm. Fixation and embedding conditions and calibrations same as for Figure 5-1. A, control slice. Note dense, regularly ordered endoplasmic reticulum (*ER*), interrupted by some swollen endoplasmic reticulum lumina (*L*). ×32,000.

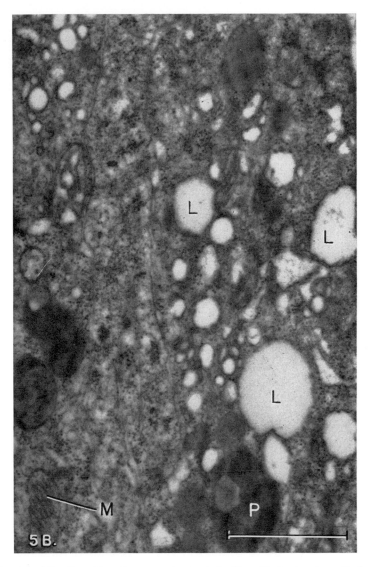

FIG. 5-5 (*Continued*). *B*, ammonia-treated slice. Endoplasmic reticulum is disorganized and interspersed with numerous swollen lumina (*L*). Mitochondria (*M*) and pigment granules (*P*) appear normal. ×32,000.

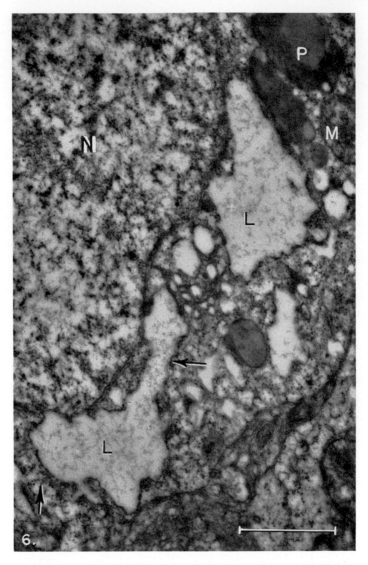

FIG. 5-6. Ammonia-treated slice. Detail, from same section as Figure 5-5*B*, of swollen endoplasmic reticulum lumina (*L*), showing luminal membranes encrusted with ribosomal granules (at arrows). Details of mitochondria (*M*), pigment granules (*P*), and neuronal nucleus (*N*) are well shown. ×25,000.

(Fig. 5-7) and myelin sheaths (Fig. 5-8). These structures were seen in comparable states of preservation in sections from both types of samples. Since the morphological appearance of these two structures is often indicative of the state of preservation of the tissue sample, the normal appearance of synaptic regions and of myelin lamellae suggests that the experimental and fixation procedures to which these tissue samples were subjected were accompanied by minimal production of methodological artifacts.

The evidence obtained from electron microscopic examination of incubated slice sections may be summarized as follows. The presence of 10 mM of NH_4Cl in the incubation medium of such slices is associated with more extensive swelling of astrocytes, with distortion of mitochondrial morphology, with extensive swelling of neuronal endoplasmic reticulum lumina, and with an apparent greater compactness of other elements. Whether these changes may be correlated directly with the chemically measured decrease of neuronal nonchloride, nonsucrose fluid space and the concomitant increase of the total chloride and sucrose space of the slice must remain for the present a moot point.

Two additional considerations are pertinent to this discussion. The morphological changes recorded here in association with exposure of cat cerebral cortex slices to excess NH_4^+ are quite different from those recently reported by Birks[15] for the effects Digoxin (a cardiac glycoside inhibitor of the Na^+ extrusion mechanism) on perfused sympathetic ganglion cells in the cat. The ganglia, fixed with osmium by perfusion and examined under the electron microscope, showed no changes from control samples in nonneuronal cells such as Schwann cells, capsule cells, fibroblasts, or endothelial cells. However, the neurons were swollen, exhibiting pale cytoplasm, greatly swollen endoplasmic reticulum lumina, shrunken dense mitochondria with loss of cristae, and swollen synaptic vesicles and axon terminals. The omission of Cl^- (by substituting sulfate) in these experiments prevented the Digoxin-induced cytoplasmic and endoplasmic reticulum luminal swelling but did not prevent other changes. All changes were prevented by lowering Na^+ concentration in the perfusion fluid from the normal 140 mEq. per liter to 20 mEq. per liter. Hence Birks has suggested that the cytoplasmic and endoplasmic reticulum swelling could be attributable to a net uptake of Na^+ and Cl^- in Digoxin-treated

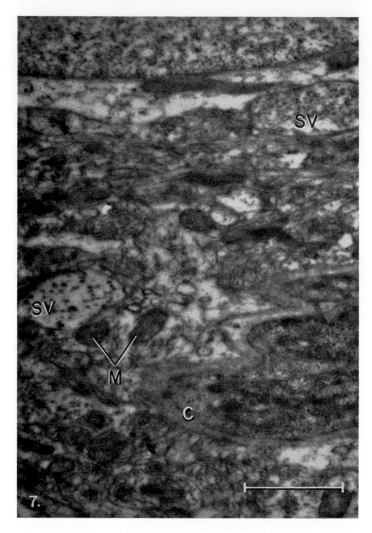

FIG. 5-7. Control slice. Detailed field showing several synaptic vesicles (*SV*), numerous mitochondria (*M*), and tangentially cut capillary (*C*). ×25,000. Fixation and embedding conditions and calibration same as for Figure 5-1.

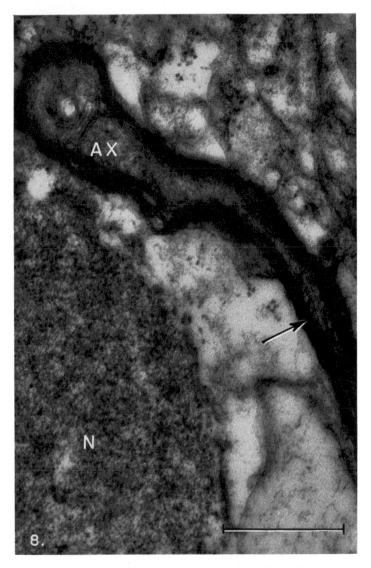

FIG. 5-8. Control slice. Typical myelinated axon (*AX*) adjacent to astrocyte nucleus (*N*). Note good preservation of lamellar structure of the myelin sheath (at arrow). ×32,000. Fixation and embedding conditions and calibration same as for Figure 5-1.

neurons and that the other changes might reflect the intracellular presence of abnormally elevated Na$^+$ concentrations.

A final consideration concerns the effects of the osmium fixation itself on fluid distributions and morphology of the slices studied here. Dr. Robert Bourke in our laboratory has recently confirmed and amplified previous observations of Pappius, Klatzo, and Elliott[16] that such fixation is associated with a significant increase of slice fluid up-

TABLE 5-1. Fluid Spaces in Slices of Cat Cerebral Cortex

| | Per cent of initial fresh weight | | |
| | | Incubated 1 hr. | |
Fluid spaces	Initial, unincubated	Control	$+NH_4Cl$
"Swelling" (13)*	30.1 ($\pm$7.2)	48.5 ($\pm$11.95)	55.0 ($\pm$9.95)
Chloride space (11)	51.5 ($\pm$3.85)	42.7 ($\pm$3.45)	46.3 ($\pm$2.4)
Sucrose space (6)	51.2 ($\pm$6.0)	42.2 ($\pm$5.5)	46.0
Calculated nonchloride, nonsucrose space:†	32.5	41.3	37.7
Glial	8.8	10.8	11.6
Neuronal	23.7	30.5	26.1

Number of experiments is indicated in parentheses after each item. Tabulated values are means ($\pm$ standard deviations).

* "Swelling" was determined as weight gain of slices after immersion in incubation media with or without incubation, compared with initial weights of slices, and includes adherent medium.[7] All swelling was confined to chloride and sucrose spaces, so that values tabulated for latter have been corrected accordingly to true net values.

† Calculations are based on separately verified dry weights (solids) of 15 to 17 per cent of initial fresh weights. Calculations of glial and neuronal fractions are described in detail elsewhere.[1,8] Astrocytes are considered to participate in chloride and sucrose space[8] and are therefore excluded from the glial fraction tabulated.

take. Dr. Bourke has found that such uptake occurs even with fixation times as short as 1 minute, but that it is progressively greater for longer periods of fixation. Thus, for the 30-minute fixation with osmium used in the present studies, he found an excess fluid uptake (slice weight gain over control weight) of 49.75 ($\pm$3.2) per cent of the initial slice weight in four experiments, or virtually a 100 per cent increase of swelling over the control values totaling 48.5 per cent for unfixed slices (Table 5-1). Measurements of chloride and sucrose spaces in these osmium-fixed slices indicated that these solutes were distributed throughout the total water of the slices and hence the permeability properties of cell membranes therein had been markedly altered. No satisfactory estimate of the changes in extracellular space as measured by the trisaccharide raffinose could be obtained since it failed to penetrate any fluid space even in unfixed slices, and the validity of using inulin to measure such spaces in brain slices incubated in vitro is open to question.[16] However, in unpublished studies, Dr. Walter Oppelt of the National Cancer Institute has found that the dog brain in vivo normally exhibits a C^{14}-inulin space of about 14 per cent,* whereas after osmium fixation *in situ*, the C^{14}-inulin space is reduced to less than 5 per cent.

It would seem, therefore, that some reservations must be invoked regarding the fluid space morphology of osmium-fixed brain sections, since the osmium-induced swelling found in the studies cited above appears to be intracellular and would thus tend to obliterate portions of tissue spaces normally present. The recent studies by Dr. Bourke in our laboratory suggest that osmium fixation of incubated cerebral cortex slices for only 1 minute provides good fixation and is attended by much less extra swelling than is encountered with longer fixation times.

Several other points in technique deserve re-emphasis. Special attention to careful handling of the slice specimens at all stages from their preparation through fixation would seem to be essential for good preservation of morphological characteristics seen under electron microscopy. This point may account for some of the differences between our preparations and those shown by Cohen and Hartmann[18] at this symposium. In addition the use of a bicarbonate-buffered incubation medium and particularly the use of this same medium during slice fixation appears to provide more normal morphology, when compared with unincubated controls, than the use of other buffered media such as phosphate or veronal, although this is admittedly an impression difficult to substantiate. It is evident that much remains to be done in this field of morphological-biochemical correlations. The studies reported here indicate some of the problems and some of the potentialities for the future.

---

* This value is considerably higher than the value of 4 per cent obtained by Woodbury[17] for rat brain, but compares favorably with his value of 10 per cent for cat brain.

SUMMARY

Cat cerebral cortex slices were incubated in vitro under carefully controlled conditions, and the effects of adding 10 mM of NH_4Cl to the incubation medium were investigated by parallel determinations of chemically definable fluid spaces (chloride and sucrose) and examinations of the morphology of such slices (after osmium fixation) under the electron microscope.

The ammonia-treated slices were found to have a significantly smaller neuronal nonchloride and nonsucrose space and a significantly larger total chloride and sucrose space than the control slices. Morphological differences between the two types of samples were seldom absolute, but it could be concluded that the ammonia-treated slice specimens characteristically exhibited more extensive swelling of astrocytes, distortion of mitochondrial morphology, extensive swelling of neuronal endoplasmic reticulum lumina, and an apparent increased compactness of other elements. Some of the problems posed by attempts to correlate these two sets of data are discussed.

REFERENCES

1. Tower, D. B., Wherrett, J. R., and McKhann, G. M. "Functional implications of Metabolic Compartmentation in the Central Nervous System," in *Regional Neurochemistry*, ed. by Kety, S. S., and Elkes, J. New York, Pergamon Press, 1961, p. 65.

2. Tower, D. B. Effects of 2-deoxy-D-glucose on metabolism of slices of cerebral cortex incubated in vitro. *J. Neurochem.* 3:185, 1958.

3. McKhann, G. M., and Tower, D. B. A modified manometric vessel for special studies on tissue metabolism. *Anal. Biochem.* 1:511, 1960.

4. Ward, R. T. Prevention of polymerization damage on methacrylate embedding media. *J. Histochem.* 6:398, 1958.

5. Peters, E. L., and Tower, D. B. Glutamic acid and glutamine metabolism in cerebral cortex after seizures induced by methionine sulphoximine. *J. Neurochem.* 5:80, 1959.

6. McKhann, G. M., and Tower, D. B. Ammonia toxicity and cerebral oxidative metabolism. *Am. J. Physiol.* 200:420, 1961.

7. Terner, C., Eggleston, L. V., and Krebs, H. A. Role of glutamic acid in the transport of potassium in brain and retina. *Biochem. J.* 47:139, 1950.

8. Tower, D. B. "Some Neurochemical Aspects of Cortical Neurobiology," in *Structure and Function of the Cerebral Cortex,* ed. by Tower, D. B., and Schade, J. P. Amsterdam, Elsevier, 1960, p. 411.

9. Farquhar, M. G., and Hartmann, F. G. Neuroglial structure and relationships as revealed by electron microscopy. *J. Neuropath. & Exper. Neurol.* 16:18, 1957.

10. Gerschenfeld, H. M., Wald, F., Zadunaisky, J. A., and De Robertis, E. D. P. Function of astroglia in the water-ion metabolism of the central nervous system. *Neurology* 9:412, 1959.

11. Luse, S. A. "Electron Microscopic Observations of the Central Nervous System," in *Inhibition in the Nervous System and γ-aminobutyric Acid,* ed. by Roberts, E. New York, Pergamon Press, 1960, p. 29.

12. Pomerat, C. M. Personal communication.

13. Siekevitz, P. "On the Meaning of Intracellular Structure for Metabolic Regulation," in *Regulation of Cell Metabolism,* ed. by Wolstenholme, G. E. W., and O'Conner, C. M. Boston, Little, Brown, 1960, p. 17.

14. Allfrey, V. G., Meudt, R., Hopkins, J. W., and Mirsky, A. T. Sodium-dependent "transport" reactions in the cell nucleus and their role in protein and nucleic acid synthesis. *Proc. Nat. Acad. Sc.* 47:907, 1961.

15. Birks, R. I. Effects of a cardiac glycoside on subcellular structures within nerve cells and their processes in sympathetic ganglia and skeletal muscle. *Canad. J. Biochem. & Physiol.* 40:303, 1962.

16. Pappius, H. M., Klatzo, I., and Elliott, K. A. C. Further studies on swelling of brain slices. *Canad. J. Biochem. & Physiol.* 40:885, 1962.

17. Woodbury, D. M. Personal communication.

18. Cohen, M. M., and Hartmann, F. G. See Chapter 4, this volume.

ALFRED POPE, HELEN H. HESS,
and EDWARD LEWIN

CHAPTER

6

Studies on the Microchemical Pathology of Human Cerebral Cortex

FOR SOME YEARS OUR LABORATORY HAS BEEN CONCERNED WITH APPLYING the principles and techniques of quantitative histochemistry, as originally developed by Linderstrøm-Lang and Holter, to certain selected problems in chemical neuropathology.

Within this context, attention has been focused upon analysis of the microchemical architecture of human cerebral cortex. This endeavor has been based both upon theoretical considerations—the intrinsic neurological importance of the neocortex and the significance of its action as complementary in the physical domain to normal and abnormal human behavior—and upon the practical fact that the laminated architecture of the cortex is an invitation to its study by means of the Carlsberg methods for microsampling and biochemical analysis. The objective has been to determine the quantitative distributions of chemical constituents within the architectonic layers and sublayers and thus to arrive at an elementary but orderly description of cortical chemo-architecture. In addition, by comparing the intra-

Supported in part by research grant B-361 from the National Institute of Neurological Diseases and Blindness, National Institutes of Health, U.S. Public Health Service.

The authors gratefully acknowledge the cooperation of Dr. E. P. Richardson, Jr., and associates of the Massachusetts General Hospital in making available cortical autopsy specimens, and the skillful technical assistance of Miss Caroline Thalheimer and Mrs. Marie Rose.

laminar profiles of chemical constituents with the nonuniform histological structure of the cortex, it is possible to infer certain general histochemical correlations applicable to human brain.

For these studies the prefrontal cortex has been selected as representative of the eugranular and eulaminate isocortex that constitutes such a unique proportion of the cerebral mantle in man. During the era of psychosurgery, we were fortunate in being able to obtain cortical biopsy specimens excised during frontal lobotomy. These were utilized for a series of investigations on the intracortical distributions of various enzymes of known importance in the general or special metabolism of brain. The results have been analyzed with respect to the neurobiological significance of the intralaminar enzyme profiles[1-4] and in relation to the psychopathological reactions of the patients in-

TABLE 6-1. Microchemical Pathology of Human Frontal Isocortex

Structural components	Ribonucleic acids
	Deoxyribonucleic acids
	Proteolipid protein
	Cerebrosides
Enzymes	Acetylcholinesterase
	Dipeptidase (vs. L-alanylglycine)
	Lipase (vs. tri-N-butyrin)

volved.[1,5] Currently, similar studies are in progress upon biochemical structural components (classes of lipids, proteins, and nucleic acids) in autopsy specimens free of neuropathological changes and obtained from patients without known neurological involvement or complications. Partly in parallel to the latter series, and in a sense ancillary to both, comparative experiments are also being carried out on postmortem specimens that are the sites of certain important cortical diseases, especially those associated with the dementias occurring in middle and late life. In this article, the potentialities and limitations of such studies are illustrated by considering the microchemical findings in single instances of Alzheimer's and Jakob-Creutzfeldt diseases, which may be taken as exemplifying characteristic but differing forms of cortical degeneration.

The chemical constituents studied microchemically in these cases are listed in Table 6-1. DNA is being measured in all such specimens to determine the total cell population at standard intracortical depths, and RNA as an index (mainly) of ribosome content (roughly equatable with Nissl bodies) and, hence, presumably of the "trophic" potential of neurons. Proteolipids are one of several protein fractions under study. The anatomical localization of these complexes remains uncertain, though a relation to membrane structures in general is probable. Cerebrosides can be considered the best single chemical index of the amount and integrity of myelin. The three hydrolytic enzymes have been found to be generally resistant to postmortem autolysis and, therefore, suitable for assay in autopsy tissue. Acetylcholinesterase (AChE), dipeptidase, and lipase activities are being studied as rough indices, respectively, of the integrity of neurons and of the tissue potential for protein and lipid breakdown such as might be anticipated in necrotizing and atrophic processes.

MATERIALS AND METHODS

Portions of the superior frontal convolutions were dissected immediately following postmortem removal of the brain, refrigerated, and transported directly to the laboratory. The site of each specimen corresponded with the architectonic area designated 9 by Brodmann, FDm by von Economo, and IEfs by Bailey and von Bonin.[6] Blocks were immediately dissected for quantitative histochemical experiments, frozen, and stored at −60°C. until used. Other blocks were placed in fixatives suitable for chromatic and metallic stains specific for nerve cells, axis cylinders, myelin, and the several species of glia.

The experimental design for determining the intracortical distributions of the constituents under study was essentially similar to that used in this laboratory for this purpose in the past.[1-4] In summary, a vertical cylinder of uniform diameter is punched from the frozen cortical block. Serial, 40-μ, horizontal microtome sections are cut from pial surface to subjacent white matter and used in consecutive groups of four sections each for histological preparation (Nissl), microchemical analyses, and determination of dry weight. For experiments revealing intracortical enzyme profiles, assays were made upon the second and fourth sections of each series. For chemical structural components,[7] sections two and three in each series were weighed and extracted with 2:1 chloroform-methanol containing 4% water. The lipid extract was partitioned according to Folch, Lees, and Sloane Stanley,[8] and cerebrosides measured in the "washed lower phase" by determination of galactose concentration. The insoluble residue was extracted with cold perchloric acid, and RNA was determined in the extract by its ultraviolet absorption.[9] DNA was determined in the residue by the method of Kissane and Robins.[10] The fourth slice was also desiccated, weighed, and extracted with chloroform-methanol, and the extract partitioned. Proteolipids were determined by measurement of the protein concentration in the lower phase using an adaptation[7] of the method of Lowry *et al.*[11] AChE, dipeptidase, and lipase activities were determined respectively by the microtitrimetric methods of Glick,[12] Linderstrøm-Lang and Holter,[13] and Glick and Biskind.[14] Concentrations of structural constituents and activities of enzymes are expressed in terms of dry weights determined by means of quartz-fiber microbalances of the sort described by Lowry.[15]

The relations of resulting intracortical distribution patterns to the cyto-architecture were estimated as previously described.[1-4] The locus of each horizontal control section stained by Nissl's method was observed directly. In addition, the actual widths of the cyto-architectonic layers were measured in reduced silver preparations of vertical sections cut from the block immediately adjacent to the site of the cylinder used for quantitative histochemistry.

RESULTS AND DISCUSSION

For this summary report, the results are presented in a simple form. For each experiment and each constituent, means have been calculated of all values obtained upon samples assignable to each of ten approximately equivalent intracortical levels coinciding with the standard cyto-architectonic designations of layers and sublayers. In the accompanying tables, the data for the pathological specimens are presented individually; those for the normal controls represent the averages of several experiments.

Normal Cortex

Values obtained in normal cortex for the structural compounds and enzymes being considered are shown in Table 6-2. Since all the ex-

TABLE 6-2. Biochemical Constituents in Cyto-architectonic Layers of Frontal Isocortex, Normal* and Alzheimer's Disease

| | Chemical structural component concentrations† | | | | | | | | Enzyme activities‡ | | | | | |
| | DNA | | RNA | | Proteolipid | | Cerebroside | | AChE | | Dipeptidase | | Lipase | |
Layer	Norm.	Alz.	Norm.	Alz.	Norm.	Alz.	Norm.	Alz.	Norm.	Alz.	Norm.	Alz.	Norm.	Alz.
I	0.31	0.42	0.42	0.58	3.7		4.1	3.0	3.2		0.35		7.2	8.8
II	0.39	0.39	0.62	0.70	2.8	2.0	3.2	3.3	2.1	1.0	0.29	0.42	8.3	6.5
IIIa	0.34	0.33	0.62	0.66	2.9	1.8	3.2	3.4	2.4	1.3	0.27	0.37	8.0	5.4
b	0.33	0.27	0.61	0.70	3.0	2.3	3.5	3.6	2.1		0.27	0.39	6.7	7.6
c	0.35	0.36	0.61	0.69	3.2	1.8	4.4	3.6	2.0	0.9	0.26	0.38	7.8	6.1
IV	0.39	0.44	0.62	0.71	2.8	2.3	6.7	4.5	1.8	0.8	0.27	0.28	5.8	
V	0.35	0.33	0.55	0.67	3.3	1.8	6.4	4.9	2.2	1.6	0.29	0.34	8.6	8.9
VIa	0.34	0.27	0.51	0.50	3.3	2.2	7.5	6.3	1.3	1.6	0.27	0.28	7.2	4.3
b	0.30	0.33	0.33	0.28	3.9	3.1	10.3	9.1	0.9	2.3	0.26	0.29	3.7	3.0
WM	0.29	0.35	0.24	0.28	5.1	4.5	12.9	13.7	0.3		0.25	0.26	3.6	4.0

* Normal values for structural components are averages of results in eight experiments on autopsy specimens. For AChE and dipeptidase they are averages in seventeen and eight experiments, respectively, on cortical biopsy specimens[1,2] for lipase, of three experiments on autopsy specimens. In three experiments on autopsy specimens corresponding AChE and dipeptidase activities were similar to those in biopsy material.

† Expressed as per cent of dry weight.

‡ Expressed as titration values in 0.05N HCl per microgram of dry weight ($\times 10^2$ for AChE and lipase).

periments represented have been or are being presented in full elsewhere, the detailed nature and anatomical significance of the laminar patterns of chemical composition will merely be summarized to serve as normal referents for the results on pathological specimens considered below.

Of the structural components, DNA shows an anticipated parallelism with total cell population. RNA concentration is quite uniform in a broad zone including layers II to VIa, corresponding with the cortical band containing abundant neuroplasm. The distributions of cerebrosides and proteolipid protein are similar in layers I to III, but the concentration of cerebrosides becomes relatively much greater in the infragranular layers and subcortical white matter. More detailed analysis of these patterns[16] reveals that cerebroside concentration correlates remarkably well with strata containing large numbers of medullated fibers in myelo-architectonic pictures. However, the distribution of proteolipid shows that these complexes cannot be a constituent of myelin alone, in keeping with other recent observations on their regional neurochemistry.[17]

The intralaminar pattern of AChE has been considered consistent with its localization in the cortical plexuses of axons and dendrites and their synaptic articulations;[1] that of alanylglycine dipeptidase as reflecting localization of proteolytic activity in the perikarya and protoplasmic expansions of both neurons and neuroglia.[2] A still incomplete series of experiments on lipase activity, as exemplified by the enzymatic hydrolysis of tri-N-butyrin, indicates that the potential for lipid breakdown is much less than that for proteolysis but is distributed in a not dissimilar fashion.

Alzheimer's Disease

The first specimen to be considered was obtained from the brain of a 61-year-old female with a 6-year history of progressive disorientation and loss of memory and judgment. Death was sudden, due to pulmonary embolism arising from a thrombosed renal vein. Grossly, the brain showed little obvious cortical atrophy, though the pia-arachnoid was thickened and stripped with difficulty. Reduced silver preparations (Fig. 6-1) revealed a very large number of argyrophilic plaques at all cortical levels; neurons containing neurofibrillar tangles could be found at will. Nissl and Luxol-fast-blue preparations showed slight cortical thinning, but minimal cell or myelin loss or distortion of architecture. In Cajal's gold stains some astrocytic hyperplasia and fibrous metaplasia were evident. Silver carbonate preparations revealed many rod cell forms of activated microglia. On both clinical

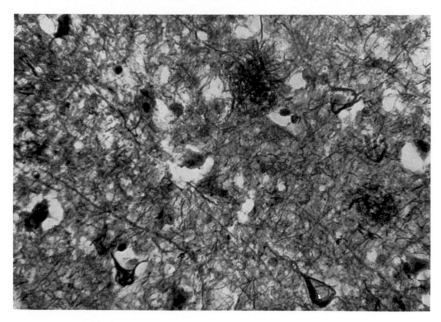

FIG. 6-1. Cerebral cortex in Alzheimer's disease. Representative field in layer IIIc showing argyrophilic plaques and neurons containing neurofibrillar tangles. Hortega-Cajal reduced silver preparation. ×320.

and pathological grounds, this was considered to be a classic instance of Alzheimer's presenile dementia.

The cortical microchemical findings are presented in Table 6-2. DNA was essentially within normal limits in all layers, corresponding with the absence of cell outfall noted in the Nissl stains. However, an unchanged DNA concentration might merely reflect a combination of neuron cell loss and glial proliferation. RNA values were not only not reduced but actually in the high normal range (layers I to V), which is surprising. Possibly, this is a reflection of the hyperplastic reaction of astrocytes and microglia with a concomitant increase in protein synthesis. Cerebroside values were unchanged in the supragranular layers, but slightly lowered in layers IV to VI, suggesting a mild degree of myelin loss in these strata, which, however, was not correlatable with any obvious change in the Luxol-fast-blue stains. The only clear-cut abnormality was in proteolipid concentration, which was reduced at all levels and well below normal limits in layers III and V. The significance of this is quite obscure, but it is noteworthy that the greatest reduction was in those layers which usually exhibit maximal changes in Alzheimer's disease.[18]

The cortical average for AChE activity was within normal limits due, in part, to an unexplained elevation in layer VIb. Unfortunately, layer I was not satisfactorily sampled, but it is clear that activity was abnormally low in layers II to V, reflecting either some measure of nerve cell outfall or diminished discharged rates, or both. In contrast, dipeptidase activity was somewhat elevated at all cortical levels, especially in the supragranular layers. Such an inverse relation to AChE has often been noted previously in both human and animal material. In this instance, it may well represent an enzymatic correlate of the astrogliosis, since there are a number of indications that proteolytic activity may be preferentially located in astrocytes.[2,19] Intracortical tributyrinase activity was not remarkable and gave no indication of increased lipolytic potential, in spite of the presence of numerous rod cells.

Jakob-Creutzfeldt Disease

The second specimen was derived from the brain of a 59-year-old refrigeration engineer. For about 1 month, the patient had shown an intermittent staggering gait and recurring episodes of bizarre, irrational behavior. On hospital admission, he displayed a confusional state with memory loss and hallucinations. Within a few days myoclonic jerks appeared, followed by a progressive, rapidly deteriorating course leading in a few weeks to cessation of mentation and a decerebrate posture. The electroencephalogram showed virtual absence of electrical signs of cortical activity. The patient survived in this essentially decorticate state for 5 months. At autopsy, the brain showed extensive wasting of the cortex, most severe in the frontal lobes. On the cut surface, the cortex consisted of an irregularly thinned, grayish-yellow, spongy-to-fibrous band. Microscopically, there was devastation of neuron population, giving the tissue a loose reticulated appearance and resulting in obliteration of the normal architecture. Some activation of microglia was in evidence, but in

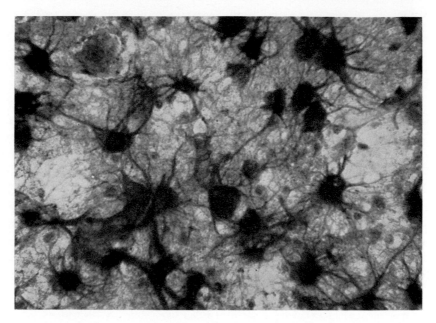

FIG. 6-2. Astrocytes in frontal cortex in Jakob-Creutzfeldt disease. Appearance of hypertrophied and hyperplastic astrocytes showing robust fibers and evidence of cell division in severely degenerated cortex. Cajal's gold chloride–sublimate stain. ×1,125.

the frontal lobe particularly, the most striking feature was conversion to a mass of actively proliferating fibrous astrocytes (Fig. 6-2). Both clinically and pathologically this case was considered a severe but classic instance of the fulminating type of cortical degeneration originally described by Creutzfeldt and Jakob.

Because of insufficient material, it was necessary to do the analyses for structural components on a sample from the midparietal lobe (area 5 or 7). The results are shown in Table 6-3. As indicated, three histological zones could be distinguished. In the outermost, layers I, II, and III could be identified but showed severe neuron loss and glial reaction. The second zone consisted of layers IV to VI, within which the neuron necrosis was so advanced that the architectonic structure was no longer recognizable. Beneath this was a third region of degenerating white matter.

The data show that the total solids per unit volume were reduced especially in the superficial zone, corresponding with its spongy ap-

TABLE 6-3. Chemical Components in Midparietal Cortex, Jakob-Creutzfeldt Disease

Zones	*Layers I–III*		*Layers IV–VI*		*White matter*	
Subpial depth	0–680 μ		680–1,320 μ		1,320–2,280 μ	
Histopathology	Severe neuron loss; gliosis; microglial activation		Rare neurons; gliosis; microglial activation		Nerve fiber and oligodendrocyte loss; gliosis; microglial activation	
		Normal*		*Normal**		*Normal**
Total solids†	12.7	17.1	23.6	19.1	24.4	28.0
Proteolipid proteins‡	3.9	3.1	8.0	3.4	6.4	5.1
RNA‡	0.61	0.59	0.36	0.48	0.28	0.24
DNA‡	0.48	0.34	0.41	0.34	0.33	0.29

* Averages for designated layers in eight experiments on normal autopsy specimens.
† Expressed as per cent of (calculated) fresh weight.
‡ Expressed as per cent of dry weight.

pearance both grossly and in microscopic preparations. A similar finding was reported by Korey, Katzman, and Orloff,[20] in a formalin-fixed brain used for biochemical studies.

A remarkable feature in our specimen was the high concentration of proteolipid protein in all three zones, especially the intermediate one. To be more precise, some constituent was present in abnormal amounts that analyzed as proteolipid protein. (In view of the severity of the neuropathological changes, it is necessary to repeat that proteolipid in these microchemical studies is defined only in operational terms as protein analyzable by the Lowry method in the washed lower phase of a chloroform-methanol extract.) There is no ready explanation for this finding. Conceivably, it may be related somehow to the fibrous astrogliosis. Curiously enough, a similar finding has been obtained in a second, less advanced case of Jakob-Creutzfeldt disease.[21]

RNA concentration was normal, or somewhat lowered (zone II), despite an increase in total cell population due to active gliosis and reflected by the increased DNA observed in zones I and II. Consequently, the RNA per cell was much reduced, corresponding

TABLE 6-4. Enzymes in Frontal Cortex, Jakob-Creutzfeldt Disease

Zones	Plexiform layer (I)		Degenerated cortex (II–VI)		Altered white matter	
Subpial depth	0–250 μ		250–900 μ		> 900 μ	
Histopathology	Axon loss; fibrous astrocytes		Profound neuron outfall and fibrous gliosis; microglial activation		Fiber degeneration; pleomorphic microglia; disappearance of oligodendrocytes	
		Normal†		Normal†		Normal†
AChE*	0	3.2	0.3	1.8	0.3	0.3
Dipeptidase*	0.49	0.35	0.20	0.27	0.34	0.25
Lipase*	6.6	7.2	2.9	7.0	4.9	3.6

* Expressed as titration values in microliters of 0.05N HCl per microgram of dry weight ($\times$ 10² for AChE and lipase).
† Average normal values for designated layers computed from same series of experiments referred to in footnote to Table 6-2.

with the loss of neurons and their replacement by the relatively RNA-poor astrocytes.

Enzyme activities were analyzed in the even more severely devastated frontal cortex. The results are summarized in Table 6-4. Histopathological examination again revealed three more or less distinguishable horizontal zones. The most superficial was relatively acellular and appeared to consist of thickened pia plus plexiform layer of cortex. Beneath was a cellular region almost devoid of neurons, in which the tissue had been converted to necrotic debris enmeshed in a dense population of fibrous glia, as depicted in Figure 6-2. This evidently represented the altered remains of cortical layers II to VI. Subjacent to it there was again a zone of severely degenerated white matter.

Inspection of Table 6-4 shows that AChE activity had virtually disappeared from the remnants of gray matter, corresponding to the electrical silence and absence of viable appearing neurons. In the subjacent white matter, activity was normal. However, the depleted lipid might have rendered this deceptive since the activities are expressed on a dry-weight basis. Furthermore, the contribution to total acetylcholine hydrolysis by pseudocholinesterase is difficult to evaluate, especially under such circumstances.[5]

Dipeptidase and lipase activities varied together (in part) in the three discernible zones. However, both activities were within the usual ranges observed in normal human cortex. This, perhaps, is not inconsistent with the histopathological evidence of continuing necrosis and glial reaction and once more points to the presence of considerable proteolytic potential in neuroglia.

The foregoing results demonstrate the applicability of quantitative histochemistry for relatively refined observations on the chemical pathology of human cortex. They show that analyses made upon microgram-sized tissue samples, hence in terms of cellular aggregates, can have considerable virtue for establishing the biochemical equivalents of morphological reactions to injury and repair. In this way, the biochemistry of disease can be explored at histopathological dimensions, and chemical description of tissue abnormalities can be established in precise quantitative terms.

It can be predicted with confidence that within such a framework, observations will eventually be made relevant for understanding the molecular mechanisms involved in the genesis of such baffling illnesses as those considered in the foregoing. However, it is essential to recognize not only the preliminary and fragmentary nature of such data as those presented but also the lack of illumination provided regarding the basic biochemical mechanisms of these obscure diseases. This difficulty is inherent in most forms of analysis upon postmortem tissues in which, by and large, it is the end stage of a pathological process that is studied, and the biochemical correlations are with the pathological consequence of disease (including reparative reactions) rather than with those molecular alterations that must originally be of etiological significance. For this reason, greater precision in delineating the biochemistry of the dementias may be anticipated from analyses upon selected biopsy specimens as currently exemplified by the comprehensive chemical and ultrastructural investigations on cerebral diseases being carried out by Korey *et al.*[22]

SUMMARY

Studies in progress on the quantitative architectonic distributions of chemical structural components and enzymes in pathological human cerebral cortex are illustrated by microchemical findings in two types of middle-life dementias.

In a case of Alzheimer's disease, DNA and RNA were within normal limits at all intracortical levels. Proteolipid protein concentration was reduced, especially in layers III and V. Cerebrosides were slightly lowered in the infragranular layers. In layers II to V the activity of acetylcholinesterase was decreased and that of dipeptidase (vs. L-alanylglycine) somewhat increased.

In a case of Jakob-Creutzfeldt disease, cortical RNA concentration per cell was considerably reduced, proteolipid protein values were elevated, and the activity of AChE was almost abolished.

Relations between these results and the histopathological findings as well as the potentialities of quantitative histochemistry for investigating chemical neuropathology in man are briefly discussed.

REFERENCES

1. POPE, A., CAVENESS, W. F., and LIVINGSTON, K. E. Architectonic distribution of acetylcholinesterase in the frontal isocortex of psychotic and nonpsychotic patients. *A.M.A. Arch. Neurol. & Psychiat.* 68:425, 1952.

2. POPE, A. Intralaminar distribution of dipeptidase activity in human frontal isocortex. *J. Neurochem.* 4:31, 1959.

3. HESS, H. H., and POPE, A. Intralaminar distribution of cytochrome oxidase activity in human frontal isocortex. *J. Neurochem.* 5:207, 1960.

4. HESS, H. H., and POPE, A. Intralaminar distribution of adenosinetriphosphatase activity in human frontal isocortex. *J. Neurochem.* 8:299, 1961.

5. POPE, A. "Brain Enzymes in Mental Disease," in *Chemical Pathology of the Nervous System* (Proceedings of the Third International Neurochemical Symposium), ed. by Folch, J. New York, Pergamon Press, 1961, pp. 388–402.

6. BAILEY, P., and VON BONIN, G. *The Isocortex of Man.* Urbana, Ill., University of Illinois Press, 1951.

7. HESS, H. H., LEWIN, E., and THALHEIMER, C. Microassay of biochemical structural components in human brain: I. Scheme of analysis and methods for cerebrosides, proteolipid proteins and residue proteins. To be published.

8. FOLCH, J., LEES, M., and SLOANE STANLEY, G. H. A simple method for the isolation and purification of total lipides from animal tissue. *J. Biol. Chem.* 226:497, 1957.

9. HESS, H. H., and THALHEIMER, C. Microassay of biochemical structural components in human brain: II. Methods for nucleic acids, gangliosides, and residue sialic acid components. To be published.

10. KISSANE, J. M., and ROBINS, E. Fluorometric measurement of deoxyribonucleic acid in animal tissues with special reference to the central nervous system. *J. Biol. Chem.* 233:184, 1958.

11. LOWRY, O. H., ROSEBROUGH, N. J., FARR, A. L., and RANDALL, R. J. Protein measurement with the Folin-phenol reagent. *J. Biol. Chem.* 193:265, 1951.

12. GLICK, D. Studies on enzymatic histochemistry: XXV. A micro method for the determination of cholinesterase, and the activity-pH relationships of this enzyme. *J. Gen. Physiol.* 21:289, 1938.

13. LINDERSTRØM-LANG, K., and HOLTER, H. Studies on enzymatic histochemistry: XI. The distribution of peptidase in the gastric and duodenal mucosa of the pig. *Compt. rend. trav. lab. Carlsberg, série chim.* 20:42, 1935.

14. GLICK, D., and BISKIND, G. R. Histochemistry of the adrenal gland: II. The quantitative distribution of lipolytic enzymes. *J. Biol. Chem.* 110:575, 1935.

15. LOWRY, O. H. Quantitative histochemistry of brain: Histological sampling. *J. Histochem.* 1:420, 1953.

16. LEWIN, E., and HESS, H. H. Intralaminar distribution of proteins and cerebrosides in human frontal cortex. *J. Neuropath. & Exper. Neurol.* 22:329, 1963 (abstract).

17. AMADUCCI, L. Distribution of proteolipids in the human nervous system. *J. Neurochem.* 9:153, 1962.

18. McMENEMY, W. H. "The Dementias and Progressive Diseases of the Basal Ganglia," in *Neuropathology*, ed. by Greenfield, J. G. London, E. Arnold, 1958, pp. 475–528.

19. POPE, A., HESS, H. H., and ALLEN, J. N. "Quantitative Histochemistry of Proteolytic and Oxidative Enzymes in Human Cerebral Cortex and Brain Tumors," in *Progress in Neurobiology. II. Ultrastructure and Cellular Chemistry of Neural Tissue,* ed. by Waelsch, H. New York, Hoeber-Harper, 1957, pp. 182–191.

20. KOREY, S. R., KATZMAN, R., and ORLOFF, J. A case of Jakob-Creutzfeldt disease: 2. Analysis of some constituents of the brain of a patient with Jakob-Creutzfeldt disease. *J. Neuropath. & Exper. Neurol.* 20:95, 1961.

21. HESS, H. H. Unpublished data.

22. KOREY, S. R., SCHEINBERG, L., TERRY, R., and STEIN, A. Studies in presenile dementia. *Tr. Am. Neurol. A.* 86:99, 1961.

CLEMENT A. FOX, KENNETH A. SIEGESMUND,
and CHITTA R. DUTTA

CHAPTER 7

The Purkinje Cell Dendritic Branchlets and Their Relation with the Parallel Fibers: Light and Electron Microscopic Observations

STUDIES OF THE CEREBELLAR CORTEX'S PURKINJE CELL HAVE PLAYED THE key role in the development of our fundamental concept of central nervous system interneuronal relations. Moreover, the date, 1837, of Purkinje's description of this nerve corpuscle makes this nerve cell historically the first of the eponymous neurons.[1] Ramón y Cajal's description, in 1888, of the basket formations about the Purkinje cell bodies was the first direct evidence of actual contact between nerve cells.[2] Also, in the same year, his discovery of the climbing fibers and their intimate association with the dendrites of the Purkinje cell dispelled Golgi's notion that the dendrites were merely elaborate nutritional devices.[2] These disclosures prompted the point of view pervading all his subsequent investigations and provided the foundation for his concept of the dynamic polarization of the nerve cell, which in substance expressed the doctrine that Waldeyer later called the "neuron theory."[3,4]

Golgi,[5] who saw the rich ramification of the Purkinje cell dendritic system in greater detail than any investigator before him, noted that this cell is easier to draw than to describe, and he indicated that its

Supported by the National League Baseball Club of Milwaukee, Inc.

112

dendrites have a first, a second, a third, and a fourth order of branching. Ramón y Cajal's discovery in 1891 of the peridendritic spines[6,7] which form a "nap-like" covering on portions of certain neurons enabled him to refine Golgi's account of the Purkinje cell by distinguishing the primary, secondary, and tertiary smooth branches (*ramure*) from the spine-laden terminal branchlets (*ramuscles terminaux*), which emerge in great profusion from the smooth branches.[8,9] This led to the important observation that specific parts of the neuron have specific afferents: The Purkinje cell bodies are contacted by the nest-like formations of the basket cell axons; the smooth branches are contacted by the climbing fibers; and the spiny branchlets are contacted by the parallel fibers.[8,9]

Various investigators have explored limited aspects of the cerebellar cortex by means of electron microscopy.[10–15] Its superficial position, and above all its well-known structure, make it ideal for such studies. Ramón y Cajal's statement[16] that "there is perhaps no nervous center in which the fine structure is better known than that of the cerebellum" is as true today as it was in 1926. Furthermore, the rigid orientation of cerebellar elements in the molecular layer—the parallel disposition of the granule cell axons; the transverse spread of the leaf-like dendrites of the Purkinje cells, which the early anatomists detected;[17–20] the similar spread of the stellate cells; the presence of medullated fibers in the most inferior portion of this layer; and the palisade arrangement of the Bergmann fibers—all supply valuable clues for the correlation of electron microscopic observations with those of light microscopy.

The present study is concerned with the structure and interrelation of the Purkinje cell spiny dendritic branchlets and the parallel fibers. Since one of the aims of electron microscopy is to extend our past knowledge, Golgi and electron microscopic preparations from the same species (*Macaca mulatta*) are presented side by side in an attempt to better correlate the information derived from these two types of investigations.

MATERIALS AND METHODS

Cerebellar cortices were fixed *in situ* in living, anesthetized (with Nembutal) adult cats and monkeys (*Macaca mulatta*) by dripping a 2% solution of chilled osmium tetroxide on their surfaces for 15 to 20 minutes. The osmium tetroxide solution was buffered to pH 7.4 to 7.5 (with acetate-veronal) and brought to a molarity of 0.02 by the addition of calcium chloride. Blackened bits of cortex were removed with a sharp, pointed scalpel, placed in a drop of osmium tetroxide on a slab of dental wax, and then cut into fragments less than a cubic millimeter in size. These fragments were transferred to chilled osmium tetroxide, further fixed for 1 hour, then dehydrated by passage through increasing concentrations of ethanol and embedded in Araldite or Vestopal. Ultrathin sections were cut by means of glass or diamond knives on a Porter-Blum or an LKB microtome. Sections were mounted on copper grids without a carbon substrate and stained with lead hydroxide.[21] At times, while surveying blocks of tissue, entire sections were mounted on formvar films over large areas of a copper grid from which some of the grid squares had been cut out with a sharp razor blade. Such sections permitted the examination of relatively large areas of tissue unobstructed by the grid bars and were useful in determining the contents and orientation of the blocks of tissue. A number of large montages made from some of these sections were invaluable aids in the present investigation.

The Golgi observations reported here are based on a long-time study of the extensive collection of Golgi preparations of the cerebellar cortex of the adult monkey (*Macaca mulatta*)[22] available in this laboratory.

MOLECULAR OR PLEXIFORM LAYER

Background Fibers

Many of the fine structural details and the relations of elements Ramón y Cajal[9] described in the molecular layer of the cerebellar cortex can be confirmed and amplified in the present material. A glance at the numerous crosscut profiles of axons of varying caliber, packed in the interdendritic space down to the summit of the Purkinje cell body, in the low-power electron micrograph montage (Fig. 7-1) shows clearly why Ramón y Cajal[9] preferred to call the outer layer of the cerebellar cortex the plexiform layer. Most of these fibers

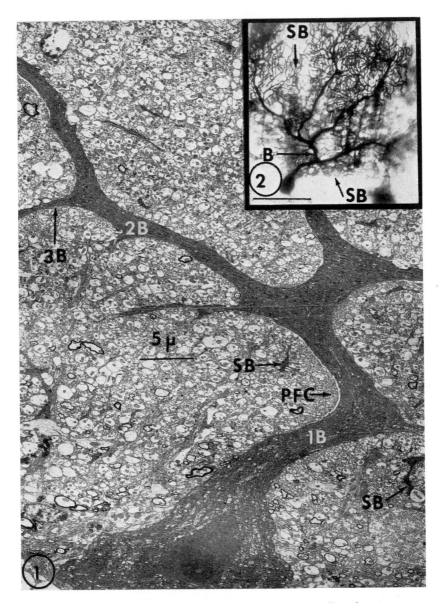

FIG. 7-1. Electron micrograph montage showing Purkinje cell with primary, secondary, and tertiary smooth branches (*1B, 2B, 3B*). (*PFC*) constricted portions of parallel fibers; (*SB*) spiny branchlets. Monkey cerebellar cortex. ×2,800.

FIG. 7-2. Purkinje cell impregnated by the Golgi method. (*B*) smooth branch; (*SB*) spiny branchlets. Monkey cerebellar cortex. Scale, 100 μ.

115

are unmedullated, and with few exceptions they are the parallel fibers resulting from the T-shaped bifurcations of the granule cell axons.

Attention is also directed to the few medullated fibers concentrated mostly in the lower portion of the montage. They belong to the well-known fiber system that Jakob[23] called the supraganglionic plexus. Ramón y Cajal[9] demonstrated that this medullated plexus is derived from the recurrent collaterals of Purkinje cells in the same folia. Incidentally, since they are found only in the most inferior portion of the molecular layer they can, at times, provide a useful clue in establishing more precisely the region from which a high-magnification electron micrograph is taken. The present material reveals that some of them are only 0.3 μ in diameter and are thus of finer caliber than some of the parallel fibers.

PURKINJE CELL DENDRITIC SYSTEM

Smooth Branches

To facilitate comparisons, a Purkinje cell impregnated by the Golgi method (Fig. 7-2) is inset on the same plate with the montage (Fig. 7-1). The latter is approximately nineteen times the magnification of the former. Both show details of the Purkinje cell dendritic system, which always emerges from the summit of the pear-shaped cell body, usually by a single, thick, vertically oblique trunk, describing an arc as it ascends. Occasionally two, and very rarely three, trunks elongate directly from the summit of the cell body. Actually, we have observed three trunks on only one occasion. The trunk divides, and the resulting subdividing branches ascend and spread out in the molecular layer in a leaf-shaped formation (Fig. 7-2) that always lies in the transverse plane of the folium. Viewed in longitudinal sections of the folium (P, Fig. 7-15) this formation shows only in profile. The successively, slimming primary, secondary, and tertiary smooth branches (1B,2B,3B, Fig. 7-1) form the basic framework of this system and sprout an enormous number of spine-laden terminal branchlets (SB, Fig. 7-2). It should be noted that the bifurcations of the smooth branches are arciform and not angular and that at the point of bifurcation the parent branch has a triangular thickening. These details, observed by Ramón y Cajal,[9] can easily be confirmed in the Golgi preparations. In the montage (Fig. 7-1) they show in an exaggerated way.

Electron Microscopy of Smooth Branches

Figure 7-3, an electron micrograph, shows a primary branch (*1B*) ascending from the bottom of the figure and dividing at the top of the figure into two secondary branches (*2B*). The fine longitudinal canaliculi which Palay *et al.*[15] illustrated in the dendrites of the rat Purkinje cell and which Palay[24,25] and others[26,27] described in other dendrites, appear in this lead hydroxide–stained section as regularly arranged dark, longitudinal striations, paralleling each other. They are about 200 A in diameter, and their tubular nature is revealed at the base of the secondary branch on the right, where some of them are sectioned transversely and obliquely as this branch changes course. Palay[24,25] regarded these structures as extensions of the endoplasmic reticulum, and Gray[26] named them dendritic tubules. At several places adjacent to the surfaces of these robust dendrites, membranes of the longitudinally disposed cisternae of the endoplasmic reticulum are prominent (*ER*, Fig. 7-3). In addition, these dendrites contain long slender mitochondria, dense granular inclusion bodies (*GB*, Fig. 7-3), and a few barely noticeable, rosette-like clusters of RNP particles (*N*, Fig. 7-3). The latter may account for the occasional flecks of Nissl substance seen in the primary branches of Purkinje cells in light microscopic preparations.

Pappas and Purpura[27] found the granular inclusion bodies (*GB*, Fig. 7-3) in the cytoplasm of neurons in the superficial portion of the cat neocortex and noted their resemblance to the "large secretory droplets" Palay[28] described in secretory neurons of the goldfish. We have seen them frequently in the cytoplasm of Purkinje cells. Palay[24,25] has also observed the sparse clusters of Nissl material (*N*, Fig. 7-3) in the dendrites of the abducens and cochlear nuclei.

Spiny Branchlets

For a short distance just at their origin from the smooth branches, the branchlets are devoid of spines. Moderately branched and roughly the

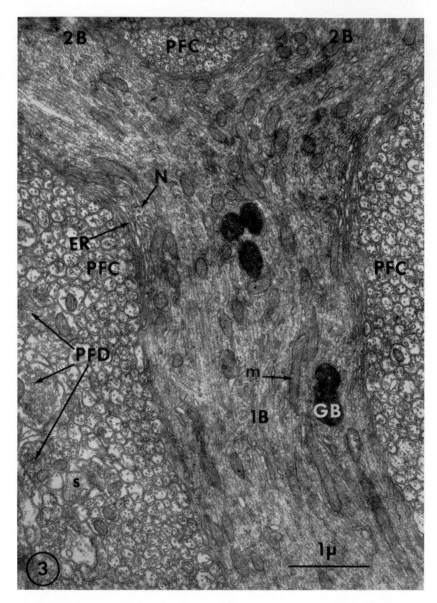

FIG. 7-3. Electron micrograph showing primary smooth branch (*1B*) bifurcating to form secondary smooth branches (*2B*). (*ER*) endoplasmic reticulum; (*GB*) granular inclusion body; (*m*) mitochondrion; (*N*) Nissl substance; (*PFC*) constricted portion of parallel fibers; (*PFD*) dilated portions of parallel fibers; (*s*) spine. Lead hydroxide–stained section. Monkey cerebellar cortex. ×21,000.

118

same in length, the branchlets arise mostly from the tertiary branches, but some of them, particularly the lowermost, take origin from secondary and primary branches (Fig. 7-2). Transversely, the branchlets extend beyond their smooth branches of origin, and in intermediate regions they span the spaces between the smooth branches. Unlike the smooth branches, which never reach the surface of the cortex and never descend, the superior branchlets ascend to the surface of the cortex, where some of them recurve inferiorly, and the inferior branchlets descend to a line running through the summits of the Purkinje cell bodies. The inferior line where the descending branchlets are arrested is clear in Figure 7-2; in preparations where a series of adjacent Purkinje cells is impregnated, it is striking. Thus the branchlets greatly extend the range of the Purkinje cell dendritic system, making it coextensive with the distribution of the parallel fibers.[29] The superior and inferior distribution of the parallel fibers can easily be confirmed by glancing at the low-power electron micrographs through the most inferior portion of the molecular layer (Fig. 7-1) and through the superficial portion of the molecular layer (Fig. 7-19). See also the Golgi impregnation (Fig. 7-15).

Some idea of the dense thicket the spiny branchlets erect in the path of the oncoming parallel fibers can be had by viewing a medium-power photomicrograph, Figure 7-4. If the focus were changed slightly, either upward or downward, more branchlets belonging to this Purkinje cell would be brought into view. Clearly the branchlets are not rigidly confined to a single plane; rather they are in planes two or three deep, and some of them veer off at slight angles to these planes. Owing to the thinness of the individual branchlets, this does not noticeably increase the thickness of the dendritic formation, which is about 10 μ in depth.[29] Ramón y Cajal[9] considered this staggered arrangement of the branchlets a further means of assuring contact with as many parallel fibers as possible. It was previously estimated that the total length of all the spiny branchlets on a Purkinje cell from the monkey cerebellar cortex is about 40 mm.[29] It was further estimated that if these branchlets were in lengths equal to the distance from the summits of the Purkinje cells to the pial surface, and were placed side by side, they would take in a much greater transverse spread than the dendritic formation,[29] which further emphasizes the necessity of the staggering of the branchlets.

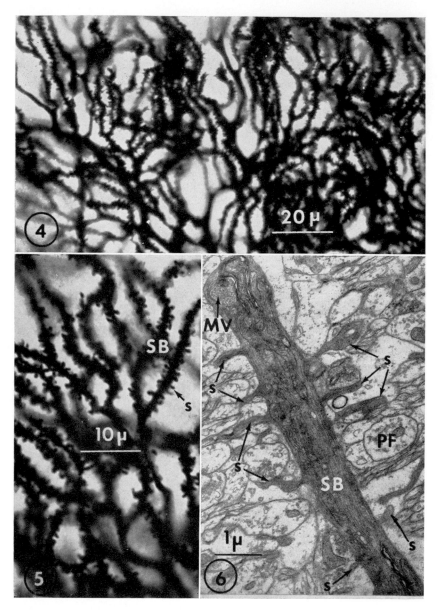

FIG. 7-4. Photomicrograph showing dense thicket of spiny branchlets. Monkey cerebellar cortex.

FIG. 7-5. Oil-immersion photomicrograph showing spiny branchlets. (*s*) spine; (*SB*) spiny branchlet. Monkey cerebellar cortex.

FIG. 7-6. Electron micrograph showing a spiny branchlet (*SB*) sectioned in mid-longitudinal plane. (*MV*) multivesicular body; (*PF*) parallel fiber; (*s*) emerging spines. Lead hydroxide–stained section. Cat cerebellar cortex. ×13,000.

Electron Microscopy of Spiny Branchlets

To simplify the transition from light to electron microscopy, an oil-immersion photomicrograph of the spiny branchlets from the monkey cerebellar cortex is shown (Fig. 7-5). These curved branchlets have the appearance of poplar tree catkins. Alongside this figure is an electron micrograph (Fig. 7-6) of an ideally sectioned branchlet from the cerebellar cortex of the cat, printed at approximately eight times the magnification of Figure 7-5. The emergence of spines is obvious in both figures.

One of our concerns in a previous study[29] was the determination of the number of spines on 10-μ lengths of the branchlets—a determination necessary to assess, roughly, the total number of spines on a Purkinje cell. This estimation was difficult to make in thick Golgi sections under oil immersion because the spines emerged from all sides of the branchlets. Now, after viewing electron micrographs, we are forced to reconsider our previous estimates. Note the branchlet (Fig. 7-6) sectioned longitudinally in the plane of its cross-sectional diameter. Here, in a distance of about 7 μ, nine spines (s, Fig. 7-6) emerge from this ultrathin section. If this branchlet had been similarly sectioned in a plane at right angles to the present plane, most likely a similar number of spines would be visible. Even these two sections, we believe, would not have revealed all the spines on this segment of the branchlet, for some of the staggered spines would have escaped the planes of section. In another electron micrograph (Fig. 7-7) two longitudinally sectioned spiny branchlets from the monkey cerebellar cortex are displayed. Figure 7-8 a transversely sectioned spiny branchlet from the same species is shown at the same magnification. The diameter of this branchlet, approximately 1 μ, accords with our previous estimates in Golgi preparations. It is obvious, then, that the branchlets in Figure 7-7 are not sectioned in the mid-longitudinal plane; only the edges of the branchlets are in view. Despite this, however, the branchlet extending diagonally from the top to the bottom of the figure reveals nine emerging spines in a stretch of about 8 μ. Furthermore, the two spines emerging from the transversely sectioned branchlet (Fig. 7-8) are about 0.5 μ apart. Although these scattered observations give some indication of the

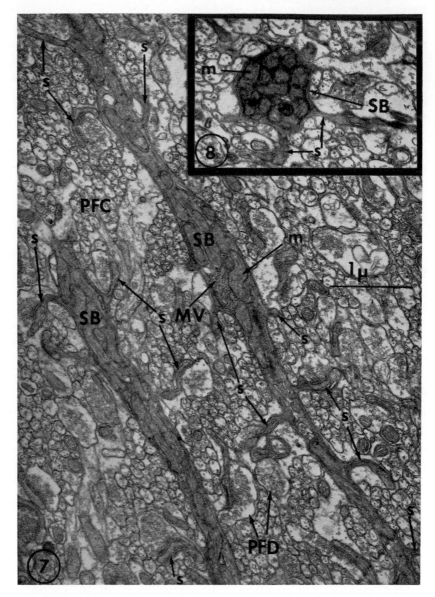

FIG. 7-7. Electron micrograph showing two longitudinally sectioned spiny branchlets (*SB*) filled with mitochondria (*m*). (*MV*) multivesicular body; (*PFC*) constricted portions of parallel fibers; (*PFD*) dilated portions of parallel fibers filled with synaptic vesicles; (*s*) emerging spines. Lead hydroxide–stained section. Monkey cerebellar cortex. ×21,000.

FIG. 7-8. Electron micrograph showing profile of transversely sectioned spiny branchlet (*SB*) filled with profiles of thirteen mitochondria (*m*). (*s*) emerging spines. Lead hydroxide–stained section. Monkey cerebellar cortex. ×21,000.

density of the spines per unit length of the branchlet, it is impossible, from these limited determinations, to estimate precisely the number of spines per unit length of branchlet. Nevertheless, these studies do indicate that our previous estimation[29] of fifteen spines per 10 μ of branchlet is rather conservative and perhaps should be revised upward.

The spiny branchlets, so different from the smooth branches in their surface morphology as revealed in Golgi preparations, are equally different from the smooth branches in their internal ultrastructure as revealed by electron microscopy. Mitochondria are so densely packed in their stroma that the simplest description that can be given is to say that the branchlets are like sacks or sausages (*SB*, Figs. 7-7, 7-8, and 7-10) filled with mitochondria. The crosscut branchlet (Fig. 7-8) 1 μ in diameter, has crowded within it the profiles of thirteen transversely sectioned mitochondria. This close packing of mitochondria obscures the dendritic tubules in most views of the branchlets. True, the dendritic tubules are rather prominent, and there are relatively few mitochondria in the branchlet from the cat cerebellar cortex (Fig. 7-6), but this is not the usual condition encountered in either our cat or monkey material. Ordinarily, the tubules are found in the outer rim of the branchlet subjacent to the surface. Dendritic tubules are seen in the spiny branchlet in the electron micrographs (*dt*, Figs. 7-9 and 7-10) taken from the monkey and cat cerebellar cortices, respectively, and reproduced here at the same magnification. Because no mitochondria show and because parallel-arrayed dendritic tubules are present, the profile of the branchlet (*SB*, Fig. 7-9) is interpreted as passing through the outer rim of the branchlet. On the other hand, there are closely packed mitochondria in the branchlet (*SB*, Fig. 7-10) and the dendritic tubules (*dt*) are near the surface of the branchlets. Our interpretation here is that this profile is deeper in the core of the branchlet.

An element frequently found in the branchlet is the multivesicular inclusion body (*MV*, Figs. 7-6 and 7-7). These membrane-bound inclusions are round or oval in shape, about 0.5 μ in diameter, and contain a number of vesicles ranging from 200 to 400 A in diameter. Their position is usually peripheral in the branchlet. We have as yet never seen these structures in the Purkinje cell cytoplasm or in the

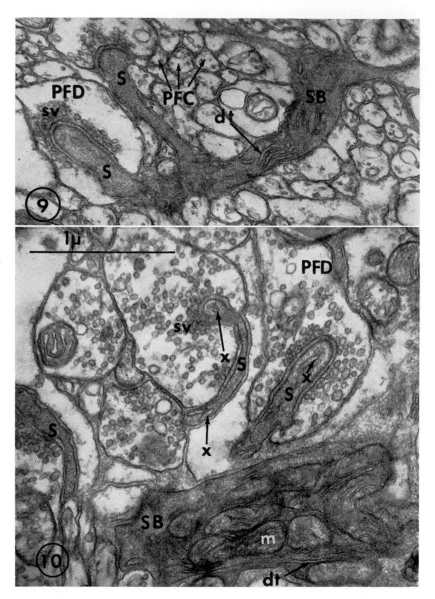

FIG. 7-9. Electron micrograph of spiny branchlet (*SB*) showing emerging spines (*S*). (*PFC*) constricted portions of parallel fibers; (*PFD*) dilated portion of a parallel fiber with synaptic vesicles (*sv*); (*dt*) dendritic tubules. Lead hydroxide–stained section. Monkey cerebellar cortex. ×38,000.

FIG. 7-10. Electron micrograph of spiny branchlet showing dendritic tubules (*dt*) and mitochondria (*m*). (*S*) spines; (*PFD*) dilated portion of a parallel fiber; (*sv*) synaptic vesicles; (*x*) paired sac-like profiles in spines. Lead hydroxide–stained section. Cat cerebellar cortex. ×38,000.

smooth dendrites. They have been observed in the dendrites of the superficial neocortex of cats.[27]

Electron Microscopy of Spines

The average length of the spines in Golgi preparations is approximately 1 μ,[29] which accords with measurements made in the present electron micrographs. Compare the spines in the Golgi preparation (s, Fig. 7-5) with the longest profiles of spines in the electron micrographs (s, Fig. 7-6; s, Figs. 7-9 and 7-10). Occasionally slightly longer spines are found.

In electron micrographs the profiles of spines present a variety of configurations. The most commonly found are profiles of spines completely within the parallel fibers (S, Figs. 7-11 to 7-13); profiles of spines invaginating the parallel fibers (S, Figs. 7-9 and 7-10); profiles of spines indenting the parallel fibers (s, Fig. 7-7; S, Figs. 7-9, 7-17, and 7-18); or profiles of spines curling to conform to the contour of the parallel fibers (s, Figs. 7-6 and 7-7; S, Fig. 7-10). Whether or not every spine invaginates a parallel fiber is impossible to say; a large number of them do. It must be remembered that only profiles are seen, and serial sections would be required to answer this question. However, to entertain the possibility that all spines invaginate parallel fibers, consider the curled spine (S) in Figure 7-10 in synaptic relation with two adjacent parallel fibers. Its complete configuration is, of course, not known. It might be bifid as some spines are in Golgi preparations. Other sections could have been made and profiles obtained that would not reveal one tip of the spine invaginating the upper parallel fiber. From such profiles the erroneous conclusion might be drawn that this spine is completely outside the axon.

The reason for suggesting the possibility that the above spine may be bifid, is the presence of the paired sac-like profiles (x, Fig. 7-10) found in each of its tips, since such profiles are frequently found in the distal end of spines. One is seen in the straight spine to the right. Gray[26] has described a structure in the spines of dendrites in the cerebral cortex which shows sac-like profiles alternating with dense bands. This structure, his spine apparatus, has only been found

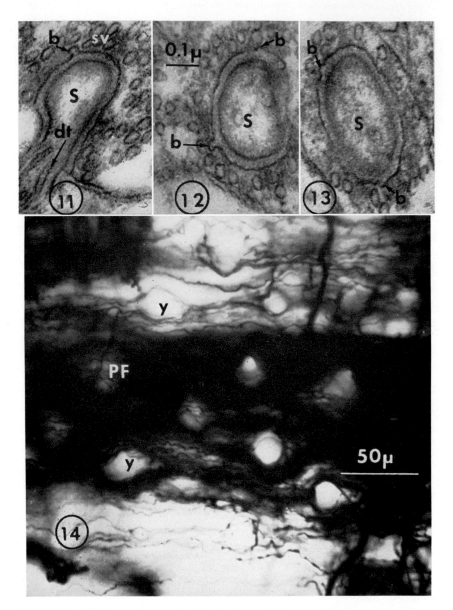

FIG. 7-11. Electron micrograph of spine invaginating parallel fiber. (*b*) bleb on presynaptic membrane; (*dt*) dendritic tubules at the base of the spine; (*S*) spine; (*sv*) synaptic vesicles. Lead hydroxide–stained section. Monkey cerebellar cortex. ×85,000.

FIG. 7-12. Electron micrograph showing profile of spine within parallel fiber.

in the cerebral cortex. We wonder if the paired sac-like profiles in the spines of Purkinje cell branchlets may represent some distant variant of Gray's spine apparatus.

The stroma of the spines in our lead hydroxide–stained sections appears to be of the same consistence and electron density as the stroma of the branchlets (Figs. 7-6 to 7-10). We have never observed mitochondria or dendritic tubules in the spines. However, we have occasionally seen dendritic tubules oriented in the direction of the spines near the bases (*dt*, Fig. 7-11).

At the synaptic junctions of the spines and the parallel fibers, the apposing membranes are thickened and separated from each other by the 300-A gap of the synaptic cleft. The thickened postsynaptic membranes of the spines may be slightly thicker than the thickened presynaptic membranes of the parallel fibers, but in our lead hydroxide–treated sections this difference is not as striking as it is in Gray's[14] phosphotungstic acid–treated sections of the same synapse in the rat cerebellar cortex. This may be due to the differences in the techniques employed. On the basis of the greater thickness of the postsynaptic membrane, Gray considered the spine and parallel fiber synapse a type-1 synapse in his system of classification.[26]

Attention is called to the blebs (*b*, Figs. 7-11 to 7-13) on the parallel fiber presynaptic membranes. We have observed these inpockets not only on parallel fiber presynaptic membranes but also on mossy fiber presynaptic membranes and have wondered if they may be related to the synaptic vesicles. The question we ask is this: Does the membrane of a synaptic vesicle fuse with the presynaptic membrane; the membranes dissolve at the point of fusion, emptying the contents of the vesicle into the intersynaptic cleft; and the bleblike remainder participate in the reconstruction of the presynaptic membrane? Of course, there is no proof for this; it is only a suggestion.

Note blebs (*b*) on presynaptic membrane. Lead hydroxide–stained section. Monkey cerebellar cortex. ×85,000.

FIG. 7-13. Electron micrograph showing the oval profile of spine (*S*) within parallel fiber. (*b*) blebs on presynaptic membrane. Lead hydroxide–stained section. Monkey cerebellar cortex. ×85,000.

FIG. 7-14. Photomicrograph of Golgi preparation through deep part of molecular layer in longitudinal plane parallel to surface of cortex. (*PF*) densely impregnated mass of parallel fibers; (*y*) spaces for upper portion of Purkinje cells. Monkey cerebellar cortex.

THE PARALLEL FIBERS

The magnitude of the unmedullated fiber plexus in the molecular layer, apparent in low-power electron micrographs (Figs. 7-1 and 7-19), is a corollary of the large number of granule cells in the granular layer. It has been estimated that there are more than 2 million granule cells per cubic millimeter of granular layer in the monkey cerebellar cortex,[29] and more recent estimates made on human material place this figure between 3 and 7 million granule cells per cubic millimeter of granular layer.[30] Another factor contributing to the density of this plexus is the length of the individual parallel fibers. Calculations based on rather fragmentary Golgi observations estimate the lengths to range from 3 mm. for the longest to 1 mm. or less for the shortest parallel fibers.[29] These measurements refer to the total length of individual parallel fibers and include both segments of the parallel fiber issuing from the point of the T-shaped bifurcation. The only other possible contributors to this plexus, i.e., unmedullated fibers with the same orientation as the parallel fibers, are the right-angle collaterals of the transversal fibers, which Estable[31] discovered; the axons of the intermediate cells of Lugaro,[32] and possibly unmedullated terminals of the supraganglionic plexus. The transversal fibers are the axons of the inferior stellate cells, i.e., the basket cells. We have observed these right-angle collaterals— Estable's[31] longitudinal fibers—and they are always seen immediately above the Purkinje cell layer, which is also the location of the axons of the intermediate cells of Lugaro.[32] Unmedullated terminals of the supraganglionic plexus have never been seen, but since this plexus shows medullated fibers as small as 0.3 μ, any unmedullated terminals must be extremely small. Considering the quantity of all the elements involved, the contributions from these sources are relatively insignificant compared with the contribution of the granule cells. Moreover, they are confined to the most inferior portion of the molecular layer. We have never observed right-angle collaterals on the superior stellate cells, so we feel perfectly confident in interpreting crosscut profiles of all unmedullated axons in the outer four-fifths of the molecular layer in transverse sections as parallel fibers.

The density of the parallel fibers is frequently revealed in Golgi preparations. Observe the band of parallel fibers, impregnated en masse, in the Golgi section deep in the molecular layer (Fig. 7-14) that slices the folium longitudinally in a plane parallel to the surface of the cortex. It shows how the course of masses of parallel fibers, such as those packed around the summit and the arched dendritic trunk of the Purkinje cell in the montage (Fig. 17-1), weave their way through the molecular layer to accommodate the upward elongations of the Purkinje cells that emerge through the oval and rounded openings (y) in Figure 7-14. Bands and streaks of parallel fibers are also impregnated in the instructive longitudinal section (Fig. 7-15), which reveals the classic orientation of the longitudinally running parallel fibers (*PF*) passing through the flattened dendritic system of a Purkinje cell (*P*) shown here in profile. This section also gives an indication of the superior and inferior distribution of the parallel fibers.

According to Ramón y Cajal,[9] the parallel fibers vary in diameter from 0.5 to 0.2 μ, and he[33] noted that only the parallel fibers in the lower third of the molecular layer are revealed in reduced silver preparations. This refractoriness of the superior parallel fibers to reduced silver suggested to him[16] that they were thinner than the inferior fibers. In this regard the fortunate section of a fortunate impregnation illustrated in Figure 7-16, a photomicrograph, is revealing. Four radially running granule cell axons ascending to different heights within the molecular layer and branching, T- or Y-shaped, to form the parallel fibers, are completely in focus. Notice the heavy parallel fiber (*HPF*) just above the unimpregnated Purkinje cells (*P*) visible in shadowy outline; then observe the successive reduction in the caliber of the parallel fibers at successively higher levels in the molecular layer. This photomicrograph also supplies other observations that facilitate the interpretation of the electron micrographs. Notice the dilations (*PFD*) and the constrictions (*PFC*) on the thinner-caliber parallel fibers. When viewed from above under oil immersion in sections parallel to the surface of the folium, these dilations appear in Golgi preparations as warty rosettes, boutons, and hook-like formations (see Fig. 9 in Fox and Barnard[29]). Before electron micrographs were available, these dilations were regarded as synaptic sites. The correctness of this surmise is now apparent.

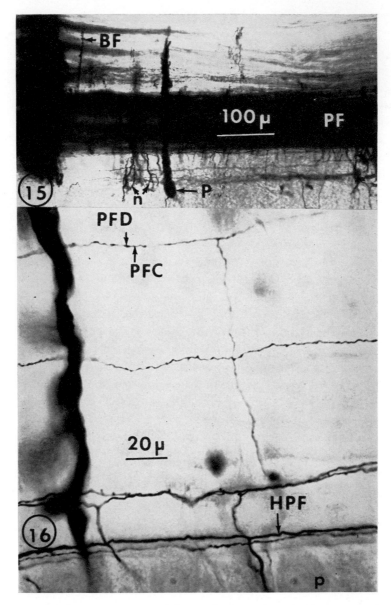

FIG. 7-15. Golgi impregnation of longitudinal section of folium perpendicular to surface of cortex, showing densely impregnated mass of parallel fibers (*PF*) and profile of a Purkinje cell (*P*). (*BF*) Bergmann fiber; (*n*) nest-like formations of basket cell axons that encompass Purkinje cell bodies. Monkey cerebellar cortex.

FIG. 7-16. High-power photomicrograph of Golgi impregnation showing axons of granule cells ascending into molecular layer and their T-shaped bifurcations. (*HPF*) heavy-caliber parallel fiber; (*PFC*) constricted portion of parallel fiber; (*PFD*) dilated portion of parallel fiber; (*P*) Purkinje cell. Monkey cerebellar cortex.

Electron Microscopy of Parallel Fibers

The electron micrographs reproduced as Figures 7-17 and 7-18 are sections from the superficial and inferior regions, respectively, of the molecular layer and are printed at the same magnification on the same plate to facilitate comparisons of these contrasting areas. Figure 7-18 shows two medullated fibers of the supraganglionic plexus and several heavy-caliber parallel fibers. The presence of both these elements immediately indicates the area from which this section is taken. A heavy-caliber fiber near the bottom of the figure has within it the profile of a spine. Another, on the left of the figure, has a spine indenting its surface, and still another, labeled (*HPF*), is invaginated by a spine. There are also a spiny branchlet and a number of profiles of constricted parallel fibers. The latter points out that not all the parallel fibers here are of heavy caliber. Actually, as far as numbers are concerned they constitute only a small fraction of this fiber population (Figs. 7-1 and 7-18). Their prominence is due only to their size. Moreover, during their course the heavy-caliber fibers constrict and become thin caliber.[29]

The absence of heavy-caliber fibers and the multitude of constricted parallel fibers (*PFC*) give the outermost region of the molecular layer its characteristic appearance (Fig. 7-17). The profiles of the dilated portions of the parallel fibers (*PFD*) usually appear smaller than they do in lower regions of the molecular layer. Moreover, the profiles of dendritic spines found here (*s*, Fig. 7-17) are usually seen indenting the parallel fibers, and rarely are such profiles found completely within the parallel fibers.

The dilated portions (*PFD*, Figs. 7-9 and 7-10) of the parallel fibers seen in electron micrographs are obviously profiles of the warty rosettes, the bouton-like swellings, and the hook-like formations seen in Golgi preparations. They are the synaptic terminals. Filled with synaptic vesicles (*sv*, Figs. 7-9 and 7-10), they are in synaptic relation with the dendritic spines. The constricted portions of the parallel fibers seen in electron micrographs are the equivalent regions seen in Golgi preparations. They have no synaptic vesicles; instead they contain several or more longitudinally running tubules—axonic tubules—the circular profiles of which are about 200 A in diameter

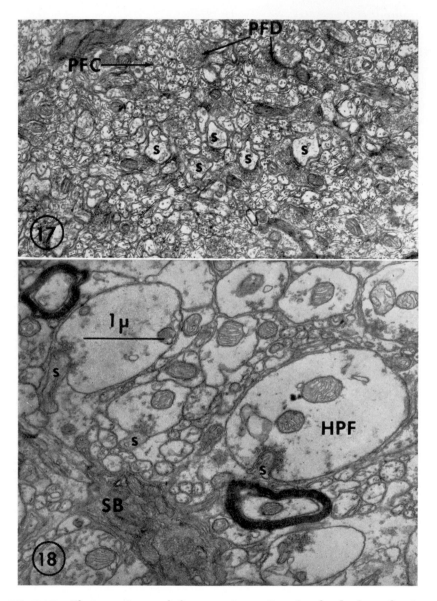

FIG. 7-17. Electron micrograph from superior portion of molecular layer showing constricted portions of parallel fibers (*PFC*) and dilated portions of parallel fibers (*PFD*) filled with synaptic vesicles. Lead hydroxide–stained section. Monkey cerebellar cortex. ×21,000.

FIG. 7-18. Electron micrograph from inferior portion of molecular layer. Note two medullated fibers and spines (*s*) indenting and invaginating heavy-caliber parallel fibers (*HPF*). (*SB*) spiny branchlet. Lead hydroxide–stained section. Monkey cerebellar cortex. ×21,000.

132

and are clearly seen in the electron micrographs (Figs. 7-3, 7-9, and elsewhere). Essentially they are the preterminals preceding the successive regions of synapse along the course of the parallel fibers. Their crosscut profiles are more or less polygonal in shape, and the smallest of them are about 0.1 μ in diameter. It is significant that these nonsynaptic regions of the parallel fibers (*PFC*) are closely packed about the smooth primary and secondary branches in the electron micrograph (Fig. 7-3) and that the synaptic regions of the parallel fibers (*PFD*) are in relation with dendritic spines (*s*) and are a micron or more away from the surfaces of the smooth branches. This affords a clear demonstration of Ramón y Cajal's[8,9] observation that the parallel fibers are not in synaptic relation with the smooth branches of the Purkinje cells.

BERGMANN FIBERS

As a prelude to interpreting the electron micrographs reproduced as Figures 7-19 and 7-20, the following essential background information is given.

The Bergmann fibers are the ascending expansions of the Golgi epithelial cells. These neuroglial elements resemble the Müller cells of the retina,[9] and there is general agreement that they are a special form of astrocyte[34] indigenous to the molecular layer of the cerebellar cortex. The Golgi epithelial cells that give rise to these expansions are situated near and slightly below the Purkinje cells. Some of these cells give off two upward expansions and others give off three, four, and even more. In Golgi preparations these expansions have what appear to be little lateral granular extensions. The upward prolongations run perpendicularly in the molecular layer, forming straight palisades, and terminate at the surface of the cortex in a conical expansion the base of which is directed toward the external surface of the folium. The ensemble of all the conical expansions, side by side, directly beneath the pia mater, forms the basal membrane of the older anatomists. Today these expansions are known as the subpial astrocytic end-feet.

The Bergmann fibers are easily impregnated by the Golgi method and they are dense in the molecular layer. One is shown in the Golgi

FIG. 7-19. Electron micrograph of superficial portion of molecular layer. Note dense packing of constricted portions of parallel fibers (*PFC*) in outer 10 μ of this layer, continuity of palisade-like Bergmann fibers (*BF*) with subpial astrocytic end-feet (*sae*), and dendrites (*D*) of stellate cells. In lower portion of this figure there are spiny branchlets (*SB*) and a vast number of dilated portions of parallel fibers (*PFD*). Monkey cerebellar cortex. ×6,800.

134

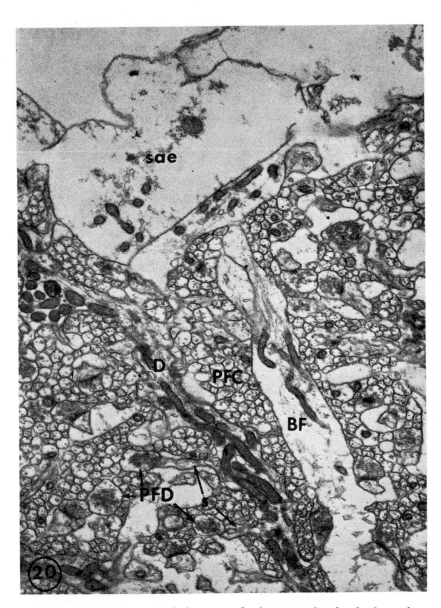

FIG. 7-20. Electron micrograph from superficial portion of molecular layer showing a Bergmann fiber (*BF*) in continuity with subpial astrocytic end-feet (*sae*) and dendrite (*D*) of stellate cell with spines (*s*) contacting dilated portion of parallel fiber (*PFD*). (*PFC*) constricted portions of parallel fibers. Monkey cerebellar cortex. ×19,000.

preparation (*BF*, Fig. 7-15). Ramón y Cajal[9] has demonstrated in longitudinal sections of the folia that the Bergmann fibers are sandwiched between the dendritic arborizations of consecutive Purkinje cells (see his Fig. 51). He has also shown, in longitudinal sections of the folia, that the stellate cells, which include the basket cells, are similarly intercalated between the dendritic spread of consecutive Purkinje cells.

The electron micrographs (Figs. 7-19 and 7-20) were taken from large survey sections prepared in the manner described under "Materials and Methods." They were photographed at 50 kv., at magnifications of 2,600 and 4,800, respectively. Lead hydroxide–treated sections might have brought out more details.

Our reasons for identifying the profiles of the elongated processes (*BF*, Figs. 7-19 and 7-20) as Bergmann fibers are the following: They are elongated; they have little lateral extensions; they are close together (2 μ or a little over 2 μ apart); they have a palisade arrangement; they expand at their upper extremities and enter into the formation of the subpial astrocytic end-feet (Fig. 7-20); and they contain fine fibrils. Moreover, the outer 8 or 9 μ of the upper portion of the micrograph contains no elements of the Purkinje cells.

The outer 9 μ of the superficial portion of the molecular layer, strikingly different than the region below, is filled with a great number of constricted parallel fibers (*PFC*). The dendrites (*D*) in Figures 7-19 and 7-20 are interpreted as dendrites of stellate cells. Two spines emerging from the dendrite in Figure 7-20 are shown in contact with dilated portions of parallel fibers. It should be recalled that these dendrites also have spines and that they are contacted by parallel fibers.[9] Recalling Ramón y Cajal's demonstration of the Bergmann fibers and the stellate cells, sandwiched between consecutive arborizations of Purkinje cells, Figure 7-19 is interpreted as follows: The upper portion of the micrograph is in the plane of the Bergmann fibers and the stellate cells, and the lower portion just slices into the plane containing elements of the Purkinje cells. Note the spiny branchlets (*SB*) here.

The above interpretation of the Bergmann fibers favors the view that the glial cells with watery or less dense cytoplasm are astrocytes.[35] They are obviously not oligodendroglia. Furthermore, Schroeder,[36] who made an exhaustive study of the glia in the cerebellar cortex, using all the classic methods, could find oligodendroglia only in the lower portion of the molecular layer and none in the outer third of this layer. Jakob,[23] whose account of the glia of the cerebellar cortex in Möllendorff's *Handbuch* is based on Schroeder's investigations, shows many of Schroeder's[36] excellent illustrations.

SUMMARY

The discussion has been given throughout this presentation in order to explain immediately the interpretations given the electron micrographs. Only a few comments are added in this summary.

The smooth branches and the spiny branchlets, easily distinguishable by their external morphology in Golgi preparations, are also readily distinguishable from each other by their internal ultrastructure. The smooth branches display longitudinally running dendritic tubules, long slender mitochondria, dense granular inclusion bodies, and occasional scattered RNP particles. At various places at the surface of the dendritic trunk longitudinally disposed cisternae of the endoplasmic reticulum are prominent. The dendritic tubules are sparse in the spiny branchlets and are usually confined to the branchlets' outer rim. The stroma of the branchlets is densely packed with mitochondria, and multivesicular bodies are present.

The dendritic spines have approximately the same electron density as the dendritic branchlets. Usually two sac-like profiles are found near the tips of the spines. Many of the dendritic spines invaginate the parallel fibers.

Correlates of the various features found in Golgi impregnations of the parallel fibers can be found in electron micrographs. Heavy-caliber parallel fibers are located in the most inferior portion of the molecular layer. The constricted portions of the parallel fibers seen in Golgi preparations are shown in electron micrographs to be the preterminals preceding the successive regions of synapse along the course of the parallel fibers. They contain axonic tubules. The warty rosettes, the bouton-like swellings, and the hook-like formations seen in the dilated portions of parallel fibers in Golgi preparations are obviously the synaptic endings on the parallel fibers. They are filled with synaptic vesicles and are in synaptic relation with the dendritic spines.

The interpretation here of the palisade-like elongated profiles, with little electron density, as Bergmann fibers favors the view that glial cells of this consistency are astrocytes.

The suggestion that the bleb-like in-pockets on the preterminal presynaptic membranes of the parallel fibers are related to the synaptic vesicles and that they may represent synaptic vesicles fusing with the presynaptic membrane and emptying their contents into the intersynaptic cleft is only a suggestion and should be regarded accordingly.

Finally, the verification in electron micrographs of many of the details seen in Golgi preparations should strengthen the confidence of the investigators who use this method in the results that this technique gives. The spines, for example, a case in point, have been considered artifacts of the Golgi method,[37-39] end-feet implanted on the dendrite,[40,41] dendritic collaterals,[7] and even as belonging to both the afferent fibers and the dendrites.[42] The spines have now been seen in the cerebral cortex[26,27,43] and on the Purkinje cell branchlets.[14,15,44] Blackstad and Kjaerheim[43] have even made wax reconstructions of dendritic spines of cells in Ammon's horn from serial ultrathin sections. Ramón y Cajal considered the spines dendritic devices for increasing the receptive surface and rendering the synapse more intimate. It is difficult to conceive of a synaptic arrangement more intimate than that of an elongated dendritic spine invaginating a parallel fiber.

We are fully aware that there is not universal agreement that the synaptic vesicles contain transmitter substance or its precursor.[45]

REFERENCES

1. Viets, H. R., and Garrison, F. H. Purkinje's original description of the pear-shaped cells in the cerebellum. *Bull. Hist. Med.* 8:1397, 1940.

2. Ramón y Cajal, S. *Recollections of My Life,* trans. by Craigie, E. H. Philadelphia, American Philosophical Society, 1937, vol. 8, part 2.

3. Ramón y Cajal, S. Les preuves objectives de l'unité anatomique des cellules nerveuses. *Trab. Lab. invest. biol., Univ. Madrid.* 29:1, 1934.

4. RAMÓN Y CAJAL, S. *Neuron Theory or Reticular Theory?* trans. by Ubeda-Purkiss, M., & Fox, C. A. Madrid, Consejo Superior de Investigaciones Cientificas, Instituto Ramón y Cajal, 1954.

5. GOLGI, C. *Untersuchungen über den feineren Bau des centralen und peripherischen Nervensystems,* trans. by Teuscher, R. Jena, Fischer, 1894.

6. RAMÓN Y CAJAL, S. Sur la structure de l'écorce cérébrale de quelques mammifères. *Cellule* 7:123, 1891. (Cited by S. Ramón y Cajal, 1909.)

7. RAMÓN Y CAJAL, S. *Histologie du système nerveux de l'homme et des vertèbres,* trans. by Azoulay, L. Paris, Maloine, 1909, vol. I.

8. RAMÓN Y CAJAL, S. *Les nouvelles idées sur la structure du système nerveux chez l'homme et chez les vertèbres,* trans. by Azoulay, L. Paris, Reinwald, 1895.

9. RAMÓN Y CAJAL, S. *Histologie du système nerveux de l'homme et des vertèbres,* trans. by Azoulay, L. Paris, Maloine, 1911, vol. II.

10. FERNANDEZ-MORAN, H. "Electron Microscopy of Nervous Tissue," in *Metabolism of the Nervous System,* ed. by Richter, D. New York, Pergamon Press, 1957.

11. PALAY, S. L. "An Electron Microscopical Study of Neuroglia," in *Biology of Neuroglia,* ed. by Windle, W. F. Springfield, Ill., Charles C Thomas, 1958.

12. HAGER, H. Elektronenmikroskopische Untersuchungen über die Struktur der sogenannten Grundsubstanz in der Gross- und Kleinhirnrinde des Säugetieres. *Arch. Psych. Ztschr. ges. Neurol.* 198:574, 1959.

13. HAGER, H., and HIRSCHBERGER, W. "Die Feinstruktur der Kleinhirnrinde des Goldhamsters." in *Fourth International Conference on Electron Microscopy,* ed. by Bargmann, W. Berlin, Springer, 1960.

14. GRAY, E. G. The granule cells, mossy synapses and Purkinje spine synapses of the cerebellum: Light and electron microscope observations. *J. Anat.* 95:345, 1961.

15. PALAY, S. L., McGEE-RUSSELL, S. M., GORDON, S. and GRILLO, M. A. Fixation of neural tissues for electron microscopy by perfusion with solutions of osmium tetroxide. *J. Cell Biol.* 12:385, 1962.

16. RAMÓN Y CAJAL, S. Sur les fibres mousseuses et quelques points douteux de la texture de l'écorce cérébelleuse. *Trab. Lab. invest. biol., Univ. Madr.,* 24:215, 1926.

17. STIEDA, L. Zur vergleichenden Anatomie und Histologie des Cerebellum. *Arch. Anat. u. Physiol.* 407–433, 1864.

18. OBERSTEINER, H. Beiträge zur Kenntniss vom feineren Bau der Kleinhirnrinde, mit besonderer Berücksichtigung der Entwicklung. *S. B. Akad. Wiss. Wien,* Bd, 60, Abt. 11, 101–114, 1869.

19. HENLE, J. *Handbuch der Nervenlehre des Menschen.* Brunswick, Vieweg, 1879, Bd. 3, Abt. 2.

20. OBERSTEINER, H. *Anleitung beim Studium des Baues der nervösen Zentralorgane im gesunden und Kranken Zustände.* Leipzig, Toeplitz & Deuticke, 1888.

21. WATSON, M. L. Staining of tissue sections for electron microscopy with heavy metals: II. Application of solutions containing lead and barium. *J. Biophys. & Biochem. Cytol.* 4:727, 1958.

22. Fox, C. A., UBEDA-PURKISS, M., IHRIG, H. D., and BIAGIOLI, O. Zinc chromate modification of the Golgi technique. *Stain Technol.* 26:109, 1951.

23. JAKOB, A. "Das Kleinhirn," in *Handbuch der microskopischen Anatomie des Menschen,* ed. by von Möllendorff, W. Berlin, Springer, 1928, vol. 4, pp. 674–916.

24. PALAY, S. L. Synapses in the central nervous system. *J. Biophys. & Biochem. Cytol.* 2 (Suppl.): 193, 1956.

25. PALAY, S. L. Morphology of synapses in the central nervous system. *Exper. Cell Res.* 5(Suppl.): 275, 1958.

26. GRAY, E. G. Axosomatic and axodendritic synapses of the cerebral cortex: An electron microscope study. *J. Anat.* 93:420, 1959.

27. PAPPAS, G. D., and PURPURA, D. P. Fine structure of dendrites in the superficial neocortical neuropil. *Exper. Neurol.* 4:507, 1961.

28. PALAY, S. L. Fine structure of secretory neurons in the preoptic nucleus of the goldfish (*Carassius auratus*). *Anat. Rec.* 138:417, 1960.

29. Fox, C. A., and BARNARD, J. W. A quantitative study of the Purkinje cell dendritic branchlets and their relationship to afferent fibers. *J. Anat.* 91:299, 1957.

30. BRAITENBERG, V., and ATWOOD, R. P. Morphological observations on the cerebellar cortex. *J. Comp. Neurol.* 109:1, 1958.

31. ESTABLE, C. Notes sur la structure comparative de l'écorce cérébelleuse, et dérivées physiologiques possibles. *Trab. Lab. invest. biol., Univ. Madrid* 21:169, 1923.

32. Fox, C. A. Intermediate cells of Lugaro in the cerebellar cortex of the monkey. *J. Comp. Neurol.* 112:39, 1959.

33. RAMÓN Y CAJAL, S. Un sencillo metodo de coloracion selective del reticulo protoplasmico. *Trab. Lab. invest. biol., Univ. Madrid* 2:129, 1903. (Cited by S. Ramón y Cajal, 1926.)

34. PENFIELD, W. "Neuroglia: Normal and Pathological," in *Cytology and Cellular Pathology of the Nervous System,* ed. by Penfield, W. New York, Hoeber-Harper, 1932, vol. 2.

35. HARTMANN, J. F. "Two Views Concerning Criteria for Identification of Neuroglia Cell Types by Electron Microscopy," in *Biology of Neuroglia,* ed. by Windle, W. F. Sprinfield, Ill., Charles C Thomas, 1958.

36. SCHROEDER, A. H. Die Gliaarchitektonik des menschlichen Kleinhirns. *J. Psychol. Neurol.* 38:234, 1929.

37. KOLLIKER, A. *Handbuch der Gewebelehre des Menschen.* Leipzig, Engelmann, 1896, Bd. 2, Aufl. 6. (Cited by A. Hill, 1897.)

38. Meyer, S. Die subcutane Methylenblauinjection, ein Mittel zur Darstellung der Elemente des Centralnervensystems von Säugethieren. *Arch. mikr. Anat.* 46:282, 1895. (Cited by A. Hill, 1897.)

39. Meyer, S. Ueber eine Verbindungesweise der Neuronen nebst Mittheilungen ueber die Technik und die Erfolge der Methode der subcutanen Methylenblauinjection. *Arch. mikr. Anat.* 47:734, 1896. (Cited by A. Hill, 1897.)

40. Held, H. Beiträge zur Struktur der Nervenzellen und ihrer Fortsätze. *Arch. Anat. u. Physiol.* 21:204, 1897.

41. Bodian, D. Further notes on the vertebrate synapse. *J. Comp. Neurol.* 73:323, 1940.

42. Hill, A. Note on "thorns," and a theory of the constitution of gray matter. *Brain* 20:131, 1897.

43. Blackstad, T. W., and Kjaerheim, A. Special axo-dendritic synapses in the hippocampal cortex: Electron and light microscopic studies on the layer of mossy fibers. *J. Comp. Neurol.* 117:133, 1961.

44. Fox, C. A. In *The Structure of the Cerebellar Cortex in Correlative Anatomy of the Nervous System,* ed. by Crosby, E. C., Humphrey, T., and Lauer, E. W. New York, Macmillan, 1962, pp. 193–198.

45. Barrnett, R. J. The fine structural localization of acetylcholinesterase at the myoneural junction. *J. Cell Biol.* 12:247, 1962.

Corticocortical Connections in the Cerebellum

DOW,[8] IN THE DECEREBRATE PREPARATIONS, STUDIED CORTICAL RESPONSES in the cerebellum following local application of electrical stimuli to adjacent folia. However, as indicated in his paper, because of technical reasons it was necessary to disregard the electrical events occurring during the 1- to 2-millisecond interval immediately after stimulation. Since then, oscillographic techniques have advanced considerably; Brookhart, Moruzzi, and Snider[4] were able to record from single units within the cerebellar cortex, and more recently Granit and Phillips[10,11] have made detailed studies of the behavior of units identified as Purkinje cells during natural and evoked discharges. Also their data indicated widespread corticocortical connections that Dow had not observed. In addition, electrophysiological experiments on intracerebellar connections by Barnard and Woolsey[2] led to the conclusions that connections exist between the anterior lobe and the ipsilateral paramedian lobule. Purpura, Girado, and Grundfest[14] recorded responses in the posterior vermis following electrical activation of the anterior lobe and contralateral crus I. Obviously, such data indicate extensive intracerebellar connections, and it is the purpose of this paper to study these details. Besides the use of gross electrodes on the pial surface, micropipette electrodes

Supported by research grants to Northwestern University from the National Institutes of Health, U.S. Public Health Service.

were inserted into various cortical layers in order to obtain data on the behavior of single cells within the cortex. As can be seen in the following experiments, not only have extensive corticocortical connections been observed but some of the electrical characteristics of these connections have been elucidated as well as their relations to the underlying white matter and cerebellar nuclei.

MATERIALS AND METHODS

The present report is based on observations obtained in work on forty-two adult cats. The animals were anesthetized with chloralosane (70 mg. per kilogram of body weight) given intraperitoneally. The posterior poles of both cerebral hemispheres were ablated, and the anterior and posterior lobes of cerebellum were exposed and explored. For experiments in which pipettes were used, the anterior lobe was exposed and a small niche was made in the pia to admit the electrodes and thus protect the tip. During all surgical procedures, both carotid arteries were kept intact and care was taken to prevent drying of the exposed brain by moistening the surface with mineral oil, except in those areas where the drugs were applied topically.

Electrical stimulations were carried out by single square wave pulses (through an isolation transformer), the duration (0.01 to 0.2 millisecond) and strength (0.5 to 20 v) of which could be altered independently within the limits stated. Bipolar silver wire (2 mm. separation) and concentric stainless steel stimulating electrodes were used. The former were utilized for the cerebellar cortical stimulation, and the latter, insulated except at the tip, were used for the nuclear and subcortical stimulations.

The gross electrodes used for surface recording consisted of silver wires, about 100 μ in diameter, beaded at the tip. Surface recordings were done either monopolarly or bipolarly. The glass micropipettes were made from ordinary glass as well as Pyrex capillary tubing. The latter had finer tips than the former. When filled with 3 M KCl, the d.c. resistance of the microelectrodes was 5 to 30MΩ. They were carefully oriented into the brain with a micromanipulator. The gross electrode was connected to the input of a differential cathode follower input and the micropipette was mounted in a probe containing one of the input tubes. The output of this stage was led both to d.c. and condenser-coupled amplifiers. An indifferent electrode was attached to the periosteum of the skull. Having been amplified, alterations in electrical activity were recorded photographically from the face of a 5-in. double-beam cathode ray oscillograph by means of a kymograph camera. In the case of both gross monopolar and micropipette recording, upward deflections indicate positive potentials at the tip of the lead electrode.

RESULTS

Cortical Responses Recorded Monopolarly and Bipolarly with Gross Electrodes

Cerebellar responses were observed following electrical stimulation of various areas in the cerebellar cortex. Figure 8-1 (*A* to *F*) shows the result of these experiments in which points in the anterior lobe and ansiform lobule (crus I) were stimulated. The records shown in *A* to *C* were obtained with bipolar leads, while those in *D* to *F* were obtained with monopolar leads. Besides the negative potentials observed by Dow,[8] which were obtained in the same folium lateral to the stimulating electrode, two kinds of action potentials of short and long latency were observed. The short-latency potentials were mostly positive, had a latency of 0.8 to 1.2 milliseconds and were observed up to three folia away from the stimulating point. The long-latency potentials displayed a more complicated wave form and had a latency of 1.8 to 3.6 milliseconds and a variable duration depending on the length of the negative phase. The average duration of the positive phase was 4 milliseconds when recorded bipolarly. With monopolar recording, the long-latency responses became progressively smaller when the distance between stimulating and recording electrodes increased, while they were bigger at the 3- to 4-folia interval when the bipolar recording method was used. These two groups of responses were observed in the anterior lobe, tuber vermis and medial part of ansiform lobule (crus I) following stimulation of the middle and lateral part of the anterior lobe. Accordingly, it was concluded that there are interfolial connections between these areas.

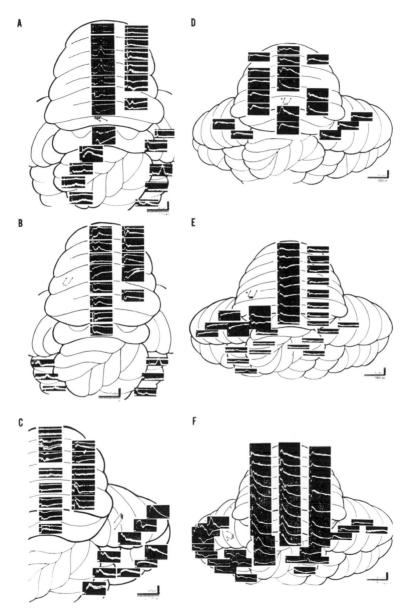

FIG. 8-1. Cerebellar corticocortical responses induced by stimulation of anterior lobe and ansiform lobule. Responses were recorded either bipolarly (*A–C*) or monopolarly (*D–F*). Upward deflection represents positivity in monopolar recording. All six traces of evoked responses were taken at same amplification and sweep time.

145

In addition to the above mentioned short- and long-latency responses, localized responses were obtained in the paramedian lobule following stimulation of the middle and ipsilateral side of the anterior lobe. These responses showed a latency of from 5.6 to 6.3 milliseconds (except in one case of 1.6 milliseconds, as shown in Fig. 8-1*B*) and a duration of 4 to 4.8 milliseconds and were similar to the intracerebellar responses observed by Barnard and Woolsey.[2]

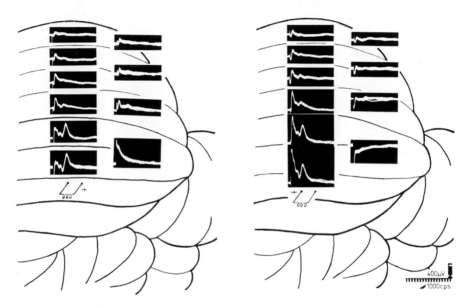

FIG. 8-2. Effect of reversing stimulus polarity on corticocortical responses. Monopolar recording electrode was placed on longitudinal line perpendicularly passing through mid-point of bipolar stimulating electrode in central part and 2 mm. lateral along paravermal vein in lateral part.

Side-to-side connections between the ansiform (crus II) and paramedian lobules were looked for but not seen. In these studies it was regularly observed that the responses were more readily recorded in the anterior lobe, and indeed this was the part of the cerebellum which received the most attention.

Figure 8-2 indicates the effect of reversing the polarity of the electrical stimulus on the corticocortical responses. Near the midline of the anterior lobe, the monopolar recording electrode was placed on successive anterior folia as shown in the figure along a longitudinal line perpendicularly passing through the mid-point of the bipolar stimulating electrode. The short- and long-latency responses were observed irrespective of the stimulus polarity, having a latency of 0.8 and 3.6 milliseconds, respectively. In the responses which were taken in the nearest site to the stimulating point, there appeared a positive notch in the falling phase of the short-latency responses. In the lateral part of the anterior lobe, the recording electrode was situated 2 mm. lateral to the paravermal vein. The responses were masked by a large stimulus artifact when recordings were taken near the stimulating point. However, both short- and long-latency responses could be identified in the distant sites even though their sizes reduced considerably. Therefore it is suggested that these two responses were induced not by the spreading artifact but by the activation of cerebellar neurons.

The left column of Figure 8-3 shows the relation between stimulus strength (indicated in arbitrary units at the right side of each record) and responses in near (*1* in the inserted schema) and far (*2* in the same schema) sites from the stimulating point. Responses were recorded bipolarly. Although both short- and long-latency responses were recorded in the near site as the stimulus strength was increased above a critical suprathreshold level, only long-latency responses appeared at site *2*. The short-latency responses possessed higher thresholds of response than the long-latency ones. Shortening of the latency of response was observed when stronger stimuli were applied.

The right column of Figure 8-3 indicates the effect of double stimuli on corticocortical responses, and the two inserted diagrams show recovery following the conditioning stimulus. Both the short- and long-latency responses were obtained via the bipolar method and are expressed as components I and II, respectively. The spike heights resulting from the test shock were plotted against those of the conditioning shock in different shock intervals. There were no obvious differences in the recovery curve of the short- and long-latency responses; both recovered in 20 to 30 milliseconds following the conditioning stimulus.

Figure 8-4 shows the results of the same experiment recorded monopolarly. Three successive potentials were photographed for each stimulus interval, and the amplitude of response was plotted against

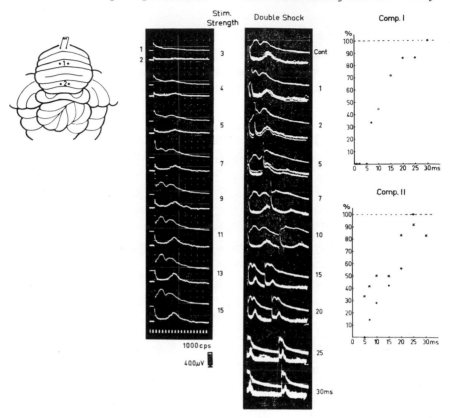

FIG. 8-3. Effects of stimulus strength (left column) and double shock (right column) on corticocortical responses. In left column, stimulus strengths are indicated in arbitrary units at right of each record, of which upper beams show responses in near (*1* in the inserted schema) and far (*2* in the same schema) sites from stimulating point. Numbers at right of double-shock responses indicate intervals between conditioning and test stimuli. Two graphs show recovery curve of response in which spike heights of test shocks are plotted against shock intervals. Short- and long-latency responses are expressed as component I and II, respectively. All records are taken bipolarly.

the intervals between two stimuli. Although responses did not recover completely in 40 milliseconds following the conditioning stimulus, the gradient of the curve was similar to that observed with bipolar recording and reached 70 per cent recovery in 15 milliseconds.

Figure 8-5 indicates cortical responses induced by cortical and fastigial stimulation. In the left column, conditioning stimulus was

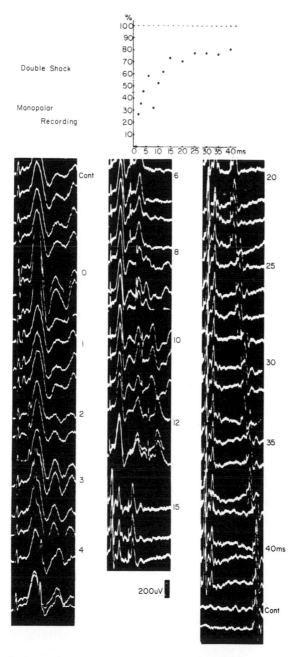

FIG. 8-4. Effect of double-shock stimuli on monopolarly recorded responses. Three successive potentials were taken for each stimulus interval (indicated at right of each record), and recovery curve was plotted against shock intervals.

149

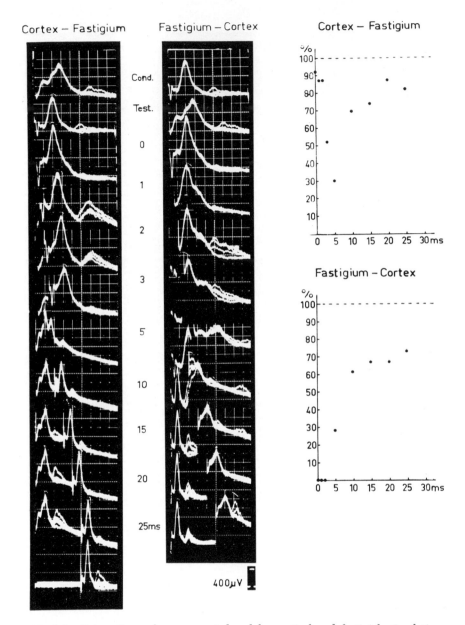

FIG. 8-5. Interactions of responses induced by cortical and fastigial stimulation. Left column, conditioning stimulus was applied to cortex and fastigial stimulation was test stimulus; right column, reverse procedure. Numbers at middle of two records indicate intervals between conditioning and test shocks. Two graphs show recovery curves. Bipolar recording.

150

applied to the cortex and fastigial test stimuli were used. In the right column, the data were collected with the stimulation procedures reversed. Since responses resulting from fastigial stimulation showed a shorter latency, the cortical responses were masked when two kinds of stimuli were given simultaneously. The fastigial responses increased in size; however, the amplitude was lower than the algebraic sum of each cortical and fastigial response, suggesting the existence of some convergence between these two kinds of responses. The small diagrams on the right show excitability curves which result after cortical (upper) and fastigial (lower) conditioning stimuli were used and the results presented as in Figures 8-3 and 8-4. The reponses induced by a test stimulus applied to the cortex were abolished completely by the fastigial conditioning stimulus and had not completely recovered in 30 milliseconds. The fastigial (conditioning) stimulation seemed to influence the amplitude of the cortical (test) responses more than was observed when the reverse procedure was used. These curves (Figure 8-5) were similar to those shown in Figures 8-3 and 8-4.

The left column of Figure 8-6 indicates the effects of topical application of 1% Novocain. The cortical responses were recorded bipolarly, after 1 by 5 mm. filter paper soaked in 1% Novocain solution was allowed to remain on the recording points for 5 minutes. The numbers on the right side show the time the record was taken after removal of the filter paper. The amplitude of the long-latency responses was decreased more than was that of the short-latency ones.

The right column of Figure 8-6 shows the effects of dry ice topically applied on folia between the stimulating and bipolar recording sites. Following application, the latencies of the responses increased and the spike heights decreased (especially in the long-latency responses). Once again the data suggest that the elements responsible for the long-latency responses are located more superficially in the cortex.

Cortical Responses Recorded with Micropipette Electrodes

In the above mentioned results, it was observed that there were corticocortical responses which could be divided into short- and long-latency groups. In order to obtain more detailed knowledge

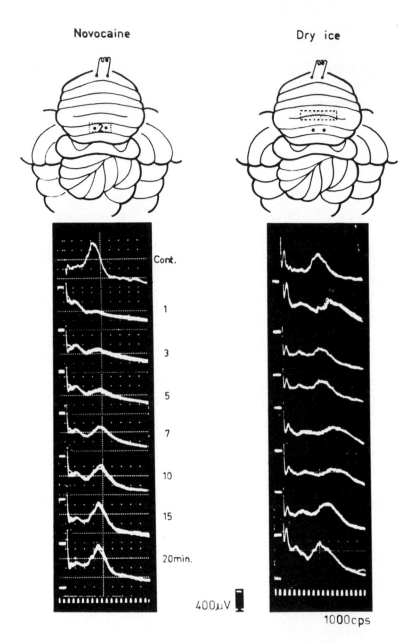

FIG. 8-6. Effects of topical application of 1% Novocain solution at recording point (left column) and of dry ice between stimulating and recording points (right column). Numbers at right of Novocain case indicate time after withdrawal of drug. Bipolar recording.

about the behavior of these responses, the electrical activity was studied following insertion of micropipettes into the cerebellar cortex.

The data shown in Figure 8-7 were collected with a medium-sized micropipette (3 μ outside diameter) inserted into the cerebellar cortex at a point midway between bipolar surface recording electrodes on the anterior lobe, and the electrical stimulus was given four folia rostral to the recording site. The surface responses were recorded on the lower beam of each record. Numbers at the right side of the record indicate the depth of the micropipette tip in microns. Although only the long-latency responses could be seen at the surface, both short- and long-latency responses were identified with micropipette recording and showed a latency of 0.8 and 3.2 milliseconds, respectively. The short-latency responses remained positive until the tip of the micropipette reached 900 μ below the surface; then they became negative and reversed to positive when the tip was deepened to 1,200 μ. The long-latency responses, on the contrary, changed polarity from positive to negative at 200 μ below the surface and remained negative to 700 μ, when they became positive once more. Superimposed on the responses were several negative spikes of 0.4 to 0.6 millisecond in duration, which often fused into larger ones. When the micropipette was inserted deeper than 700 μ, the amplitude of the positive responses became larger, and a second negative wave appeared preceding the response. This negative wave disappeared at the 1,300 μ level, and the long-latency response reversed polarity and became negative again. However, this negativity did not persist long, and the tip became positive again at 1,400 μ. Soon after (1,500 μ), the third positive wave appeared between short- and long-latency responses. It is suggested that the short-latency responses were induced by electrical dipoles situated between 900 and 1,200 μ below the surface and the long-latency ones were formed by those situated between 200 and 700 μ below the surface.

It is emphasized that these values are micromanipulator readings on the manipulator, and the movement of the cerebellum during various respiratory and circulatory functions makes it difficult to localize accurately the origin of these responses other than to say that the mechanism responsible for the long-latency ones is situated more superficially than is that of the short-latency one.

Figures 8-8 to 8-10 show various patterns of the corticocortical

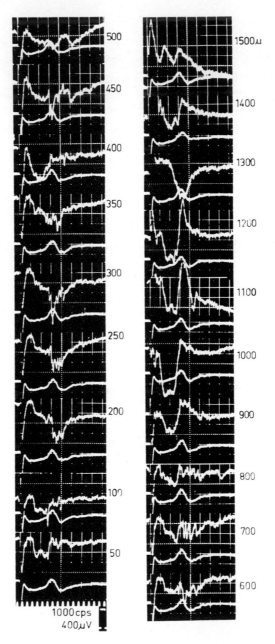

FIG. 8-7. Cerebellar responses recorded by medium-sized micropipette (upper beam of each record). Micropipette was inserted at mid-point of bipolar surface recording electrode. Numbers at right of each record indicate depths of tip of electrode in micromanipulator reading. Lower beam of each record is surface response. Stimulus was given four folia rostral to recording site.

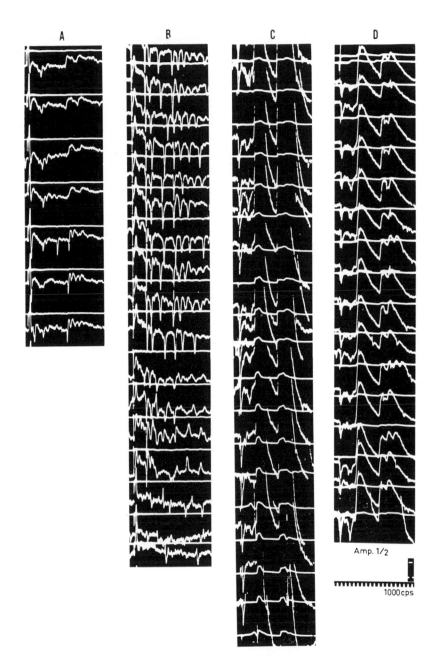

Amp. 1/2

1000cps

FIG. 8-8. Cerebellar corticocortical responses recorded by fine micropipette. Micropipette was slowly inserted into cortex, and recording starts from bottom of column *A* to top of column *D*. Unit voltage indicates 16 mv for d.c. amplification and 400 μv for C-R amplification. C-R amplification was reduced to a half in column *D*.

155

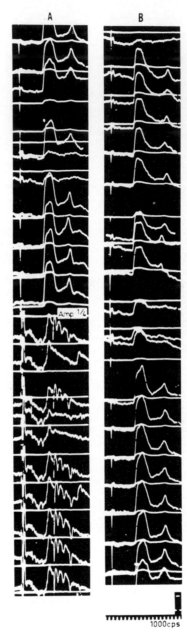

FIG. 8-9. Same as Figure 8-8. Micropipette was approached to cell and then inserted into cell. Membrane potential, 25 mv. Recording was done from bottom of column A to top of column B. Unit voltage indicates 16 mv for d.c. amplification, 400 μv for C-R amplification, and 1,600 μv for the upper half of column A and whole of column B.

156

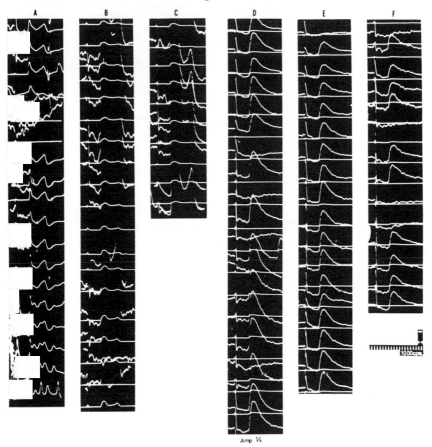

FIG. 8-10. Sequence of intracellularly recorded corticocortical response. Record was taken every 670 milliseconds from beginning of penetration (bottom, column A) until deterioration (top, column F) except for a slight interruption to reduce C-R amplification to one-fourth between columns C and D. Unit voltage indicates 16 mv for d.c. amplification, 400 μv for C-R amplification in columns A–C, and 1,600 μv in columns D–F.

responses recorded by fine micropipettes (less than 1 μ outside diameter). When the micropipettes were inserted slowly into the cortex, responses consisted of several negative spikes which appeared as shown in Figure 8-8B. They responded in an all-or-none fashion. Following electrical stimulation, the latency of the first spike was 3.0 to 3.2 milliseconds and within the limits of the long-latency responses.

The long latency and the all-or-none character of these spikes suggest that they are unitary discharges activated multisynaptically. The short-latency responses were still positive at this depth, which suggest that they arise from a deeper origin. With a slightly deeper insertion of the electrode, there occurred a sudden negative shift of d.c. potentials (up to 20 mv), and the above mentioned negative spikes reversed their polarities and increased in amplitude. Although the potential and the spike height was smaller than is usually the case, the authors suggest that these indicate that the micropipette was inserted into the cell. Figures 8-8C and D, and 8-10 show the sequence of the intracellular recordings. The condenser-coupled amplification was reduced to a half in Figure 8-8D, and to a quarter in Figure 8-10D to F. At the early stage of the penetration, repetitive firings, whose intervals ranged from 1.5 to 3.2 milliseconds and which correspond to the extracellularly recorded unitary discharges, were initiated (Fig. 8-10A.) The second and fourth spikes were smaller than the first, third, and fifth in the bottom record of Figure 8-10A, suggesting that they were in a relatively refractory period following the first and third spikes. After this stage, repetitive firing decreased in frequency and usually consisted of two broad-based spikes, as shown in Figure 8-10B and C, with an interval of 5 milliseconds between them.

Occasionally two successive spikes were recorded soon after penetration of the cell membrane, as shown in Figures 8-8C and 8-9A. In the later stage of penetration, only one spike of low amplitude was recorded, and this gradually became smaller until it disappeared (Fig. 8-10D to F). The latency of this spike corresponded to the first spike of repetitive firings.

Following further insertion of the micropipettes, another type of response was recorded. The short-latency responses were diphasic (positive-negative) as shown in Figure 8-11. The latency of the spike was 1.0 milliseconds and the duration was 1.0 to 1.5 milliseconds. With slightly deeper insertion, two new events were observed. The first was a sudden appearance of repetitive spikes, as shown in the third record from the top of Figure 8-11. The duration of these spikes was 0.8 to 1.0 millisecond, and the frequency was 500 per second. They were independent of the stimuli and usually were observed for a short period. When they disappeared, the previously

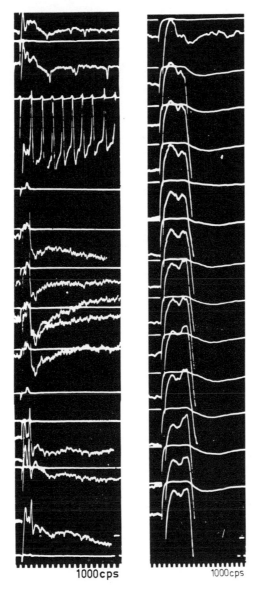

1000cps   1000cps

FIG. 8-11. *Left.* Changes of short-latency corticocortical responses following micropipette insertion into cerebellar cortex. Third record from top is supposed to show injury discharges. Recording was done from bottom to top. Unit voltage indicates 16 mv for d.c., and 400 μv for C-R, amplification.

FIG. 8-12. *Right.* After-potentials of short-latency responses. Maximum value of hyperpolarization was 10 mv. Top record was extracellular recording. Unit voltage shows 16 mv for d.c., and 400 μv for C-R, amplification.

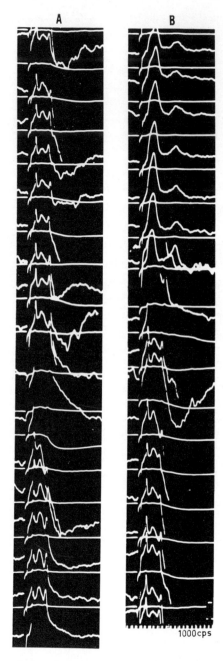

FIG. 8-13. Changes of short-latency responses along with micropipette penetration. Recording was done from bottom of column *A* to top of column *B*. Unit voltage indicates 16 mv for d.c., and 400 μv for C-R, amplification.

noted spike potentials also vanished. The absence of d.c. potential shift and the sudden appearance and disappearance of these spikes suggest that the micropipette was attached to the cell momentarily, thus causing slight injury. The second event is shown in Figures 8-12 and 8-13. Superimposed on the positive wave of long duration were three smaller positive spikes. The intervals between these spikes ranged from 1.2 to 2.2 milliseconds and seemed to resemble those observed in the repetitive firing shown in Figure 8-10. Soon these spikes disappeared, and two small waves remained which were followed by a negative potential shift. The negative shift to 10 mv suggested that the micropipette was in the cell and that the after-hyperpolarization occurred during the short-latency responses. Thus by means of micropipette recording the two events responsible for the corticocortical short- and long-latency responses were identified.

Figure 8-14 indicates a different type of unit discharge. These units were usually observed at slightly deeper levels than were the short-latency responses and appeared as negative, then positive-negative, and finally as positive discharges, as the electrode was inserted into the cortex. The duration of these spikes was slightly longer than of those described above and varied from 1.2 to 1.8 milliseconds. The frequency ranged from 220 to 300 discharges per second. They were neither induced nor changed in form by cortical and fastigial stimulation. Despite numerous attempts, this kind of discharge was never observed with intracellular recording techniques. The possibility that these discharges arise from small granule cells is being investigated.

In the above mentioned results, three kinds of cerebellar cortical activities were observed. In the hope of gaining additional information on the origin of these discharges, responses induced by fastigial stimulation were recorded and compared with those induced by cortical stimulation. Figures 8-15 to 8-17 indicate patterns of these responses when altered by electrical excitation of the ipsilateral nucleus fastigii. In the train of negative spikes which appeared (having a latency of 2.8 milliseconds, as shown in Fig. 8-15*B*), several spikes succeeded the first one, the largest one of which was observed at 6.2 to 6.8 milliseconds after the first. Occasionally a negative spike with a latency of 0.3 to 0.5 millisecond was observed which often fused with the shock artifact and was difficult to analyze. With slightly deeper insertion of the recording micropipette, the above mentioned negative spikes became positive-negative and increased in amplitude as shown in Figure 8-16. The short-latency spike, which could not be differentiated from the shock artifact in the previous description, was clearly identified as the first spike of the train

Spontanous Discharge Cortical Stimulation Fastigial Stimulation

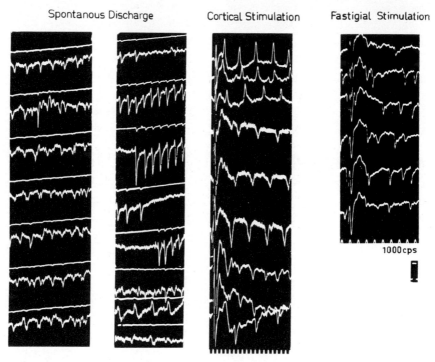

1000 cps

FIG. 8-14. Another type of unitary discharge in cerebellar cortex. These were neither induced nor changed in pattern by cortical and fastigial stimulation. Records were taken by C-R amplification in cortical and fastigial stimulation. Unit voltage shows 16 mv for d.c., and 400 μv for C-R, amplification. Right column used faster sweep speed.

discharges. The latency of this spike was 0.6 to 0.7 millisecond. Following the first spike, there were four to five discharges; the interval between each ranged from 2.0 to 2.5 milliseconds and was similar to those induced by cortical stimulation. The first spike often failed to appear, and the discharge began with the so-called second spike as shown in the middle record of Figure 8-16A.

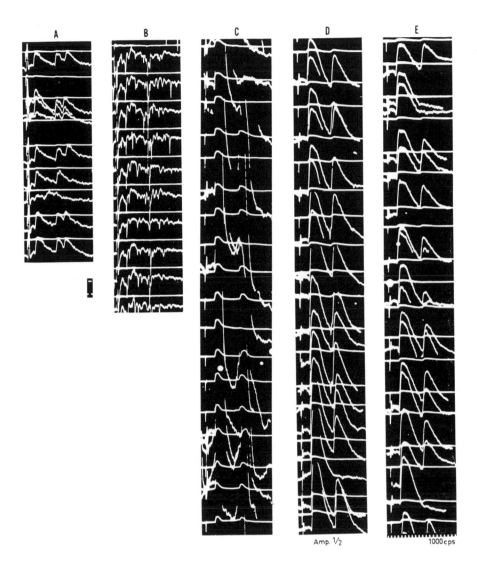

FIG. 8-15. Cerebellar responses induced by fastigial stimulation. Micropipette was inserted into cortex; recording was done from bottom of column A to top of column E. Unit voltage indicates 16 mv for d.c., and 400 μv for C-R, amplification. C-R amplification was reduced to one-half in columns D and E.

163

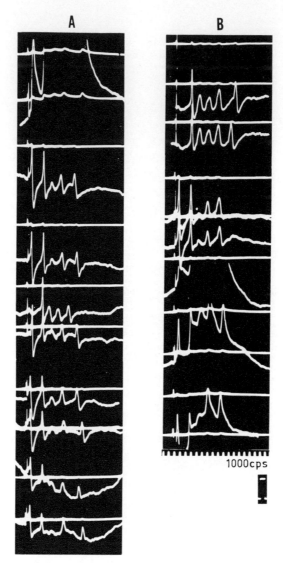

FIG. 8-16. Same as Figure 8-15. Recording was done from bottom of column A to top of column B. Unit voltage indicates 40 mv for d.c., and 1,600 μv for C-R, amplification.

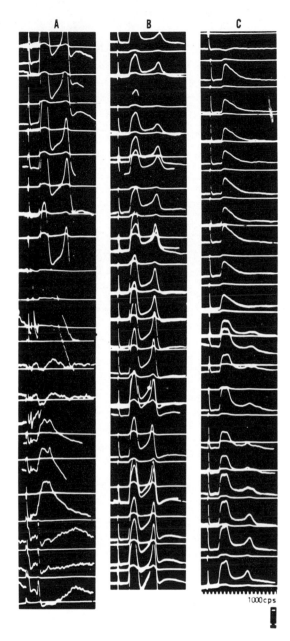

FIG. 8-17. Changes of response pattern induced by fastigial stimulation along with micropipette insertion. Recording was done from bottom of column *A* to top of column *C*. Intracellular recordings are for every 670 milliseconds. Unit voltage indicates 40 mv for d.c., and 1,600 μv for C-R, amplification.

165

Following further insertion of the electrode, there appeared a negative potential shift to more than 13 mv, and the repetitive discharges increased in amplitude and positivity accompanied by loss of the negative component. It was regularly observed that the first spike appeared alone, but when followed by other discharges it was lower in amplitude than the other spikes. Figures 8-15C to E and 8-17A and B illustrate this point. The latency and the spike intervals were 2.8 and 5 to 6.8 milliseconds, respectively, and correspond to the first and most prominent successive negative spike recorded in Figure 8-15B.

The authors suggest that the short-latency responses were the antidromic or monosynaptic firings of the cortical cells and the successive responses were the multisynaptic firings of single cells in which the synaptic delay within the cerebellar cortex was not unusually long. The fact that the first short-latency spike was isolated from the successive spikes and easily disappeared probably favors the view of the antidromic origin of it. If this is the case, one might suppose this represents Purkinje cell activities, since this is the only cortical element which can be activated by fastigial stimulation.

Figure 8-18 shows the long-latency responses induced by the fastigial stimulation. Following the insertion of the recording micropipette into the cerebellar cortex, the diphasic positive-negative responses increased in amplitude and became positive monophasic when the electrode was very near to the cells (Fig. 8-18A). The latency of the response was 7.2 milliseconds, and the intervals of repetitive firings were 2.8 to 3.6 milliseconds. The later spikes were broader than the first. When the electrode was inserted slightly deeper, there appeared a sudden negative potential shift to 57 mv and the responses suddenly increased in amplitude (35 mv in Fig. 8-18B). The authors interpret this to indicate that the electrode was inserted into the cell. At the early stages of penetration, repetitive discharges were recorded in which cellular firings became progressively smaller and broader.

In the above mentioned experimental results, it was observed that the pattern of cerebellar cortical responses induced by fastigial stimulation was quite similar to that induced by the cerebellar cortical stimulation. Thus short latency, short duration, and difficulty of recording by means of the micropipette technique were the common

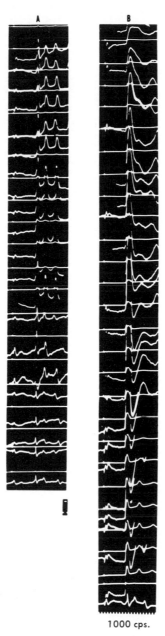

1000 cps.

FIG. 8-18. Same as Figure 8-17 except responses have long latency. Changes of response pattern were clearly shown from bottom of column *A* to top of column *B*. Membrane potential, 57 mv. Unit voltage indicates 40 mv for d.c., and 1,600 μv for C-R, amplification.

properties of the short-latency responses, and longer duration plus characteristic patterns of repetitive firing were the properties of the long-latency responses. Therefore one might suppose that the cortico-cortical short-latency responses were antidromic firings of Purkinje cells and long-latency responses were multisynaptic firings of the same cells. In order to obtain information on this assumption the data shown in Figure 8-19 were obtained.

Figure 8-19 shows the cerebellar cortical responses induced by fastigial stimulation. All-or-none unitary discharges were recorded following fastigial stimulation and are shown in the lower half of Figure 8-19A. The latency of response was 0.5 millisecond, and the intervals of repetitive discharges ranged from 2.0 to 2.5 milliseconds. When the electrode approached the cell membrane, the responses increased in amplitude. The upper half of Figure 8-19A and the lower part of 8-19B indicate the responses induced by threshold fastigial stimuli. The latency of responses was 2.2 milliseconds, and the activity consisted of three successive positive-negative spikes. When stronger stimuli were applied, the latency of the first discharge shortened to 0.5 millisecond, as shown in the middle part of Figure 8-19B.

Following fastigial stimulation, stimuli were applied to the cerebellar cortex, and electrical alterations were recorded from the same unit in nearby folia; these responses are shown in the upper part of Figure 8-19B and the lower part of 8-19C. Except that the latency was 3.8 milliseconds, the pattern of discharges was quite similar to that induced by fastigial stimulation. The upper part of Figure 8-19C shows the result of fastigial stimulation followed closely by cortical stimulation. The same response pattern occurred which followed previous fastigial stimulation. It is concluded that these Purkinje cells were activated equally either by fastigial or by cortical stimulation.

Figure 8-20 presents the results of interactions of responses induced by cortical and fastigial stimulation when the data are recorded from intracellular electrodes. Responses induced by the fastigial stimulation showed a latency of 2.8 milliseconds, suggesting that more than two synapses were involved. Two successive spikes separated by 6.3-millisecond intervals were observed in the later stage of penetration (Fig. 8-20A, B, and lower record in C). By switching the stimuli to the cerebellar cortex, single positive monophasic responses of 6-millisecond latency were recorded (middle of Fig. 8-20C). Although

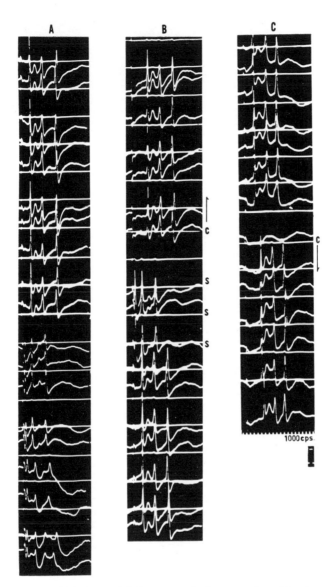

FIG. 8-19. Extracellularly recorded unitary discharges induced by fastigial stimulation. When micropipette was very near to cell, threshold stimuli were applied (from upper half of column *A* to lower part of column *B*), then stronger stimuli were given (s in middle of column *B*). Stimuli then switched to cortical stimulation (upper part of column *B* to lower half of column *C*) and indicate that same unit was activated either by fastigial or by cortical stimulation. Upper half of column *C* shows responses induced by fastigial stimulation and shows no excitability change during this experiment. Unit voltage indicates 40 mv for d.c., and 1,600 μv for C-R, amplification.

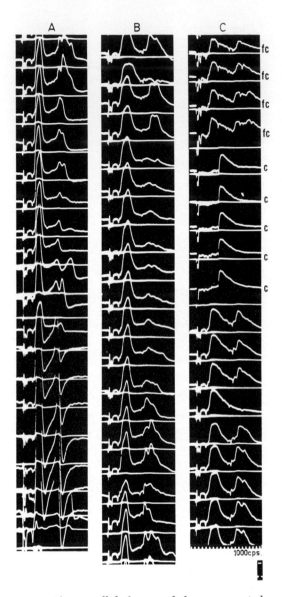

FIG. 8-20. Sequence of intracellularly recorded responses induced by fastigial stimulation. Recording was done every 670 milliseconds from beginning of penetration (bottom of column *A*). Stimuli were switched to cortical stimulation (c in column *C*), and then fastigial and cortical stimulation were applied simultaneously (fc in column *C*). Convergence of responses initiated by fastigial and cortical stimulation are shown. Unit voltage indicates 40 mv for d.c., and 1,600 μv for C-R, amplification.

the activity of the penetrated cell was beginning to deteriorate, these data indicated that fastigial and cortical impulses can converge upon the same cerebellar cortical cells. When fastigial and cortical stimuli were applied simultaneously (upper four records in Fig. 8-20C), the response patterns were similar to that induced by the fastigial stimulation alone, except that a negative notch which corresponds to the above mentioned cortical responses was observed. Since the micropipette was in the cell, this negative notch suggests outward flow of current, probably due to the incoming impulses. However, it is doubtful that this would initiate cell firing. Thus it appeared that both fastigial and cortical impulses converged on the same Purkinje cell and interacted with each other in such a way as to be recorded intracellularly.

DISCUSSION

Some of the electrophysiological properties of cerebellar activity evoked by direct cortical stimulation were analyzed experimentally by Dow[8] and by Purpura, Girado, and Grundfest.[14] These authors concluded that the cerebellar electrocortical activity was markedly deficient in a surface-positive component. The corticocortical responses in the present study had a prominent surface-positive component except when the responses were recorded in the same folium as the stimulating electrode. Considering that Dow's responses were confined to the same folium as the stimulating electrode, and that Purpura, Girado, and Grundfest's responses (cf. their Figs. 4:5 to 4:8 and 4:9 to 4:12) actually showed surface-positive components when recorded in the posterior vermis or crus I following stimulation of the anterior vermis and contralateral crus I, respectively, the present authors were not surprised to see a surface-positive component in this study. It was not surprising that the polarity of the potentials changed from positive to negative when the medium-sized micropipette was pushed deeper into the cerebellar cortex as shown in Figure 8-7. Since the polarity changes occurred deeper than the molecular layer, the suggestion is made that we were recording from Purkinje cell bodies or granule cells.

In the present study, corticocortical responses were divided into three groups: (1) short-latency responses, (2) long-latency responses, and (3) localized evoked surface responses. The former two responses were recorded in folia adjacent to the stimulating point, and the size decreased gradually as the distance between stimulating and recording electrodes increased. The response recorded farthest away seemed to correspond to the intracerebellar potentials observed by Barnard and Woolsey.[2]

An obvious difference between the corticocortical responses recorded via bipolar techniques as contrasted with the monopolarly recorded ones was that the short-latency responses were bigger when monopolar recording was used than when bipolar recording was used. The long-latency responses became smaller as the distance between stimulating and recording point increased with monopolar recording, while they were largest three to four folia away from the stimulating point when recorded bipolarly. Since bipolar recording picks up potential differences between two points on the cortical surface, differences of distance from the stimulating point to the near and far bipolar recording electrodes influence potential differences at each electrode tip, and the slow conducting elements tend to separate out more clearly than do the fast conducting ones.

The long latency of these responses indicate slow impulse conduction since it is likely that there are few, if any, synapses involved. On the contrary, if impulse conduction is very fast and the altered potential arrives at the bipolar recording points almost simultaneously, as a result of the peculiarity of conduction fibers recorded by bipolar methods, they will not be clearly shown however big the responses as recorded monopolarly. This is a possible explanation of the fact that the short-latency responses are larger when the monopolar recording techniques are used.

Before the use of the fine micropipettes in this study, two kinds of cerebellar cortical elements were considered as responsible for the origin of the short- and long-latency responses. One, located in the deeper part of the cerebellar cortex, was supposed to be responsible for the short-latency responses, and the other, more superficially located, was considered responsible for the long-latency responses. However, the facts that two kinds of responses, which seemed to correspond to the short- and long-latency corticocortical responses were recorded in the same cerebellar unit following fastigial stimulation (Figs. 8-16 and 8-17) and that both cortical and fastigial stimulation were equally effective in initiating the activity of the same unit and interacted with each other (Figs. 8-19 and 8-20) suggest that both short- and long-latency responses can be induced by the activity of the same cerebellar cells. Furthermore, the short latency indicates that antidromic firing of Purkinje cells may have occurred. Accordingly, the long-latency responses may result from multisynaptic firing of Purkinje cells. In few cases there appeared a breaking point in the rising phase of the responses which suggests the participation of the prepotential in the cell firing. However, the mechanism of cell firing is beyond the scope of this study, and only the discharges which responded in an all-or-none fashion were described. Ramón y Cajal[6] described two types of recurrent collaterals of Purkinje cell axons. They were *plexus sous-cellulaire* and *plexus suscellulaire*. The former spreads among the cells below the Purkinje cell body, and the latter traverses the molecular layer giving off branches along the way. It is probable that the Purkinje cells are activated antidromically by way of these collaterals.

According to Granit and Phillips,[10] the shortest-latency cerebellar cortical responses (0.35 to 0.6 millisecond) induced by fastigial stimulation were attributed to antidromic activation of the Purkinje cells. In the present study, the short-latency responses induced by the fastigial stimulation had a latency of 0.5 millisecond, and this is considered confirmatory of the data of Granit and Phillips. The longer-latency response of the short-latency group (0.8 to 1.2 milliseconds resulting from cortical stimulation) suggest monosynaptic or slow antidromic conduction. Granit and Phillips also encountered "giant extracellular responses" as large as 60 mv in amplitude; such giant responses were never observed in the present experiments.

The extracellularly recorded unitary responses were positive-negative when the micropipettes were supposed to be very near the cells. Recently, Hild and Tasaki[12] recorded action potentials from neuron somata and dendrites both extra- and intracellularly in tissue cultured cat and rat cerebellum and stated that these diphasic action potentials were never observed unless the recording electrode was actually dimpling the neuronal membrane. One of the phenomena described in Figure 8-11 indicated that the micropipette was attached to the cell membrane, thus causing injury discharges. When the electrode was pushed slightly deeper, the cell slipped away and the discharges disappeared.

When the micropipettes were inserted into the cell, there appeared a negative potential which varied from 13 to 57 mv, and the action potentials became positive monophasic but deteriorated very fast. Although these values were much smaller than the usual membrane and action potentials recorded intracellularly, the first intracellular record of cerebellar units taken by Buser and Rouguel[5] showed 20 to 45 mv. These workers also commented on the difficulty of maintaining the resting and action potentials of the Purkinje cells, as did Granit and Phillips[10] and Hild and Tasaki.[12] The former attributed the difficulty to the "double membrane" of the Purkinje cells, and the latter to the presence of some fibrous material on the neuronal surface.

The action potentials induced by the cortical and fastigial stimulation showed repetitive firing when recorded extracellularly (Figs. 8-16 and 8-19) or in the early period of cell penetration (Figs. 8-10, 8-18, and 8-20). In the intracellular recording of the hippocampal neurons, Kandel and Spencer[13] described the interplay of the sustaining and limiting mechanisms of repetitive firings. The intracellularly recorded repetitive firings in this study were similar to those of Kandel and Spencer and suggest that similar neuronal mechanisms may be present in Purkinje cells also.

Concerning Purkinje cell activity, there is an obvious difference between the results of the present report and that of Granit and Phillips.[10] Purkinje cells were silent unless stimulated either antidromically or orthodromically in this study except in the case shown in Figure 8-10. On the contrary, in the experiments of Granit and Phillips, Purkinje cells generally fired at 30 pulses per second. However, in the latter experiments decerebrate animals were used and Purkinje cells were activated by the tonic regulatory impulses from the musculature, which was not the case in the present study. Brookhart, Moruzzi, and Snider[3,4] also observed very high rates of spontaneous firings within the Purkinje–granular cell layer. Since larger electrodes were used in their experiments (12.5 μ), it seems likely that damage to the richly bifurcated dendrites around the Purkinje cells may have occurred, thus triggering high-frequency discharges. Although not shown in the paper, spontaneous discharges of 230 to 260 per second were recorded when medium-sized micropipettes (10 μ) were used in the initial experiments.

According to Granit and Phillips,[10] the so-called D-potential was supposed to represent massive synchronous activation of dendrites of individual Purkinje cells or of Golgi II cells. The positive monophasic polarity, long latency, and broad duration was somewhat similar to the responses shown in Figures 8-8, 8-9, 8-12, and 8-20 in this study. However, since the same kind of response was recorded following repetitive firings, these were more reasonably supposed to be initiated by slightly deteriorated cells. Dendritic potentials have been recorded in many places in the central nervous system,[1,7,9,15,16] but no evidence was obtained in the present studies of D-potentials in the dendrites.

SUMMARY

An electrophysiological study was undertaken to investigate the events occurring in the cerebellar cortex following local electrical stimulation. Both gross cortical surface recording and extra- and intracellular micropipette recordings were utilized to identify the origin of responses and their general properties and behavior during excitation induced by the stimuli applied to the cerebellar cortex as well as to the cerebellar nuclei or the subcortical structures surrounding the nuclei.

1. Besides the classic short laterally conducting surface-negative responses which were recorded only in the same folium as the stimulating electrode, three kinds of corticocortical responses were observed. They were the short-latency, long-latency, and the localized responses.

2. The short-latency responses showed a latency of 0.8 to 1.2 milliseconds, and the long-latency ones showed 1.8 to 3.6 milliseconds. These two responses were recorded in the anterior lobe, tuber vermis, and middle part of crus I following stimulation of the middle and lateral part of the anterior lobe, and obtained in the anterior lobe, neighboring ansiform lobule, and ipsilateral paramedian lobule following ansiform lobule stimulation. Their sizes were biggest in the folia adjacent to the stimulating point and gradually decreased in the far recording points.

3. The localized responses had a latency of 5.6 to 6.3 milliseconds and were obtained in the paramedian lobule following stimulation of the middle and ipsilateral side of the anterior lobe.

4. The cortical surface responses were recorded by gross electrodes and the extra- and intracellularly recorded unitary discharges by micropipettes. The cortical short-latency responses were induced by antidromic or monosynaptic firing of the Purkinje cells by way of the axon collaterals; the long-latency responses were induced by multi-synaptic firing of the Purkinje cells.

5. Repetitive Purkinje cell firings were induced by cortical and fastigial stimulation and recorded both extra- and intracellularly. The intervals of repetition ranged from 1.5 to 3.2 milliseconds. In the intra-cellular recordings, the repetitive firings gradually decreased in number. In the later stage of penetration, one broad wave was recorded which gradually deteriorated.

6. Convergence of impulses initiated by cortical and fastigial stimulation of the Purkinje cells was observed.

REFERENCES

1. ANDERSON, P. Interhippocampal impulses: I. *Acta physiol. scandinav. 47*:63, 1959.

2. BARNARD, J. W., and WOOLSEY, C. N. Interconnections between the anterior lobe and the paramedian lobule of the cerebellum. *Anat. Rec. 106*:173, 1950.

3. BROOKHART, J. M., MORUZZI, G., and SNIDER, R. S. Spike discharges of single units in the cerebellar cortex. *J. Neurophysiol. 13*:465, 1950.

4. BROOKHART, J. M., MORUZZI, G., and SNIDER, R. S. Origin of cerebellar waves. *J. Neurophysiol. 14*:181, 1951.

5. BUSER, P., and ROUGUEL, A. Réponse électrique du cervelet de pigeon à la stimulation de la voie optique et son analyse par microélectrodes. *J. Physiol., Paris 46*:287, 1954.

6. RAMÓN Y CAJAL, S. *Histologie du système nerveux de l'homme des vertèbres.* Paris, Maloine, 1911, vol. 2.

7. CHANG, H.-T. Dendritic potential of cortical neurons produced by direct electrical stimulation of the cerebral cortex. *J. Neurophysiol. 14*:1, 1951.

8. DOW, R. S. Action potentials of cerebellar cortex in response to local electrical stimulation. *J. Neurophysiol. 12*:245, 1949.

9. FATT, P. Electric potential occurring around a neurone during its antidromic activation. *J. Neurophysiol. 20*:27, 1957.

10. GRANIT, R., and PHILLIPS, C. G. Excitatory and inhibitory processes acting upon individual Purkinje cells of the cerebellum in cats. *J. Physiol. 133*:520, 1956.

11. GRANIT, R., and PHILLIPS, C. G. Effect on Purkinje cells of surface stimulation of the cerebellum. *J. Physiol. 135*:73, 1957.

12. HILD, W., and TASAKI, I. Morphological and physiological properties of neurons and glial cells in tissue culture. *J. Neurophysiol. 25*:277, 1962.

13. KANDEL, E. R., and SPENCER, W. A. Electrophysiology of hippocampal neurons. II. After-potentials and repetitive firing. *J. Neurophysiol. 24*:243, 1961.

14. PURPURA, D. P., GIRADO, M., and GRUNDFEST, H. Synaptic components of cerebellar electrocortical activity evoked by various afferent pathways. *J. Gen. Physiol. 42*:1037, 1959.

15. TASAKI, I., POLLEY, E. H., and ORREGO, H. Action potentials from individual elements in cat geniculate and striate cortex. *J. Neurophysiol. 17*:454, 1954.

16. TERZUOLO, C. A., and ARAKI, T. An analysis of intra- versus extracellular potential changes associated with single spinal motoneurons. *Ann. New York Acad. Sc. 94*:547, 1961.

OLIVER H. LOWRY

CHAPTER 9

Biochemical Studies on Layered Structures

THE OBJECTIVES OF THE NEUROCHEMIST ARE TO ACQUIRE FULL UNDER-
standing of the chemical constitution and chemical events in the
nervous system. Brain as a whole is so complex that to reach these
objectives it will be necessary in general to bring chemical studies
down to the level of the individual neuron.[1] There are, however,
regions of brain where nervous structures have been sorted out to a
certain extent, and where chemical studies may be worth while at
grosser levels than that of the single neuron. Some analytical results
will be presented that were obtained in three of these regions: cerebellum, Ammon's horn, and retina.

The analyses were made on frozen sections cut in a cryostat
and dried at −40°C. The tissue was given no opportunity to thaw
at any time after the initial rapid freezing.[2] The sections from
cerebellum and Ammon's horn were cut at 20 μ, the retinal sections
at 5 or 6 μ. The easiest way found to cut retina is to freeze the entire
eyeball (in CCl_2F_2 at −150°C.) and take sections from the intact
eye after chipping away a small portion of the sclera.[3] From the
freeze-dried sections samples for analysis were dissected under low
magnification. Clean samples of each of the three major layers of
cerebellum and each of the six layers of Ammon's horn were obtained.

Supported by grants NB00434-10 and B-1352 from the U.S. Public Health
Service and grant P-78-E from the American Cancer Society.

These weighed about 1 μg. Similarly, clean samples were obtained from each of the eight major layers of retina. These weighed about 0.1 μg. Retina from both monkey (rhesus) and rabbit were used in order to capitalize on the fact that the inner four layers have a rich blood supply in monkey, but none in rabbit.

Clean dissections are made possible because in the freeze-dried material, even though it has not been fixed, embedded, or stained, the various layers are easily visible (Fig. 9-1).

After the dissection, which was carried out at room temperature, the samples were weighed, transferred to micro test tubes, and analyzed by direct chemical procedures. Many of the methods have been described in detail.[3-5] Adenylokinase was measured by allowing the enzyme to act on ADP in the presence of glucose, excess hexokinase, excess glucose 6-phosphate dehydrogenase, and TPN[+]. The fluorescence of the TPNH formed in a 30-minute incubation was used as measure of adenylokinase activity. Creatine kinase was measured in a similar manner starting with phosphocreatine and ADP. In this case the values obtained were corrected for adenylokinase activity. Malic enzyme and isocitrate dehydrogenase were measured by the TPNH formed from TPN[+] plus either malate or isocitrate.

RESULTS

Hexokinase, Phosphofructokinase, and Other Enzymes of Glycolysis

In retina the hexokinase present in the photoreceptor neuron is almost entirely concentrated in the inner segments (Figs. 9-2 and 9-3). In monkey (Fig. 9-2) it is possible to show that it is concentrated in the outer portion of the inner segment where cytologists have found a dense congregation of mitochondria. Hexokinase was shown by Crane and Sols[6] to be present in brain in an insoluble fraction which would include mitochondria. In the rest of the retina, hexokinase is richer in fiber or synaptic layers (layers 5*b*, 7, and 9 of Fig. 9-2; layer 7 of Fig. 9-3) than in cell body layers.

Phosphofructokinase (P-fructokinase) is distributed quite differently from hexokinase in the photoreceptor neuron (Figs. 9-2 and

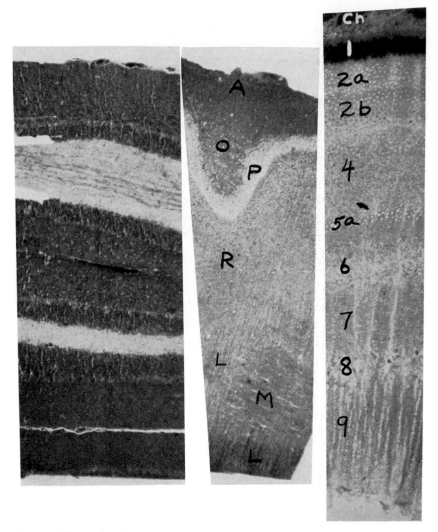

FIG. 9-1. Freeze-dried sections of cerebellum (rabbit), Ammon's horn (rabbit), and retina (monkey). These are original unfixed, unstained dry sections. Two folia of cerebellum are shown in figure on left. In Ammon's horn (center) layers are alveus (A), oriens (O), pyramidalis (P), radiata (R), lacunosum (L), and molecularis (M). In retina (*right*) the layers are numbered as follows: pigment epithelium (1), outer segments of rods and cones (2a), inner segments (2b, several sublayers are visible), outer nuclear (4), outer reticular (5, 5a is axonal portion), inner nuclear (6), inner reticular (7), ganglion cell (8), and fiber (9). As a rule, samples of layer 8 were obtained that were more densely populated with cell bodies than shown here.

9-3). P-fructokinase is a soluble enzyme in brain, and the distribution of this enzyme within a given neuron may correspond to the non-particulate cytoplasmic phase. All the other enzymes on the Embden-Meyerhof glycolytic pathway (except hexokinase) tend to parallel

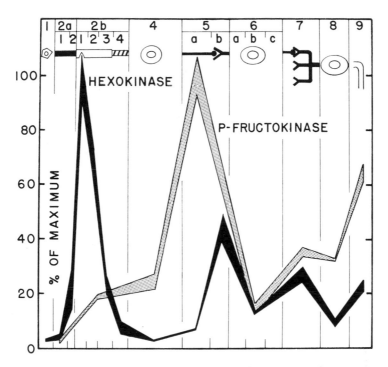

FIG. 9-2. Distribution of hexokinase and P-fructokinase in monkey retina. Line widths at center of each layer equal 2 standard deviations for that layer. Points have been connected for better visualization, but this does not imply gradual transition of values from one layer to next. Layer widths are drawn roughly proportional to actual layer thicknesses. Peak values for hexokinase and P-fructokinase were, respectively, 27 and 32 M per kilogram of fat-free dry weight per hour. (From Lowry *et al.*[3])

P-fructokinase in all layers of the retina.[3,4] The relative (and absolute) levels of P-fructokinase are higher in the avascular inner layers of rabbit retina than in the homologous vascularized layers in monkey. (Layer 9 of Fig. 9-2 is not comparable to layer 9*b* of Fig. 9-3.) The species difference suggests that glycolysis plays a greater or lesser role for a given cell type, depending on the blood supply.

In Ammon's horn and cerebellum, hexokinase and P-fructokinase, as in retina, tend to be lower in cell body layers than in synaptic layers, and the distribution of the two likewise tends to be dissociated (Fig. 9-4). The method of plotting in Figure 9-4 may obscure the close parallelism between alveus, pyramidalis, and molecular layers

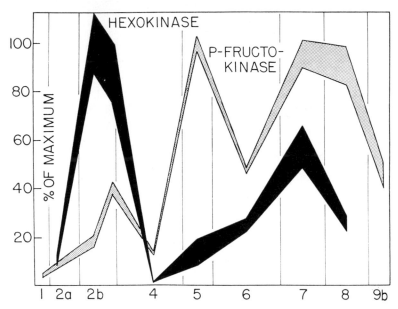

FIG. 9-3. Hexokinase and P-fructokinase in rabbit retina. Peak values were, respectively, 14.2 and 31.4 M per kilogram of fat-free dry weight per hour. Data are plotted as stated for Figure 9-2. (From Lowry *et al.*[3])

of Ammon's horn on one hand and white, granular, and molecular layers of cerebellum on the other. The most striking feature is perhaps the very high P-fructokinase value in the layer of dendrites (radiata of Ammon's horn).

As in retina, lactic dehydrogenase (Fig. 9-5) and other enzymes of glycolysis[6] tend to parallel P-fructokinase rather than hexokinase, although the ratio between activities is not strictly constant.

Enzymes of the Citric Acid Cycle

Malic dehydrogenase, like hexokinase, is most concentrated in retina in the inner segments of the rods and cones (Figs. 9-6 and 9-7) and may therefore be concentrated in mitochondria. It is known that malic dehydrogenase exists both inside and outside mitochondria, and this may explain the lack of exact parallelism between hexokinase and malic dehydrogenase in the rest of the retina.

The distribution of malic dehydrogenase is very similar to that of fumarase[4] and succinic dehydrogenase (not shown), but it bears

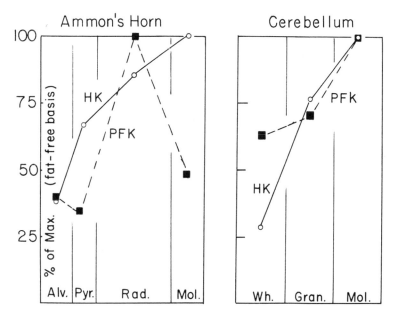

FIG. 9-4. Hexokinase (*HK*) and P-fructokinase (*PFK*) in Ammon's horn and cerebellum. Peak values (moles per kilogram of fat-free dry weight per hour) were 6.4 and 6.7, respectively, for *HK*, and 32.5 and 21.3, respectively, for *PFK*. (From Buell *et al.*[7])

little relation to that of isocitric dehydrogenase (Figs. 9-6 and 9-7). This lack of parallelism, plus the fact that malic dehydrogenase and glutamic-aspartic transaminase parallel each other very closely,[4] suggest that the portion of the citric acid cycle from α-ketoglutarate to oxalacetate, together with transaminase, may constitute a subcycle for emergency conversion of glutamate to aspartate plus CO_2:

$$\alpha\text{-ketoglutarate} \rightarrow \ldots \rightarrow \text{oxalacetate} + CO_2 \qquad (1)$$
$$\text{oxalacetate} + \text{glutamate} \rightarrow \text{aspartate} + \alpha\text{-ketoglutarate} \qquad (2)$$

Isocitrate dehydrogenase, but not malic dehydrogenase, may then be representative of the true capacity of the citric acid cycle as a whole. The values for isocitric dehydrogenase in layers 6 to 9 were nearly the same, on an absolute basis, in monkey and rabbit, in spite of the difference in blood supply. Malic dehydrogenase in

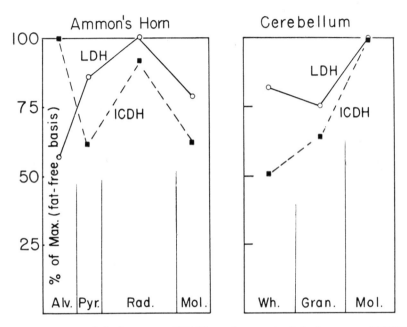

FIG. 9-5. Lactic dehydrogenase (*LDH*) and isocitric dehydrogenase (*ICDH*) in Ammon's horn and cerebellum. Peak values (moles per kilogram of fat-free dry weight per hour) were 32.2 and 28.3, respectively, for *LDH*, and 6.0 and 9.3, respectively, for ICDH. (*LDH* data from Buell *et al.*[1] *ICDH* data from Lowry and Lewis, to be published.)

contrast was about twice as high in these layers in monkey as in rabbit.[4]

The distribution of malic enzyme parallels that of isocitrate dehydrogenase in monkey very closely but is only roughly parallel in rabbit (Figs. 9-6 and 9-7). A rather surprising finding is that the absolute activities of malic enzyme in layers 5 to 8 of rabbit retina are two to three times greater than in average rabbit brain. Peak values are much lower in monkey retina.

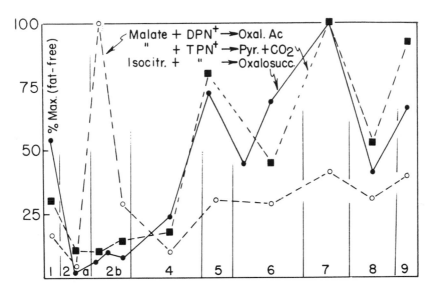

FIG. 9-6. Malic and isocitric dehydrogenases and malic enzyme in monkey retina. Peak values were, respectively, 280, 2.87, and 1.39 M per kilogram of fat-free dry weight per hour. (Malic dehydrogenase data from Lowry *et al.*[4] Isocitric dehydrogenase and malic enzyme data from Lowry, Schulz, and Ause, to be published.)

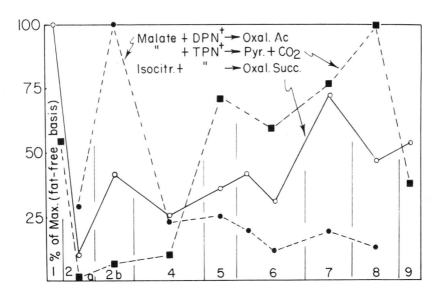

FIG. 9-7. Malic and isocitric dehydrogenases and malic enzyme in rabbit retina. Peak values were, respectively, 199, 3.62, and 2.87 M per kilogram of fat-free dry weight per hour. (Data from sources given in Fig. 9-6.)

185

In Ammon's horn the lack of parallelism between isocitric and malic dehydrogenases is borne out, although in cerebellum they appear to vary together (Fig. 9-8). Young (unpublished results) found that the distribution of malic enzyme in Ammon's horn is similar to that of malic dehydrogenase, but the peak absolute activity was only 1.92 M per kilogram of fat-free weight per hour. In

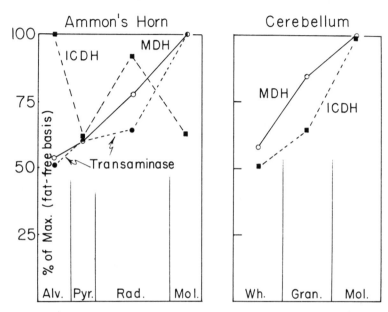

FIG. 9-8. Malic and isocitric dehydrogenases in Ammon's horn and cerebellum and glutamic-aspartic transaminase in Ammon's horn. Peak activities (moles per kilogram of fat-free dry weight per hour) were 522 and 400, respectively, for malic dehydrogenase (measured in direction of malate formation); 6.0 and 9.3, respectively, for isocitric dehydrogenase; and 50 for transaminase. (Data from Lowry and Lewis, to be published.)

cerebellum he found malic enzyme activity to be 0.93, 1.38, and 1.00 M per kilogram fat-free dry weight per hour; i.e., the distribution did not parallel that of malic and isocitric dehydrogenases.

Adenylokinase and Creatine Kinase

The capacity to mobilize high-energy phosphate from ADP and phosphocreatine in emergency is dependent on the enzymes adenylokinase and creatine kinase. Adenylokinase in both monkey and rabbit is richer in layers 5 to 7 than in layers 2b and 4, whereas creatine kinase is if anything higher in 2b and 4 than in layers 6 and 7 (Figs. 9-9 and 9-10). In general the values concur for monkey and rabbit except that the outer reticular layer (layer 5a) is very high in creatine kinase in monkey. The significance of these differences will be better understood when measurements have been

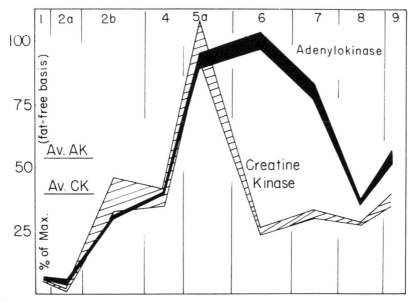

FIG. 9-9. Adenylokinase and creatine kinase in monkey retina. Peak values were, respectively, 75 and 657 M per kilogram of fat-free dry weight per hour. (Data from Lowry and Reynolds, to be published.)

made of the changes in phosphocreatine and adenylic acid derivatives in the various layers when the oxygen or glucose supply has been cut off.

In Ammon's horn there are only modest differences in the distribution of creatine kinase and adenylokinase among the various layers (Fig. 9-11). ATP and phosphocreatine were measured in Ammon's horn from a brain of an anesthetized rabbit. The brain was frozen *in situ*. The ATP levels ranged from 27 to 47 mM per kilogram of fat-free dry weight and were closely parallel to the adenylokinase activities of Figure 9-11. Phosphocreatine levels ranged from 42 to 66

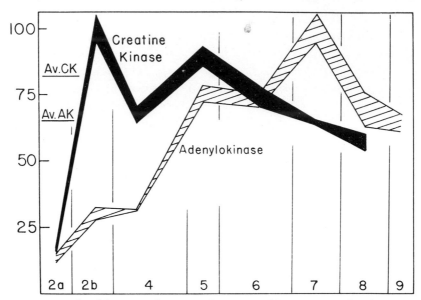

FIG. 9-10. Adenylokinase and creatine kinase in rabbit retina. Peak values were, respectively, 49 and 401 M per kilogram of fat-free dry weight per hour. (Data from same sources as in Fig. 9-9.)

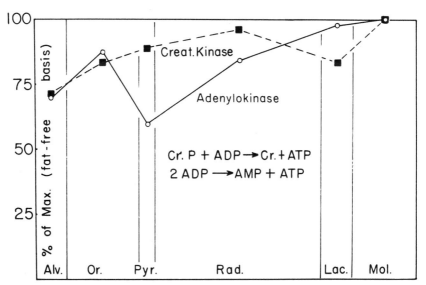

FIG. 9-11. Adenylokinase and creatine kinase in Ammon's horn. Peak values were, respectively, 47 and 249 M per kilogram of fat-free dry weight per hour. (Data from same source as in Fig. 9-9.)

mM per kilogram of fat-free dry weight and showed a strong tendency to parallel creatine kinase activities.

Inorganic Pyrophosphatase

The enzymes discussed above all have known functions in metabolic sequences. A useful function for inorganic pyrophosphatase is

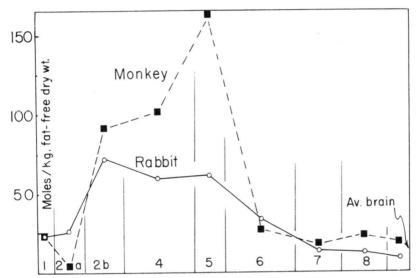

FIG. 9-12. Inorganic pyrophosphatase in monkey and rabbit retina. (Data from Lowry, Schulz, and Bausler.)

not established, but values for this enzyme are presented here because of the exceedingly high levels found in retina (Fig. 9-12). The peak value in monkey retina is fifteen times that found in average brain. The highest levels are limited to the photoreceptor neuron in both rabbit and monkey. In Ammon's horn this enzyme has its highest activity in the pyramidal cell layer (Fig. 9-13). For contrast, another phosphatase, 5′-nucleotidase, is included, which is distributed in a nearly reciprocal manner. Kornberg[8] has pointed out that many synthetic reactions yield inorganic pyrophosphate and that inorganic pyrophosphatase action would tend to pull such synthetic reactions to completion and stabilize the products. This might explain the moderately high level in the pyramidal cell layer of Ammon's horn, where protein synthesis is presumably very active, but in the

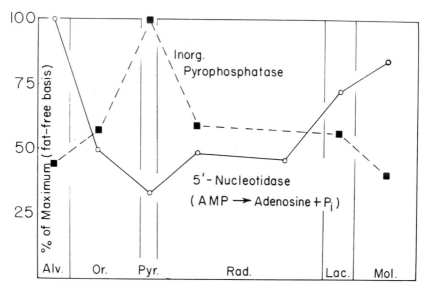

FIG. 9-13. Inorganic pyrophosphatase and 5′-nucleotidase in Ammon's horn. Peak values were, respectively, 11.1 and 6.5 M per kilogram of fat-free dry weight per hour. (Data from Lowry and Bausler.)

retina it seems more likely that the exceedingly high values are related to a metabolic rather than a synthetic function.

SUMMARY

The distribution of a number of enzymes among the discrete histological layers of retina, cerebellum, and Ammon's horn has been described. The enzymes concerned are hexokinase; phosphofructo-kinase; lactic, malic, and isocitric dehydrogenases; malic enzyme; transaminase; adenylokinase; creatine kinase; and inorganic pyrophosphatase. Cerebellum and Ammon's horn were from rabbit brain. Retina was from both rabbit and monkey.

REFERENCES

1. LOWRY, O. H., ROBERTS, N. R., and CHANG, M.-L. W. Analysis of single cells. *J. Biol. Chem.* 222:97, 1956.

2. LOWRY, O. H. Quantitative histochemistry of the brain: Histological sampling. *J. Histochem.* 1:420, 1953.

3. LOWRY, O. H., ROBERTS, N. R., SCHULZ, D. W., CLOW, J. E., and CLARK, J. R. Quantitative histochemistry of retina: II. Enzymes of glucose metabolism. *J. Biol. Chem.* 236:2813, 1961.

4. LOWRY, O. H., ROBERTS, N. R., and LEWIS, C. Quantitative histochemistry of the retina. *J. Biol. Chem.* 220:879, 1956.

5. LOWRY, O. H. "Micromethods for the Assay of Enzymes," in *Methods in Enzymology*, ed. by Colowick, S. P., and Kaplan, N. O. New York, Academic Press, 1957, vol. 4, pp. 366–381.

6. CRANE, R. K., and SOLS, A. Association of hexokinase with particulate fractions of brain and other tissue homogenates. *J. Biol. Chem.* 203:273, 1953.

7. BUELL, M. V., LOWRY, O. H., ROBERTS, N. R., CHANG, M.-L. W., and KAPPHAHN, J. I. Quantitative histochemistry of the brain: V. Enzymes of glucose metabolism. *J. Biol. Chem.* 232:979, 1958.

8. KORNBERG, A. Pyrophosphorylases and phosphorylases in biosynthetic reactions. *Advances Enzymol.* 18:191, 1957.

CHAPTER **10**

R. E. BASFORD, WILLIAM L. STAHL, _____

DIANA S. BEATTIE, HOWARD R. SLOAN, J. C. SMITH, and L. M. NAPOLITANO

*Enzymic Properties of Brain Mitochondria**

THE EXTENT TO WHICH GLUCOSE CAN BE METABOLIZED BY ISOLATED brain mitochondria has been studied by a number of workers. No glycolytic activity was exhibited by the mitochondrial preparations of Brody and Bain[3] and Aldridge.[4] Balazs and Lagnado[5] showed one-tenth of the glycolytic activity of brain to be associated with their mitochondrial preparation, while Gallagher, Judah, and Rees[6] have reported that brain mitochondria oxidize glucose completely to carbon dioxide and water. Rat brain mitochondria prepared by Brunngraber and Abood[7] glycolyzed at one-quarter the rate of the nonparticulate material. Addition of mitochondria to the supernatant fraction, enriched with an optimal amount of hexokinase, caused a twofold increase in the rate of lactate formation. This increase could also be achieved by the addition of aldolase. Johnson[8] has criticized the experimental procedure on which these findings were based. In his preparation, Johnson[9] located three-quarters of

Supported in part by research grant B-1984 from the National Institute of Neurological Diseases and Blindness, National Institutes of Health, U.S. Public Health Service, and in part by grant RG 210 from the National Multiple Sclerosis Society.

The authors are indebted to H. G. Flock, H. M. Glick, J. T. Brown, and M. L. Evans for technical assistance. The cooperation of Armour and Co. in obtaining brains from kosher-killed animals is greatly appreciated.

* The material presented here in summary form is covered more fully elsewhere.[1,2]

the total hexokinase of rat brain in the mitochondria and all the other enzymes of glycolysis mainly in the nonparticulate fraction.

The methods which have been used for the isolation of mitochondria from brain have been based almost exclusively on the method of Schneider and Hogeboom[10] for the isolation of mitochondria from liver. Our own preliminary experiments, together with the findings of Petrushka and Giuditta[11] and Dahl, Jacobs, and Samson[12] indicated that mitochondria prepared from rat or beef brain by this fractionation procedure in either 0.25 or 0.88 M sucrose were grossly contaminated by nonmitochondrial particulate matter of the cell. The high lipid content of brain, principally myelin, is responsible for the difficulty in obtaining pure mitochondrial fractions from homogenates of brain.

The discrepancies in the data on the glycolytic capacity of brain mitochondria may be due to the impurity of the mitochondrial preparations used. It seemed desirable, therefore, to develop a method for preparing brain mitochondria which were relatively free of contamination by other subcellular particles and to compare the enzymic properties of this preparation with those reported in the literature.

The purpose of this communication is to summarize the method of isolation of a relatively pure mitochondrial fraction from bovine brain as well as our findings on the glycolytic ability of this mitochondrial preparation.

PREPARATIVE METHODS

Undamaged calf or beef brains were obtained at the slaughter house from kosher-killed animals. The brains were removed within 5 to 10 minutes of the death of the animal and placed in ice-cold medium for transport to the laboratory.

The gray matter was scraped from the cortices, leaving as much of the white matter behind as possible without spending undue time for careful dissection. All steps in the procedure were carried out at 0 to 4°C. Two brains yielded about 100 gm. of wet tissue. The tissue was then homogenized with a Teflon-glass homogenizer, using 2 ml. of Medium A per gram of tissue. Medium A was composed of 0.4 M sucrose, 0.001 M EDTA,* and 0.02% polyethylene

* The abbreviations used are: EDTA, ethylenediaminetetraacetate; Tris, (tris-) hydroxymethylaminomethane; TCA, trichloroacetic acid; RNA, ribonucleic acid;

sulfonate (average molecular weight 5,900, Lloyd Bros., Cincinnati), pH 7.4.

The homogenate so obtained (adjusted to pH 7.4 with Tris if necessary) was either (Method I) more thoroughly homogenized in a ground-glass homogenizer or (Method II) treated with the bacterial proteinase, Nagarse (Biddle Sawyer Corp., New York) as described by Hagihara[13] and Hatefi, Jurtshuk, and Haavik.[14] Medium A was added to the homogenate obtained by Method I or II to give a suspension of 1 gm. of original tissue per 10 ml. of medium. The homogenate was then centrifuged at 3,000 × g for 20 minutes to remove debris (R_1). All centrifugal forces are given as g_{max}.

The supernatant fraction, S_1, was centrifuged again under the same conditions. The crude mitochondrial fraction, R_2, was separated from S_1 by centrifugation at 12,000 × g for 15 minutes, then homogenized in 6 ml. of Medium F per gram of original tissue and centrifuged at 12,000 × g for 30 minutes. Medium F contained 8% (w/v) Ficoll (Pharmacia, Uppsala, Sweden) in addition to the components of Medium A.

The resulting brown pellet, R_3, was visibly free of contaminating white fluffy material (probably myelin fragments). The pellet, R_3, was washed by resuspension, homogenization, and centrifugation in Medium A, to yield the final mitochondrial fraction, R_4, which was homogenized in Medium A to give a suspension of about 10 mg. of protein per milliliter. The average yield of the mitochondria from 100 gm. of tissue (wet weight) was 100 mg. of protein (biuret). The schema for fractionation is shown in Figure 10-1.

For comparison, mitochondria from beef brain were prepared in 0.25 M sucrose by the method of Schneider and Hogeboom.[10]

The supernatant fraction, S_2, contained the major portion of the fluffy material, microsomes, and soluble components of the homogenate. The presence of the fluffy material prevented a clear-cut separation of microsomes from the homogenate. S_2 was separated either into S_5 (soluble components) and R_5 (microsomes and fluff) by centrifugation at 105,000 × g for 60 minutes or into a fluffy fraction, R_6, with some microsomes entrapped, and a supernatant fraction, S_6, containing mainly microsomes and soluble material, by centrif-

---

DNA, deoxyribonucleic acid; ATP, adenosine triphosphate; GDP, guanosine diphosphate; DPN, diphosphopyridine nucleotide; INT, 2-(p-iodophenyl)-3-p-nitrophenyl-5-phenyl tetrazolium; ChE, cholinesterase; ACh, acetyl choline.

ugation at 46,900 × g for 60 minutes. S_6 was further fractionated into R_7 and S_7 (microsomal and supernatant fractions, respectively) by centrifugation at 105,000 × g for 60 minutes.

ANALYTICAL METHODS

Protein was determined by the biuret method, essentially as described by Gornall, Bardawill, and David,[15] except that the protein

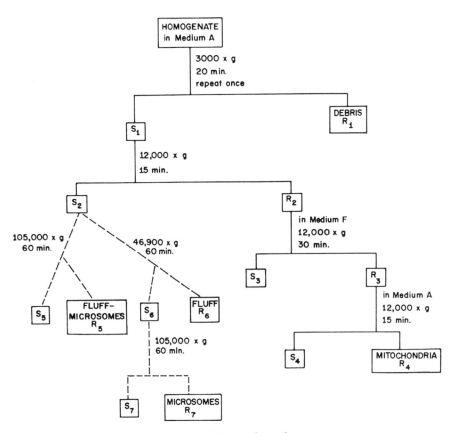

FIG. 10-1. Schema of fractionation of bovine brain homogenates.

was first precipitated with TCA and dissolved in 3% NaOH prior to the addition of biuret reagent and sodium deoxycholate.

Nucleic acids were extracted and determined in the manner recommended by Hutchinson and Munro.[16] Ribonucleic acid (RNA) was determined by its absorbancy at 260 mμ or as ribose by the procedure of Schmidt, Thannhauser, and Schneider,[17] using yeast RNA as a standard. Deoxyribonucleic acid (DNA) was estimated by the method of Burton,[18] using salmon sperm DNA as a standard.

Cholinesterase (ChE) activity was measured by the null-point potentiometric titration method of Smith, Foldes, and Foldes[19] using ACh as substrate.

Oxidative capacity was determined manometrically. The composition of the assay medium was: KH_2PO_4, 25 μmoles; cytochome c, 5×10^{-3} μmoles; DPN, 0.25 μmoles; ATP, 1.0 μmoles; glucose, 12 μmoles; hexokinase (Sigma, Types III, 0.5 mg., or crystalline, 23 to 30 KM units); $MgCl_2$, 20 μmoles; dialyzed bovine serum albumin, 10 mg.; sucrose, 360 μmoles; substrate 50 to 60 μmoles; mitochondrial fraction, 3 to 5 mg. of protein; final volume, 2.5 ml., pH 7.4.

Phosphorylative efficiency was calculated from the disappearance of inorganic phosphate as determined by the Dryer modification[20] of the method of Fiske and Subbarow,[21] or by the appearance of glucose 6-phosphate as determined with glucose 6-phosphate dehydrogenase.[22]

Mitochondrial pellets were fixed for electron microscopy in buffered 1% osmium tetroxide, pH 7.4, at 4°C. for 1 hour, dehydrated with increasing concentrations of alcohol in water, followed by acetone, and embedded in Vestopol W.[23] Samples of cortex underwent a preliminary treatment in 10% acrolein in phosphate buffer, pH 7.4, at 4°C. for 10 minutes[24] and were subsequently treated as described for the mitochondrial pellets. Electron micrographs of thin sections (Porter-Blum microtome) were taken with a Phillips Model 100B or 200 electron microscope.

Glycolytic activity was determined manometrically with 95% N_2 and 5% CO_2 as the gas phase in the following medium: ATP, 1 μmoles; $MgCl_2$, 20 μmoles; KH_2PO_4, 20 μmoles; nicotinamides, 60 μmoles; DPN. 1 μmoles; $KHCO_3$, 50 μmoles; glucose, 25 μmoles; mitochondrial and supernatant fractions and hexokinase (see Tables 10-4, to 10-8); final volume, 2.5 ml., pH 7.4. The supernatant fraction (S_{hs}) used was the high-speed (105,000 $\times$ g) supernatant fraction of the total homogenate and was comparable to S_5 or S_7.

Lactate formation was followed by CO_2 evolution from bicarbonate. At the end of the manometric determination, usually of 60 minutes duration, the reaction was stopped by addition of TCA and the deproteinized supernatant fraction was assayed for lactate by the method of Barker and Summerson.[25] Individual enzymes of the glycolytic pathway were measured by standard methods[8,26,27] employing the change in absorbancy at 340 mμ due to oxidation or reduction of pyridine nucleotide.

RESULTS

Electron Microscopy

The amount of time which elapses between the death of an animal and the chilling of the tissue can be an important factor in the preservation of the morphology of subcellular particles. An electron micrograph of a thin section of beef cortex (Fig. 10-2A) indicates that the mitochondria have not undergone more extensive morphological changes than those observed when laboratory animals are used as the source.[11]

An electron micrograph of a thin section of the mitochondrial fraction, R_4, is shown in Figure 10-2B. The preparation is nearly free of contamination by nonmitochondrial subcellular particles. For comparison an electron micrograph of a thin section of a mitochondrial fraction from beef brain prepared in 0.25 M sucrose[10] is shown in Figure 10-2C. It is apparent that the preparation is heavily contaminated with nonmitochondrial elements, especially fragmented myelin sheaths (cf. Petrushka and Giuditta[11]).

Figure 10-2D shows a higher magnification of the enclosed area in Figure 10-2B. The mitochondria do not appear to have undergone appreciable swelling during isolation, but the orientation of the cristae is more random than is seen *in situ* (Fig. 10-2A).

Oxidative Phosphorylation

As an indication of the integrity of the mitochondria, the preparations were routinely monitored for their ability to carry out oxidative phosphorylation and to exhibit respiratory control as defined by Lardy and Wellman[28] and Chance and Williams.[29]

Representative data for mitochondria isolated by Method II are

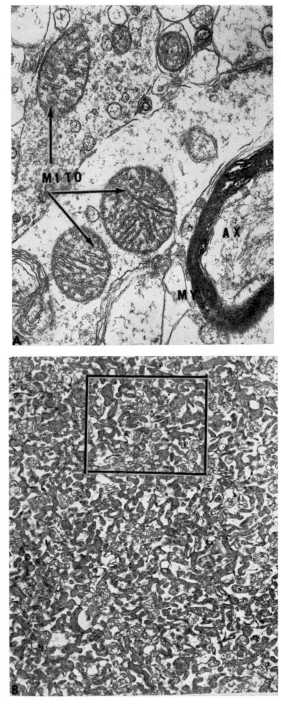

FIG. 10-2. *A,* electron micrograph of beef cortex. (*MITO*) mitochondria; (*AX*) axon; (*MY*) myelin. ×65,000. *B,* electron micrograph of the mitochondrial fraction, R₄, Method II. ×5,300.

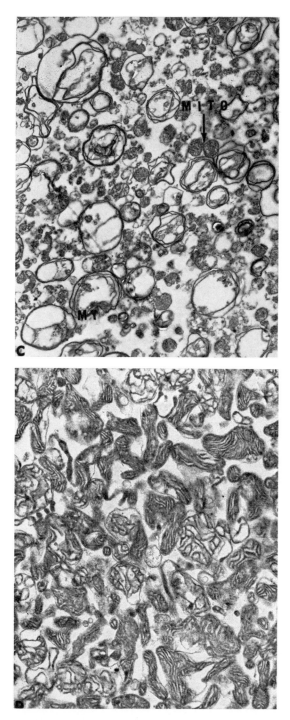

FIG. 10-2 (*Continued*). *C*, electron micrograph of a bovine brain mitochondrial fraction prepared in 0.25 M sucrose. (*MY*) myelin fragment. ×5,300. *D*, outlined portion of *B*. ×14,000.

shown in Table 10-1. Corresponding data for mitochondria prepared by Method I are only slightly lower. The P/O ratios for pyruvate, glutamate, and succinate are reasonably close to the theoretical values. With α-ketoglutarate as substrate, ratios approaching 4.0 were obtained occasionally but not routinely, and exogenous GDP did not improve phosphorylation. Addition of DPN was not required for a maximal rate of oxygen uptake or phosphorylation with DPN-linked substrates; however, exogenous cytochrome c was required for a maximal rate of oxidation of all substrates tested.

The phosphorylative ability of R_4 was not stable to freezing ($-20°$C.) and thawing but was unchanged after storage in ice for 24 hours. After storage in ice for 72 hours, the P/O ratios diminished 25 per cent.

The increased rate of oxygen uptake with pyruvate as substrate exhibited by R_4 compared with mitochondria prepared in 0.25 M sucrose (Table 10-1) appears to be a reflection of the increased purity of the preparation.

The respiratory control ratio, calculated as the rate of oxidation in the presence of glucose and hexokinase divided by the rate in the absence of phosphate acceptor, indicates that the mitochondrial preparation is fairly "tightly coupled." Respiratory control ratios with substrate concentrations of ADP measured either manometrically or with the oxygen electrode are comparable to those obtained with glucose and hexokinase.

It can be concluded that, although the electron micrographs show some fine-structure alteration of the mitochondria, enzymatically the organelles have not been affected adversely during isolation. The over-all recovery of mitochondria from the homogenate, based on succinic-INT reductase activity[30] is only 7 to 10 per cent. About 60 per cent of the total activity appears in R_1. Attempts to improve the yield of mitochondria by fractionation of R_1 or by more drastic homogenization of the tissue have been unsuccessful.

Contamination

Visual examination of electron micrographs of mitochondrial fractions prepared by the Schneider-Hogeboom procedure in 0.25 M sucrose (Fig. 10-2C) and by Method II (Fig. 10-2D) would indicate

TABLE 10-1. Oxidative and Phosphorylative Ability of Mitochondrial Preparations from Bovine Brain

Method of preparation	No. of experiments	Substrate	Rate*	P/O†	R.C.‡
0.25 M sucrose	2	Pyruvate	0.045 ± .009	3.06 ± 0.44	
Method II	6	Pyruvate	0.157 ± .039	3.02 ± 0.03	3–6
	4	Glutamate	0.154 ± .066	2.86 ± 0.20	4–5
	5	Succinate	0.137 ± .031	2.18 ± 0.34	2–3
	2	Succinate 3–4 mM Amytal	0.214 ± .027	1.39 ± 0.17	2–4
	4	α-Ketoglutarate	0.053 ± .031	2.71 ± 0.32	2–6

* Microatom of oxygen uptake per minute per milligram of protein; ± standard deviation.
† Ratio of phosphate disappearance to oxygen uptake ± standard deviation.
‡ Respiratory control ratio: rate of oxygen uptake with phosphate acceptor/rate of oxygen uptake without phosphate acceptor.

a contamination by nonmitochondrial subcellular particles of about 50 and 10 per cent, respectively.

Since contamination as judged from electron micrographs can give only a rough approximation, more accurate means of determining the degree of contamination were sought.

The total contamination in the mitochondrial fraction will be the sum of that derived from the less dense subcellular particles (microsomes and fluff) and fragments of denser particles which appear in the debris (R_1).

Glucose 6-phosphatase activity, often used as a microsomal marker, cannot be used with brain tissue owing to the low activity of the enzyme in this organ.[31]

Although a number of previous workers have shown that their brain mitochrondrial preparations contain large amounts of ChE, the highest specific activity was found in the microsomal fraction.[32-34] Although De Robertis *et al.*[35] located ChE in the mitochondrial fraction (M) of rat brain homogenates prepared in 0.32 M sucrose, fraction M could be separated into five distinct fractions by density gradient centrifugation. The ChE activity was found to be highest in fractions containing mainly pinched-off nerve endings and synaptic vesicles and the lowest in the fraction with high succinic dehydrogenase activity (mainly mitochondria). Preliminary results of the distribution of ChE in the various fractions of bovine brain homogenates indicated that ChE activity was low in the mitochondrial fraction. It was therefore decided to explore further the possibility of using ChE activity as a measure of contamination of the mitochondrial fraction by the microsomes (R_7) and fluff (R_6). The results of such determinations on fractions prepared by Method I are shown in Table 10-2. These data indicate that the specific activity of ChE in R_6 and R_7 was more than twentyfold higher than the activity in R_4. In the initial separation of mitochondria the material superincumbent to the mitochondrial pellet, R_2, was composed of fluff with entrained microsomes. Two fractions of this contaminating particulate material were prepared. One, designated fluff, R_6, still retained a large proportion of the microsomal material; the other, microsomes, R_7, was considerably contaminated with fluff. The impurities in the mitochondrial preparation included both these components. While the ChE is concentrated in the microsomal fraction, the ChE activity of highly purified microsomes is not suitable for calculation of contamination by both fluff and microsomes. Table 10-2 presents the calculated contamination using the specific ChE activity of both R_6 and R_7. The results are similar in each case, lying between 3 and 5 per cent.

The ChE activities for mitochondrial, microsomal, and fluff fractions prepared in 0.25 M sucrose are also shown in Table 10-2. These data would indicate a contamination of 18 to 27 per cent. No hydrolysis of ACh was observed in preparations treated with Nagarse (Method

TABLE 10-2. Cholinesterase Activity of Subcellular Particles from Bovine Brain

Type of preparation	Mitochon- dria (R_4) specific activity*	Fluff (R_6) specific activity*	$\dfrac{R_4}{R_6} \times 100$	Micro- somes (R_7) specific activity*	$\dfrac{R_4}{R_7} \times 100$
Method I	0.21	6.4	3.3	4.45	4.7
	0.29	8.0	3.6	6.88	4.2
0.25 M sucrose	0.52	1.94	27	2.79	18.7

* Micromoles of ACh hydrolyzed per milligram of protein per hour.

II), presumably due to proteolysis of the ChE. The assumption that ChE is not an integral constituent of the mitochondrion would seem to be a logical inference, since the specific activity of ChE decreases with increasing purity of the mitochondrial preparation as judged both by electron microscopy and the increase in the rate of oxidation of substrate.

The amount of contamination due to fragments of particles denser than the mitochondria (R_1) has been calculated from the DNA content of R_1 and R_4. The results of these determinations are shown in Table 10-3. It can be seen that the contamination from this source

TABLE 10-3. DNA Content of Subcellular Particles from Bovine Brain

Type of preparation	Mitochondria DNA content*	Debris (R_1) DNA content*	Per cent contamination
Method I	0.67	12.9	5.2
Method II	0.29	10.8	2.7
	0.30	9.0	3.3

* Microgram per milligram of protein.

is of the same order as that from R_6 or R_7. Thus, the total contamination from both sources is approximately 10 per cent.

Similar studies were undertaken using RNA as an indicator of microsomal contamination of R_4. Calculation of the contamination on this basis gave much higher values than those obtained from ChE and DNA data. Further work is in progress to establish whether or not RNA is an integral part of the mitochondrion.

Lipid analyses of both the fluff and mitochondrial fractions, when available, may give a better indication of contamination by myelin fragments.

Glycolytic Activity and Mitochondria

Enzymic studies were undertaken to determine whether the mitochondrial fraction, R_4 (Method I), was capable of glycolysis. The data shown in Table 10-4 indicate that less than 5 per cent of the

TABLE 10-4. Glycolytic Activity of Subcellular Fractions

Fraction	*Protein added to each flask (mg.)*	*Specific activity* * *(μM lactate produced/ mg. protein/hr.)*
High-speed supernatant (S_{hs})	2.7	3.15
	3.5	3.46
Mitochondria (R_4)	3.7	0.20
	7.0	0.16
	9.0	0.14

*Each figure represents the mean specfic activity calculated from the amount of lactate produced in three reaction vessels containing the standard glycolytic assay medium plus 25 KM units, type III hexokinase, after a 60 minute incubation.

glycolytic activity of the supernatant fraction (S_{hs}) was present in R_4.

This lack of glycolytic ability could be due to the absence of one or more enzymes of the glycolytic scheme. Brunngraber and Abood[7] have shown a stimulatory effect by the mitochondrial fraction of the glycolytic rate of the supernatant fraction both in the absence and presence of exogenous hexokinase.

The effect of exogenous hexokinase on the glycolytic capacity of both S_{hs} alone and on S_{hs} plus R_4 is shown in Table 10-5. These data indicate that R_4 stimulated lactate formation to about 250 per cent of the rate of S_{hs} alone. In the presence of optimal amounts of yeast hexokinase, the stimulation was 4 to 20 per cent. Therefore most of the enhancement of the glycolytic activity of S_{hs} was due to the hexokinase in R_4.

TABLE 10-5. Effects of Exogenous Hexokinase

KM units	μM lactate/hr.	
	S_{hs}	S_{hs} plus R_4
Type III hexokinase		
0	2.8	7.8
15	5.6	8.7
30	9.4	10.4
50	10.5	13.2
75	12.1	12.6
95	10.1	9.5
Crystalline hexokinase		
0	4.3	10.1
10	6.3	13.6
30	13.0	17.4
60	16.5	19.4
100	17.4	18.2

Each flask contained 3 mg. of S_{hs} protein and, when added, 4 mg. of R_4 protein.

The distribution of hexokinase activity was determined in all the fractions of the homogenate. As can be seen from the data presented in Table 10-6, a large percentage of the total hexokinase activity was sedimented in the initial centrifugation, which removes a considerable proportion of the mitochondria together with debris. Although hexokinase activity was found in all the remaining fractions, the highest specific activity was observed in R_4.

The presence of glycolytic enzymes other than hexokinase in R_4 was indicated by the use of various intermediates of the glycolytic pathway as substrates (Table 10-7). With glucose 6-phosphate, fructose 1,6-diphosphate, and glyceraldehyde 3-phosphate as substrate, slight stimulation of S_{hs} by R_4 was seen, indicating the presence of small amounts of several of the glycolytic enzymes in addition to hexokinase.

TABLE 10-6. Distribution of Hexokinase

Fraction	Total activity*	Per cent of total	Specific activity†
Homogenate	2,895	100	0.508
R_1	1,370	48	0.368
S_1	1,505	52	0.478
S_2	611	21	0.372
R_2	872	30	0.793
S_3	442	15	0.557
R_3	528	18	1.81
S_4	97	3	0.360
R_4	416	14	4.08
S_5	484	17	0.343
R_5	96	3	0.421

* Micromoles of glucose 6-phosphate per 30 minutes at 30°C.
† Micromoles of glucose 6-phosphate per 30 minutes per milligram of protein at 30°C.

TABLE 10-7. Glycolytic Intermediates as Substrates

		μM lactate produced/hr.		
			S_{hs} plus R_4	
Substrate	S_{hs}	2.5 mg.	3.8 mg.	5.1 mg.
Glucose 6-phosphate	9.2	13.8		15.6
Fructose 1,6-diphosphate	5.9	7.1	10.1	
Glyceraldehyde 3-phosphate	3.9	4.0	5.1	6.3

All substrates were substituted for glucose in equimolar amounts in standard glycolytic medium.

In order to investigate more fully the stimulation afforded by R_4, the individual crystalline enzymes of the glycolytic scheme were added to either S_{hs} alone or S_{hs} plus R_4 in the presence of optimal levels of hexokinase. If R_4 stimulates lactate formation because it contains a particular enzyme, then addition of that enzyme to the assay medium containing S_{hs} should reproduce the stimulation of glycolysis by R_4.

An example of the enzymes tested is shown in Table 10-8. It can be seen that although aldolase stimulated the production of lactate by S_{hs} to the same extent as did R_4, it also enhance the production of lactate by S_{hs} plus R_4 to the same extent. A similar pattern was observed with all the crystalline enzymes of the glycolytic pathway. These data indicate that the small stimulation of glycolytic activity afforded S_{hs} by R_4 with optimal amounts of exogenous hexokinase is due to the presence of small amounts of all the glycolytic enzymes in R_4.

TABLE 10-8. Effect of Aldolase on Glycolysis

	μM lactate produced/hr.	
Enzyme	S_{hs}	S_{hs} *plus 3.0 mg.* R_4
Hexokinase*	13.4	15.0
Hexokinase plus aldolase†	15.0	17.7

  * 60 KM units of crystalline hexokinase.
  † 60 KM units of crystalline hexokinase plus 20 μg. of crystalline aldolase.

The mitochondrial fraction was therefore tested directly for all the enzymes of glycolysis by using specific substrates for the individual enzymes. When it was necessary to couple the enzyme being tested to a reaction involving pyridine nucleotide (for ease of assay), purified coupling enzymes were added in excess, with proper controls to ensure the added enzymes were devoid of the enzymes being assayed. The data summarized in Table 10-9 indicate that the only enzyme other than hexokinase which was concentrated in R_4 was phosphofructokinase. The specific activity of phosphofructokinase in R_4 was six times greater than in the homogenate and two and one-half times greater than in S_{hs}, while the specific activity of hexokinase in R_4 was eight and eleven times greater than in the homogenate and S_{hs}, respectively. The values shown for aldolase and pyruvate kinase are representative of all the other glycolytic enzymes.

The amount of each enzyme present in S_{hs} and R_4, expressed as percentages of the total homogenate, cannot be considered as signif-

icant as the specific activity values owing to sedimentation of mitochondria with debris.

It is interesting to note that the hexokinase activity of R_4 is the
same whether prepared by Method I or II, whereas the Nagarse
treatment in Method II destroys ChE activity. Therefore Nagarse is
either not effective in destroying brain hexokinase or the hexokinase

TABLE 10-9. Distribution of Glycolytic Enzymes

Enzyme	Homogenate		S_{hs}		R_4	
	Per cent	S.A.*	Per cent	S.A.*	Per cent	S.A.*
Hexokinase	100	0.508	17	0.343	17	4.08
Phosphofructokinase	100	0.460	68	1.18	7	2.92
Aldolase	100	0.054	40	0.100	0.5	0.019
Pyruvate kinase	100	0.122	53	0.217	0.5	0.051

* Specific activity (S.A.): micromoles of substrate consumed per minute per
milligram of protein at 27°C.

is situated in or on the mitochondrion in a manner which is inac-
cessible to the enzyme.

DISCUSSION

Brain is unique in depending predominately on glucose for energy.
There is no reason to believe that brain mitochondria differ in any
significant respect from mitochondria from other tissues in regard to
citric acid cycle oxidations and terminal electron transport.

One facet of our study was to establish if brain mitochondria
possess an armamentarium of enzymes different from that of mitochondria of other tissues to allow more effective utilization of glucose as the energy source.

Our approach to this problem was to elaborate a method which
would allow the isolation from brain of relatively large quantities
of mitochondria which were intact by the established criteria invoked
for preparations from other tissues. These criteria include the rate
of oxidation of substrate, the lack of requirement for added DPN and
cytochrome c for oxidation of substrate, the ability to couple the

oxidation to phosphorylation, the degree of respiratory control, and the morphological integrity as observed in electron micrographs.

Our preparation satisfied all these criteria except for a requirement for small quantities of exogenous cytochrome *c* for a maximal oxidation rate. Mitochondria with this degree of integrity metabolize glucose at such a low rate that it is difficult to infer that the process of glycolysis is inherent in brain mitochondria.

However, the mitochondria have associated with them a considerable proportion of the total brain hexokinase and phosphofructokinase in contradistinction to mitochondria from other tissues. This unusual location of the two ATP-requiring enzymes of the glycolytic scheme could be an adaptation allowing efficient integration of ATP production and utilization for the metabolism of glucose.

All the other enzymes of glycolysis are present in trace amounts in the mitochondrial fraction, suggesting that their presence is adventitious. The possibility does remain that these enzymes might be loosely bound to the mitochondria in vivo and lost during the isolation procedure without major alteration of the properties of the particles.

The results summarized in this paper illustrate that mitochondria comparable to those from other tissues can be prepared from brain. The success of the isolation depends on special procedures designed to obviate the difficulties imposed by the high lipid content of this tissue.

Mitochondria prepared by such a procedure are deficient in most of the enzymes of glycolysis, and it seems unlikely that glycolysis is a function of brain mitochondria.

REFERENCES

1. STAHL, W. L., SMITH, J. C., NAPOLITANO, L. M., and BASFORD, R. E. Brain mitochondria: I. Isolation of borine brain mitochondria. *J. Cell Biol.* in press.

2. BEATTIE, D. S., SLOAN, H. R., and BASFORD, R. E. Brain mitochondria: II. Relationship between brain mitochondria and glycolysis. *J. Cell Biol.* in press.

3. BRODY, T. M., and BAIN, J. A. A mitochondrial preparation from mammalian brain. *J. Biol. Chem.* 195:685, 1952.

4. ALDRIDGE, W. N. Liver and brain mitochondria. *Biochem. J.* 67:423, 1957.

5. Balazs, R., and Lagnado, J. R. Glycolytic activity associated with rat brain mitochondria. *J. Neurochem.* 5:1, 1959.

6. Gallagher, C. H., Judah, J. D., and Rees, K. R. Glucose oxidation by brain mitochondria. *Biochem. J.* 62:436, 1956.

7. Brunngraber, E. G., and Abood, L. G. Mitochondrial glycolysis of rat brain and its relationship to the remainder of cellular glycolysis. *J. Biol. Chem.* 235:1847, 1960.

8. Johnson, M. K. Inactivation of anaerobic glycolysis in fractions of rat brain homogenates. *Biochem. J.* 82:281, 1962.

9. Johnson, M. K. Intracellular distribution of glycolytic and other enzymes in rat-brain homogenates and mitochondrial preparations. *Biochem. J.* 77:610, 1960.

10. Umbreit, W. W., Burris, R. H., and Stauffer, J. F. *Manometric Techniques*, ed. 3, Minneapolis, Burgess, 1957, p. 194.

11. Petrushka, E. and Giuditta, A. Electron microscopy of two subcellular fractions isolated from cerebral cortex homogenates. *J. Biophys. & Biochem. Cytol.* 6:129, 1959.

12. Dahl, D. R., Jacobs, R. J., and Samson, F. E., Jr. Characterization of two "mitochondrial" particulates from rat brain. *Am. J. Physiol.* 198:467, 1960.

13. Hagihara, B. Twelfth Symposium on Enzyme Chemistry, Japan, 1960, p. 140.

14. Hatefi, Y., Jurtshuk, P., and Haavik, A. G. Studies on the electron transport system: XXXII. Respiratory control in beef heart mitochondria. *Arch. Biochem., Biophys.* 94:148, 1961.

15. Gornall, A. G., Bardawill, C. J., and David, M. M. Determination of serum proteins by means of the biuret reaction. *J. Biol. Chem.* 177:751, 1949.

16. Hutchison, W. C., and Munro, H. N. Determination of nucleic acids in biological materials. *The Analyst* 86:768, 1961.

17. Volkin, E., and Cohn, W. E. In *Methods of Biochemical Analysis*, ed. by Glick, D. New York, Interscience, 1954, vol. 1, p. 290.

18. Burton, K. A study of the conditions and mechanism of the diphenylamine reaction for the colorimetric estimation of deoxyribonucleic acid. *Biochem. J.* 62:315, 1956.

19. Smith, J., Foldes, V., and Foldes, F. F. The distribution of cholinesterase in normal human muscle. *Cam. J. Biochem. Physiol.* in press.

20. Dryer, R. L., Tammes, A. R., and Routh, J. I. Determination of phosphorus and phosphatase with N-phenyl-p-phenylenediamine. *J. Biol. Chem.* 225:177, 1957.

21. Fiske, C. H., and Subbarow, Y. Colorimetric determination of phosphorus. *J. Biol. Chem.* 66:375, 1925.

22. Horecker, B. L., and Wood, W. A. In *Methods in Enzymology*, ed. by Colowick, S. P., and Kaplan, N. O. New York, Academic Press, 1957, vol. 3, p. 152.

23. RYTER, A., and KELLENBERGER, E. L'inclusion au polyester pour l'ultra-microtomie. *J. Ultrastructure Res.* 2:200, 1958.

24. LUFT, J. Use of acrolein as a fixative for light and electron microscopy. *Anat. Rec. 133*:305, 1959.

25. BARKER, S. B., and SUMMERSON, W. H. Colorimetric determination of lactic acid in biological material. *J. Biol. Chem. 138*:535, 1941.

26. WU, R., and RACKER, E. Regulatory mechanisms in carbohydrate metabolism: III. Limiting factors in glycolysis of ascites tumor cells. *J. Biol. Chem. 234*:1029, 1959.

27. KORNBERG, A. In *Methods in Enzymology,* ed. by Colowick, S. P., and Kaplan, N. O. New York, Academic Press, 1955, vol. 1, p. 441.

28. LARDY, H. A., and WELLMAN, H. Oxidative phosphorylation: Role of inorganic phosphate and acceptor systems in control of metabolic rates. *J. Biol. Chem. 195*:215, 1952.

29. CHANCE, B., and WILLIAMS, G. R. The respiratory chain and oxidative phosphorylation. *Advances Enzymol. 17*:65, 1956.

30. PENNINGTON, R. J. Biochemistry of dystrophic muscle. *Biochem. J. 80*:649, 1961.

31. DIXON, M., and WEBB, E. C. *Enzymes.* New York, Academic Press, 1958, p. 644.

32. TOSCHI, G. A biochemical study of brain microsomes. *Exper. Cell Res. 16*:323, 1959.

33. ALDRIDGE, W. N., and JOHNSON, A. Choline esterase, succinic dehydrogenase, nucleic acids, esterase, and glutathione reductase in sub-cellular fractions of rat brain. *Biochem. J. 73*:270, 1959.

34. HOLMSTEDT, B., and TOSCHI, G. Enzymic properties of cholinesterases in sub-cellular fractions from rat brain. *Acta physiol. scandinav. 47*:280, 1959.

35. DE ROBERTIS, E., PELLEGRINO DE IRALDI, A., RODRIGUEZ DE LORES ARNAIZ, G., and SALGONICOFF, L. Cholinergic and non-cholinergic nerve endings in rat brain: I. Isolation and sub-cellular distribution of acetylcholine and acetylcholinesterase. *J. Neurochem. 9*:23, 1962.

Some Factors Involved in the Use of Glucose and Hexokinase as a Trap for ATP in Cerebral Mitochondrial Studies

IN ANY STUDY CONCERNING OXIDATIVE PHOSPHORYLATION IN MITO-
chondrial systems, a trap is usually added to transform the synthesized ATP into a more stable compound.[1] Glucose or glucose-hexo-
kinase additions are most commonly used, since it was established
early by the pioneering studies of Ochoa,[2] Green,[3] and others that
the phosphorylative efficiency of a cell-free tissue extract or respiring
mitochondrial system was thereby considerably increased. In the
presence of this trap, glucose 6-phosphate piles up, and P/O ratios
are commonly obtained by measuring the disappearance of inorganic
phosphate or the increase in Glc 6-P* or in the total acid-soluble
organic phosphate. The purpose of this presentation is to discuss
some problems associated with the addition of glucose and hexokinase primarily to cerebral mitochondrial systems, since most of the
studies were carried out with cerebral preparations. However, it

---

* Abbrevations used in this paper include: Glc 6-P, glucose 6-phosphate; Pi,
orthophosphate; ATP, adenosine 5′(pyro)-triphosphate; DNP, 2,4-dinitrophenol;
Fru 6-P, fructose 6-phosphate; ADP, adenosine 5′(pyro)-diphosphate; NAD,
oxidized nicotinamide-adenine dinucleotide; NADH₂, reduced nicotinamide-adenine
dinucleotide.

Supported by grant B3364 from the Neurological Research Center in Cere-
brovascular Disease, U.S. Public Health Service.

is the author's view that the problems discussed may also apply, in part, to mitochondrial studies in general.

The problems referred to arise primarily out of the assumption that, except for ATP trapping, glucose and hexokinase are essentially nonparticipants in the complex of cerebral mitochondrial metabolism. Several aspects of the glucose-oxidizing cerebral mitochondrial system will be discussed and related to our belief that the above assumption is essentially false.

MATERIALS AND METHODS

Cerebral mitochondria (P-2) were prepared and the oxidative phosphorylation measurements carried out as previously described.[4] The inorganic salts used were Merck or equivalent reagent grade. All nucleotides and substrate materials were the highest grade obtainable from Pabst Laboratories, Sigma Chemical Co., or California Corporation for Biochemical Research and were checked before use for freedom from significant contamination. Glucose and glutamic acid uniformly labeled with C^{14} were obtained from the Nuclear Chicago Corporation.

Lactic acid, pyruvic acid, and glucose were determined by enzyme analysis as previously reported.[4] For the respiration studies using C^{14}-labeled glucose or glutamate, the C^{14}-labeled CO_2 was trapped in 0.2 ml. of freshly prepared 0.125N NaOH. At the end of the run, perchloric acid was tipped in to the main vessel compartment to stop the reaction and free the fluid of all CO_2. The vessels were quickly removed from the manometers, stoppered, and allowed to stand in an ice bath for at least 15 minutes before the center-well material was quantitatively removed with a Pasteur pipette and brought to 10 ml. in a volumetric flask with CO_2-free glass-distilled water. Five-milliliter aliquots were then placed in an all-glass titration cell and back-titrated with 0.0155N HCl under nitrogen to pH 8.2. The equipment used was the automatic Metrohm titrator with a 1.0 ml. buret. One-milliliter aliquots were also removed for scintillation counting in a water-ethanol-toluene system, using a Packard Tricarb scintillation spectrometer. A 50 per cent counting efficiency was obtained.

The differential spectra studies were carried out with the Bausch and Lomb 505 recording spectrophotometer, using the 5-mμ fixed slit to obtain adequate reference energy throughout the scan. Two 3.0-ml. quartz cuvettes were filled with media and mitochondria and balanced immediately in the absence of glucose or yeast enzyme concentrate. At zero time, glucose and bovine serum albumin were added to the reference cuvette, the yeast material to the other, and the automatic scanning begun. A complete scan from 330 to 650 mμ took about 6 and one-half minutes, but some were run in approximately half that time. Repeat scans were run immediately after mixing the cuvette contents by gently inverting them several times. This was done to minimize settling out of mitochondria as well as to add oxygen to the system. It is probable, however, that a condition of partial anoxia existed during the latter part of the 6 and one-half-minute scan.

RESULTS

Metabolism of Glucose by Cerebral Mitochondrial Preparations

The complete metabolism of glucose to CO_2 and H_2O has been reported by others, and the coupling of this metabolism to net phosphorylative processes was established by Cohen.[4] Recent studies using a slightly modified medium provide a pattern of metabolism as shown by Figure 11-1. Respiration is linear for at least 3 hours and probably longer, while net phosphorylation levels off after 90 minutes. Lactate formation is linear during the 3-hour period. However, 90 per cent of the glucose added is utilized by 90 minutes, and the fall off in phosphorylation parallels the almost complete utilization of the added glucose. The decrease in phosphorylative activity cannot be prevented by increasing the initial concentration of glucose. Moreover, glucose utilization under these circumstances still levels off at about 90 minutes. The lag in utilization of glucose during the first 30 minutes, while respiration and phosphorylation proceed in an essentially linear manner, must mean that there is significant oxidation of endogenous substrate during this period and that this is coupled to net phosphorylative processes. The addition of hexokinase to a system similar to the above results in an increase in net phosphorylation and P/O ratios. That this effect is variable, and that the variability is probably due to the presence of contaminating materials, is shown in Figure 11-2. It can be seen that the most effective Sigma preparation, per unit of hexokinase, is their type II—the least pure material available. The two most active preparations (and probably

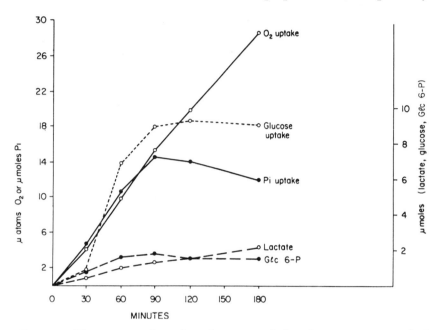

FIG. 11-1. Time course of aerobic glucose metabolism by guinea pig cerebral mitochondrial system. Incubation after 10-minute equilibration period was carried out in Warburg vessels at 25°C., air atmosphere. Incubation mixture contained, in final volume of 3.0 ml., following concentration of materials: 1×10^{-2} M K phosphate buffer, pH 7.4; 1×10^{-2} M $MgCl_2$; 8.33×10^{-4} M NAD; 4×10^{-2} M nicotinamide; 1 mg. bovine serum albumin (Armour); 8.33×10^{-4} M ADP; 3.33×10^{-3} M glucose; and 0.4 ml. mitochondria tipped in at zero time. Vessels were removed at times indicated. Reaction was stopped with addition of 0.4 ml. 3 M perchloric acid.

the purest) provide the least stimulation of net phosphorylation per unit of hexokinase activity.

Inhibition of Cerebral Mitochondrial Metabolism

Certain peculiarities of cerebral mitochondrial metabolism as it pertains to phosphate-linked respiratory activity have been brought

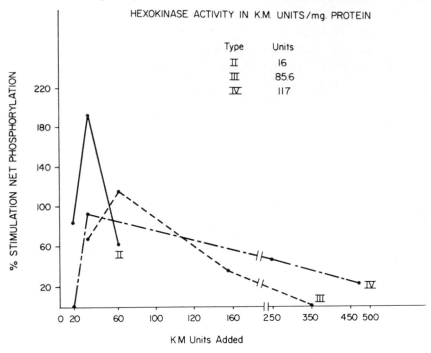

HEXOKINASE ACTIVITY IN K.M. UNITS/mg. PROTEIN

Type	Units
II	16
III	85.6
IV	117

FIG. 11-2. Stimulation of net phosphorylation of respiring cerebral mitochondria by yeast hexokinase preparations. Incubation after 10-minute equilibration period was carried out in Warburg vessels at 25°C., air atmosphere. Incubation mixture contained, in final volume of 3.0 ml., following concentration of materials: 1×10^{-2} M K phosphate buffer, pH 7.4; 1×10^{-2} M $MgCl_2$; 8.33×10^{-4} M NAD; 1 mg. bovine serum albumin (Armour); 8.33×10^{-4} M ADP; 3.33×10^{-3} M glucose; and 0.4 ml. mitochondria tipped in at zero time. Sigma crude yeast hexokinase preparations added as indicated. Reaction was stopped 30 minutes after equilibration by addition of 0.4 ml. 3 M perchloric acid. Results were obtained over a period of many months, and each point represents *maximum* stimulation obtained with indicated amount of hexokinase, from minimum of four runs made at different times. Same lot number of each preparation was used throughout this series of experiments, and total protein added to each vessel was same (additional bovine serum albumin was added, as needed, to bring total to 5.0 mg.).

to light with the use of inhibitor substances. Examined singly, there are probably some circumstances where similar results could be obtained using other tissue mitochondrial preparations. Taken as a whole, the experiments provide a picture of an active metabolic system different in some significant aspects from other mitochondrial preparations. Table 11-1 shows the effect of DNP on certain aspects of cerebral mitochondrial metabolism in the absence of exogenous hexokinase. With glucose as substrate, 3×10^{-5} M DPN reduces respiration by 50 per cent and inhibits phosphorylation. The inhibition of glucose uptake is probably directly related to the decrease in net phosphorylation and Glc 6-P formation. At the same time, however, net aerobic glycolysis, as indicated by lactic acid formation, remains unchanged. On the other hand, when pyruvate is substrate, DNP addition causes a 70 per cent increase in respiration, with no change

TABLE 11-1. Effect of DNP on Cerebral Mitochondrial Metabolism

Substrate	DNP	O_2 uptake ($\mu atoms$)	Pi uptake ($\mu moles$)	Pi/O	Glucose uptake ($\mu moles$)	Pyruvate uptake ($\mu moles$)	Lactate ($\mu moles$)
Glucose	—	6.39	9.6	1.5	5.6	—	1.68
Glucose	+	3.04	1.9	0.63	1.5	—	1.66
Pyruvate and fumarate	—	9.93	3.5	0.35	—	3.7	0.0
Pyruvate and fumarate	+	16.9	2.2	0.13	—	3.8	0.1

Incubation media same as for Figure 11-2. Pyruvate and fumarate, when present, were at concentration of 1×10^{-2} M and 1×10^{-3} M, respectively. DNP, 3×10^{-5} M. Incubation at 25°C. for 30 minutes after 10 minutes temperature equilibration.

in net disappearance of pyruvate, indicating a stimulation of oxidation of endogenous substrates. The effect of DNP additions on oxidative phosphorylation in the presence of yeast hexokinase is shown in Table 11-2. It can be seen that as little as 6×10^{-6} M DNP causes a significant inhibition of respiration in the presence of glucose, and net phosphorylation is completely inhibited within the range of 1×10^{-5} to 3×10^{-5} M DNP. The addition of hexokinase completely *reverses* the effect of DNP on respiration in the presence of pyruvate. When α-ketoglutarate is substrate, the typical stimulation of respiration is noted.

Inhibition of cerebral mitochondrial metabolism by the sulfate ion is discussed briefly elsewhere.[4] It is important to note that this inhibition was discovered through use of an ammonium sulfate suspension of crystalline hexokinase and that experiments with other salts indicated that sulfate was primarily responsible for the effect. The author knows of no such effect of sulfate (at the concentrations used) on tissue mitochondrial metabolism other than that prepared from the brain. Care must be taken to remove ammonium sulfate completely from hexokinase preparations before additions are made to cerebral mitochondrial systems.

Inhibition of oxidative phosphorylation by fluoride[4] could be considered unique were it not for the fact that the metabolism of glucose

TABLE 11-2. Effects of DNP on Cerebral Mitochondrial Oxidative Phosphorylation

Addition	DNP (M)	O_2 uptake (μatoms)	Pi uptake (μmoles)	Pi/O
None	0	4.10	7.6	1.9
None	6×10^{-6}	3.47	2.4	0.69
None	1×10^{-5}	2.97	0.7	0.24
None	3×10^{-5}	2.40	+0.6	—
None	6×10^{-5}	1.16	+1.2	—
Pyruvate and fumarate	0	16.9	46.8	3.1
	3×10^{-5}	9.3	11.1	1.2
α-Ketoglutarate and	0	9.0	29.9	3.3
malonate	3×10^{-5}	10.3	14.1	1.4

Incubation after 10-minute equilibration period carried out in Warburg vessels at 25°C., air atmosphere. For experiments run in absence of added substrate, incubation mixture contained, in final volume of 3.0 ml., following concentration of materials: 1×10^{-2} M K phosphate buffer, pH 7.4; 1×10^{-2} M MgCl$_2$; 8.33 $\times$ 10^{-4} M NAD; 1 mg. bovine serum albumin (Armour); 8.33×10^{-4} M ATP; yeast hexokinase (Sigma type III) 4 mg.; and 0.4 ml. mitochondria tipped in at zero time. Incubation time 30 minutes. Yeast hexokinase contained considerable invertase activity, which provided glucose substrate. DNP concentrations as indicated. Experimental conditions for other data were similar to above except that twice as much buffer was used and incubation time was 20 minutes in the presence of pyruvate and fumarate. Substrate concentrations were as follows: 1×10^{-2} M Na pyruvate; 1×10^{-3} M Na fumarate; 1×10^{-2} M K α-ketoglutarate; 1×10^{-2} M Na malonate.

by cerebral mitochondria proceeds in part through aerobic glycolysis. Inhibition of glycolysis would lead to inhibition of respiratory and therefore of phosphorylative activity. However, it must be noted that fluoride inhibition is still present when hexokinase is added to the system, even though glycolysis is primarily limited to the net formation of Glc 6-P and some Fru 6-P, and the system is still sensitive to the addition of cyanide, DNP, and pentobarbital. Fluoride, beside the effect it may have on glycolysis, must also be inhibiting some aspect of the oxidatively coupled phosphorylative complex.

Glucose Metabolism and Endogenous Respiration

Glucose is oxidized by the cerebral mitochondrial system in the presence of considerable endogenous respiration. Table 11-3 presents some typical data taken from recent experiments and compares the utilization of glucose with that of glutamate. While almost all the CO_2 formed when glutamate is the sole added substrate derives from glutamate, only 65 per cent of the CO_2 comes from glucose when it is the sole exogenous substrate. The range of several experiments is 95 to 103 per cent for glutamate and 59 to 65 per cent for glucose.

TABLE 11-3. Utilization of Substrate by Cerebral Mitochondrial System

Exper.	*Substrate*	O_2 *uptake* *(μatoms)*	$C^{14}O_2$ *forma-tion* *(μmoles)*	*R.Q.*	*S.A.* $(C^{14}O_2)$ *(cts/min/* *μmoles)*	*S.A.* *(substrate)* *(cts/min/* *μmoles* *carbon)*	*R.S.A.*
1	Glucose	7.76	3.74	0.96	1,299	2,040	0.65
2	Glutamate	15.76	6.75	0.86	5,570	5,899	0.95

Incubation media same as for Figure 11-1. Sixty-minute incubation period after 10-minute temperature equilibrium. Representative results from two experiments run on different days are presented. Glucose (3.33×10^{-3} M) and glutamate (3.33×10^{-3} M) each contained 1 to 3 $\times$ 10^{-5} counts of their respective uniformly labeled C^{14} radioisotopes.

The endogenous respiration of brain mitochondria is presumed to be the result primarily of oxidation of glutamic and aspartic acids and glutamine.[5] The results obtained with glutamate support this view and indicate moreover that glutamate may be the chief endogenous metabolite of guinea pig cerebral mitochondria. A recent experiment comparing endogenous respiration with that obtained in the presence of substrate quantities of glucose (containing trace amounts of uniformly labeled glucose-C^{14}) shows that in the presence of glucose the CO_2 formed from the oxidation of endogenous substrate accounts for 110 per cent of the O_2 uptake determined in the absence of added substrate, assuming an R. Q. of 1. This would indicate either no effect on, or only slight stimulation of endogenous respiration by, glucose. As in the case of rat liver mitochondria,[6,7] the endogenous respiration of guinea pig brain mitochondria is also associated with esterification of inorganic phosphate (see Fig. 11-1 and previous discussion) but only in the presence of glucose added as substrate or ATP trap. In the experiment just discussed and in all previous work with phosphorylating cerebral mitochondrial systems, the author has never observed inorganic phosphate uptake in the absence of glucose. Even if we ignore the effect of hexokinase for a moment, the use of glucose as part of a presumably inert trapping system in cerebral mitochondrial systems provides for the coupling of a base level of endogenous respiratory activity to net phosphorylative processes. It has been found also that certain substrates affect the level of endogenous respiration in rat brain, pyruvate stimulating and succinate inhibiting oxidation of endogenous metabolites.[5] Thus, even the study of substrate oxidation by cerebral mitochondrial preparations involves more than the measurement of respiratory activity. Disappearance of substrate should be correlated with oxygen uptake, and studies should be undertaken to determine the effect of substrate additions on the oxidation of endogenous metabolites. The determination of P/O ratios in the presence of various metabolites conceivably is even more of a problem, for it is possible that some may be acting, in part, by stimulation of endogenous respiration and, in the presence of glucose, coupling this to an active phosphorylating system.

Electron Transport Activity in Presence of Yeast Hexokinase

Preliminary studies have been carried out to determine the effect of the addition of crude hexokinase preparations to the mitochondrial system on electron transport activity by means of differential spectra analysis.[8] The original equipment used for these studies had low sensitivity but gave reproducible results in this and other work carried out at the same time. Ten minutes after addition of the crude yeast enzyme preparation to the system, definite maxima appeared at approximately 330 mμ, 390 mμ, and 420 mμ. The band at 390 then disappeared, and one was observed at 460 mμ. In time the 330 band shifted to 340 mμ, and at 100 minutes after addition of the yeast material a large band was observed at 340 mμ and a considerably smaller band at 460 mμ. Figure 11-3 presents the spectra redrawn from the original records. While not warranting

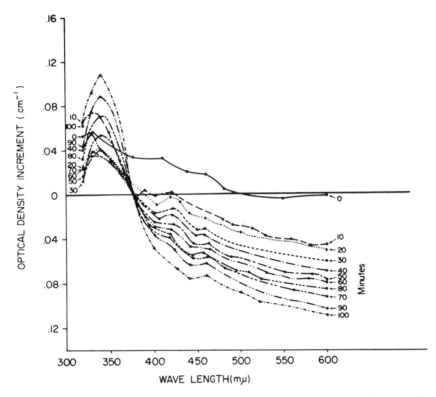

FIG. 11-3. Sample (glucose plus hexokinase) minus reference (glucose) differential spectra of respiring guinea pig brain mitochondrial system. Initially each cuvette was filled with solution containing following concentration of materials in final volume of 3.0 ml.: 1×10^{-2} M K phosphate buffer, pH 7.4; 1×10^{-2} M $MgCl_2$; 8.33×10^{-4} M NAD; 4×10^{-2} M nicotinamide; 1 mg. bovine serum albumin (Armour); 8.33×10^{-4} M ADP; and 0.4 ml. mitochondria added just before placing the cuvette in the spectrophotometer. After adjusting to instrument zero, glucose (3.33×10^{-3} M) and 2.0 mg. bovine serum albumin (Armour) were added to reference cuvette, and 2.0 mg. yeast enzyme concentrate (Sigma lot No. 20B-780-2) containing 100 KM units of hexokinase to the other. Cuvettes were mixed and scanning begun. Yeast enzyme contained considerable invertase activity. As control, aerobic metabolism of system was checked manometrically for respiratory and phosphorylative activity in presence of glucose. P/O ratio of 1.6 was obtained. It is known from other studies that yeast enzyme preparation used was capable of at least a 50 per cent stimulation of net phosphorylation. Time (minutes) represents interval between start of particular scan and addition of glucose and hexokinase.

full interpretation, the evidence obtained so far clearly indicates a definite effect by the yeast material on the electron transport activity of a cerebral mitochondrial system with glucose as sole added substrate. The slow but steady increase in the size of the 340 maxima indicates a piling up of reduced pyridine nucleotide (presumably $NADH_2$). The data also indicate a relative block in the span $NADH_2 \rightarrow fp$ (reduced) in the presence of the yeast hexokinase. More frequent mixing of the cuvettes (see under "Materials and Methods") did not seem to affect the results. Whether these results are due in part to contaminants of the yeast material is not known but is presently under investigation with crystalline hexokinase samples and more sensitive techniques.

DISCUSSION

The question whether or not the brain mitochondrion contains the complete glycolytic sequence of enzymes as an integral part of its structure still remains unresolved, although recent evidence tends to strengthen the view of those who believe that it does not.[9,10] It must be noted, however, that rather exhaustive treatment is required to prepare mitochondria which do not metabolize glucose and that these preparations do not respire (in the presence of Kreb's cycle intermediates such as pyruvate and fumarate) at a level obtained by the author with his preparation (60 μmoles per gram of equivalent fresh brain per hour).[11] Regardless of the final solution of this problem, studies carried out in this and other laboratories concerning the interaction between glycolytic activity and the basic oxidative metabolism of cerbral mitochondria have been and continue to be fruitful.

The addition of glucose and hexokinase to cerebral mitochondrial systems which glycolyze at a low rate, or not at all, provides maximum P/O ratios but results in the rapid removal of ATP through the transformation of ATP to inert Glc 6-P. This could conceivably mask significant metabolic interrelations since it is doubtful that this situation obtains during the steady state give and take between mitochondrial and other cellular metabolic activity. Certainly two of the most striking effects of the addition of hexokinase to respiring mitochondria, i.e., the reversal of the stimulation of respiration by DNP and the changes observed in electron transport activity, could be related to changes in system kinetics as a result of the rapid removal of ATP. There is some evidence that the phosphorylative efficiency of mitochondria within the living cell is equivalent to the best values obtained with isolated mitochondrial preparations.[12] It is interesting to note, however, that these data were obtained with glucose as substrate. While it is clear that some of the effects observed with crude yeast hexokinase preparations are the result of contaminant activity, it must be remembered that until the last year or so most investigators used either crude yeast hexokinase preparations or partially purified crystalline material (presumably in ammonium sulfate) in their studies. This may account for some of the early reports on the instability of cerebral mitochondrial preparations and metabolism.

The development of interest in the endogenous respiration of mitochondria has brought to light several interesting aspects of mitochondrial metabolism, some of which have already been mentioned. It must be remembered, however, that whether or not a cerebral mitochondrial system oxidizes glucose, it does oxidize endogenous glutamate, and this is coupled to net phosphorylation in the presence of glucose.

It appears, therefore, that the addition of glucose and hexokinase to cerebral mitochondrial systems produces extensive metabolic changes in the respiring system. Some of the changes are probably related to the rapid removal of ATP from the system, and others, like the glucose effect, to the stimulation of ATP synthesis. It is the author's opinion that if we are ever to understand fully the complexities of the interaction in vivo between the metabolism of mitochondria and that of the other constituents of the cell the role played by addition of glucose and hexokinase to mitochondrial systems in order to obtain maximum P/O ratios must be more clearly understood and taken into account.

SUMMARY

The use of glucose and hexokinase as a trap for ATP formation in respiring cerebral mitochondrial systems has been discussed. The primary endogenous substrate of guinea pig cerebral mitochondria is probably glutamic acid, and its oxidation is coupled to net phosphorylation in the presence of glucose.

The addition of yeast hexokinase preparations of varying purity to a respiring mitochondrial system results in an increase in net phosphorylation, but the extent of the increase depends more on the purity of the material than on the absolute number of units of hexokinase added, the least pure material being the most active. Hexokinase addition reverses the effect of DNP on mitochondrial respiration when pyruvate is substrate and, in the presence of glucose, has considerable effect on electron transport activity, which changes in time. These last are presumed to be related to changes in system kinetics as a result of the rapid removal of ATP.

REFERENCES

1. HUNTER, F. E. "Coupling of Phosphorylation with Oxidation," in *Methods in Enzymology*, ed. by Colowick, S. P., and Kaplan, N. O. New York, Academic Press, 1955, vol. 2, p. 610.

2. OCHOA, S. Efficiency of aerobic phosphorylation in cell-free heart extracts. *J. Biol. Chem. 151*:493, 1943.

3. CROSS, R. J., TAGGART, J. V., COVO, G. A., and GREEN, D. E. Studies on the cyclophorase system: VI. The coupling of oxidation and phosphorylation. *J. Biol. Chem. 177*:655, 1949.

4. COHEN, H. P. Phosphorylation coupled to glycolytic and oxidative metabolism in cerebral mitochondrial systems. *Arch. Biochem. 92*:449, 1961.

5. BELLAMY, D. Endogenous citric acid-cycle intermediates and amino acids of mitochondria. *Biochem. J. 82*:218, 1962.

6. MINNAERT, K. Endogenous respiration of rat-liver mitochondria. *Biochem. et biophys. acta 44*:595, 1960.

7. WEINBACH, E. C. Oxidative phosphorylation with endogenous substrates of mitochondria. *J. Biol. Chem. 236*:1526, 1961.

8. CHANCE, B., and WILLIAMS, G. R. Respiratory enzymes in oxidative phosphorylation: II. Difference spectra. *J. Biol. Chem. 217*:395, 1955.

9. BASFORD, R. E., STAHL, W. L., BEATTIE, D. S., SLOAN, H. R., SMITH, J. C., and NAPOLITANO, L. M. See Chapter 10, this volume.

10. LØVTRUP, S. Chemical properties of brain mitochondria. *Acta neurol. scandinav. 38*(Suppl. 1):6, 1962.

11. COHEN, H. P. Unpublished observations.

12. HESS, B., and CHANCE, B. Phosphorylation efficiency of the intact cell: I. Glucose-oxygen titration in ascites tumor cells. *J. Biol. Chem. 234*:3031, 1959.

MARGARET R. MURRAY,
EDITH R. PETERSON, and CHARLES N. LOESER

CHAPTER *12*

Localization of Several Fluorochromes in Cultured Neurons

THIS REPORT OF CORRELATION BETWEEN CHEMISTRY AND MORPHOLOGY will deal with some preliminary attempts to apply photometric methods to living cultures of organized nervous tissue which have been exposed to the fluorochromes chlorpromazine, acridine orange, and two convulsant acridones.

MATERIALS AND METHODS

During the last decade one of us (C.N.L.) has been concerned in a series of absorption and fluorescence studies on biological systems. Originally the method employed quartz-rod illumination of the subject in the near or true ultraviolet coupled with special electronic methods of quantitating light that came to the eye through the microscope from a quartz rod or other illuminating devices.[5,6] Most recent developments of the instrumentation involve television fluorescence spectroscopy which employs in appropriate arrangement a Leitz spectroscope, an RCA image-intensifier Orthicon tube, a picture

Supported by grants B-858, A-2301, and A-1909 from the U.S. Public Health Service.

For varied and valuable aid, the authors are indebted to Dr. Lucille Loeser, Mrs. Helena Benitez, Drs. Richard Bunge, Michael Dreyfuss, Ronald Reivich, and Seymour West, and Mr. Eric Grave.

225

monitor, and a special line selector which oscillographically registers the spectrum as an intensity-versus-wave-length curve of the light transmitted through different regions of cells.[16] By these means a beginning has been made for measuring the very feeble emissions produced by cells "stained" in vivo or in vitro with various biologically interesting substances at low concentration. These agents include acridine orange, several acridones, and chlorpromazine. Though some

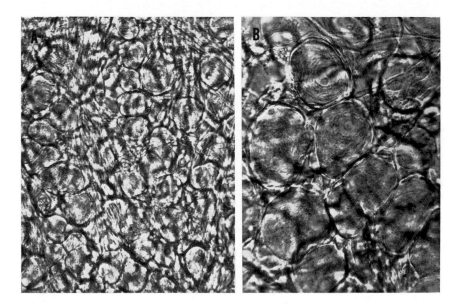

FIG. 12-1.   *A*, appearance of chick dorsal root ganglion culture living; 3 days in vitro. *B*, high-power visualization of similar culture living; 26 days in vitro. Note smooth, rather nongranular texture of cytoplasm which contains refractile filaments (neurofibrils?).

of the acridine orange work has been published,[7] most of the observations still are in the pilot stage, as are those to be reported here. For several years our two laboratories in New York and in Cleveland have been in communication to the end that when it should become technically feasible we should combine forces to analyze on an individual cell basis the fluorescence emission spectra produced by various types of nervous tissues maintained in essentially normal organization[13] in a culture assembly which was thin enough (Fig. 12-1) to allow transillumination in the above measuring system and examination at high powers of the microscope.

The ultimate aim is to analyze central nervous system material by means of fluorescent drugs, such as chlorpromazine and the convulsant acridones, which have known biological effects and which appear to select cell types and cell regions for binding. When ascites cells and slices of rat cortex (rat injected with compound at physiological levels) were used by Loeser as test objects, the spectra showed definitive maxima, certain of which appeared to be different from the peaks of the compounds measured in the pure state. If such a shift should also be observed with the cultured nerve cells as test objects we should hope to be able to hazard suggestions about the mechanism of combination between nerve cells and the compound. Absence of shift would be meaningful also.

So much for rationale and long-range objectives. Initial tests have been run on cultured dorsal root (sensory) ganglia of embryonic chick and rat, because for these nerve cells we possess the most substantial and detailed frame of reference in cytological structure, developmental behavior, and function in vitro,[4,10,13,14] having already established a series of norms for the disposition of Nissl substance, some enzymes, mitochondria, nucleus and nucleolus, satellite cells, sheaths, etc. Also, the neurons are very easily identified and can be induced to dispose themselves in culture quite advantageously from the standpoint of visualization, so that this tissue seems presently to afford the most favorable base line against which to evaluate the intracellular distribution of biologically active compounds. It was thought that the use of both chick and rat material might provide an internal check, because Nissl bodies, and therefore mitochondria which lie between them, present a somewhat different pattern in the two species; these linked patterns also shift during development and maturation of the neuron in vitro. Some attributes of the myelin sheath show interspecies differences (Fig. 12-2A to D). Preliminary tests have been run on this material with chlorpromazine, two convulsant acridones, and acridine orange.

Chlorpromazine

At a molar concentration of 7×10^{-5}, blue-green fluorescence images of adequate intensity and detail for spectral as well as for morphological analysis can be produced from chlorpromazine-stained

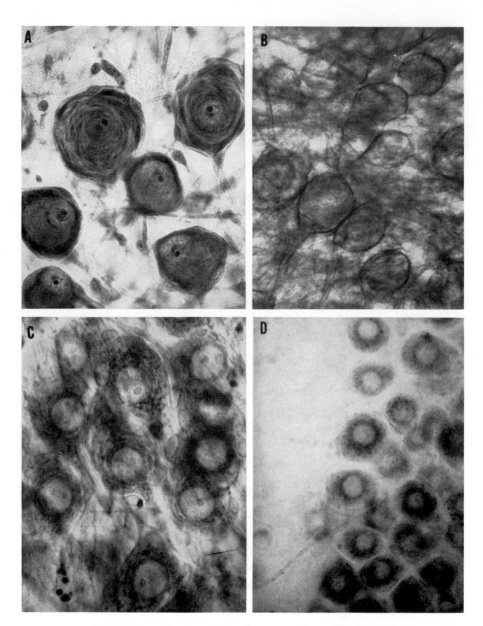

FIG. 12-2. Morphology of cultured dorsal root ganglion cells. *A,* Nissl pattern of developing chick neurons 15 days in vitro. Erythrosin–toluidine blue stain after mercuric chloride fixation. In small, immature cells Nissl substance is accumulated at periphery and nucleus is eccentric; in larger, more advanced neurons Nissl particles are arrayed concentrically around central nucleus. Note satellite cells closely applied around neuron soma. *B,* fibrous capsule distal to neuron–satellite

sensory ganglion cells which have been exposed to the solution for 6 minutes, then thoroughly rinsed in balanced salt solution. When administered at this concentration, the compound appears to be bound in the vicinity of mitochondrial aggregates; it also stains the myelin sheath in *rat* preparations, showing staining gaps at the nodes. (Fig. 12-3A and *D*) At double this concentration the drug stains many of the cellular constituents, excluding, however, the nucleus. There may be some faint nucleolar fluorescence. At both concentrations the drug is perceptibly but reversibly toxic, whether the cells are subjected to exciting radiation or not. Six minutes' continuous irradiation is immediately and irreversibly damaging to the culture in the beam but not to a sister culture 2 mm. away in the same preparation. A direct photodynamic effect is thus indicated. A short irradiation period (30 seconds) produces no immediate detectable damage. However, all cultures exposed to the drug, whether irradiated or not, show a delayed toxic response which, after 24 hours, is visualized by ordinary transmitted light as a change in shape and refractivity of materials in the mitochondrial zone (Fig. 12-4A to *D*). It appears that mitochondria may have become granular and swollen. They do not stain as usual with Sudan black B. Myelin appears undamaged. Fluorescence is still sharply localized after 24 hours and is very much more intense than in preparations examined immediately or within an hour or so after exposure to the drug (Figs. 12-3A and 12-4A to *D*). In cultures irradiated immediately after drug administration, the myelin retains its fluorescence at 24 hours, but in unirradiated cultures the myelin is no longer fluorescible by this time. In the neuron soma, are we perhaps dealing with a flavinoid fluorescence— from mitochondrial breakdown? At 48 hours, localization is becoming a little fuzzy, and intensity is somewhat less than in cultures examined immediately after exposure. Such cells continue on to complete recovery. This is a sequence to whose analysis electron microscopy could contribute; such studies are under way.

Some biochemical evidence from the test tube indicates that the

cell complex, and to axis cylinder and Schwann sheath. Foot-Bielschowsky silver impregnation after formalin fixation; 14 days in vitro. *C*, chick neurons and satellite cells stained with Sudan black B after formalin fixation. Fatty particles stained are mainly mitochondria, which are scattered between discrete Nissl bodies; 6 days in vitro. *D*, cytochrome oxidase reaction in rat neurons 80 days in vitro. (Preparation by Dr. T. Yonezawa.)

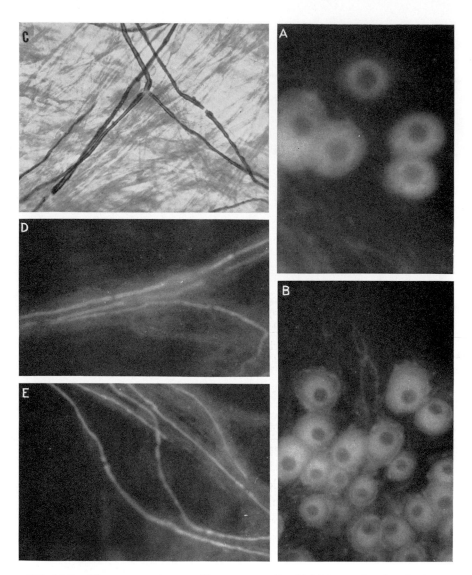

FIG. 12-3. Fluorescence image, chlorpromazine 7×10^{-5} M, visualized in fetal rat dorsal root ganglion cultures, with Reichert fluorescence microscopy assembly. *A*, living neurons examined within an hour after administration of drug. *B*, sister culture fixed in formalin before exposure to drug and subsequent examination. *C*, untreated culture, viewed by ordinary light microscope, showing myelinated fibers, stained with Sudan black B. Internodal segments take fat stain, leaving gaps at nodes. *D*, living myelinated fibers examined within an hour after exposure to chlorpromazine. Note nodal gaps in staining, comparable to Sudan black image. *E*, myelinated fibers after formalin fixation and subsequent exposure to drug.

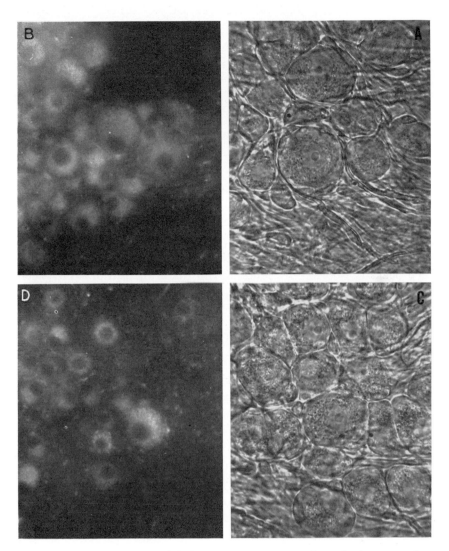

FIG. 12-4. Fluorescence and light microscope images from fetal rat ganglion cultures exposed to chlorpromazine for 24 hours in dark, before examination. *A* and *B*, light and fluorescence microscope images from same culture treated with 7×10^{-5} M chlorpromazine. *C* and *D*, light and fluorescence microscope images from sister culture treated with double above concentration of chlorpromazine. Note swollen and brightly fluorescing particles in mitochondrial zone. Compare with Figure 12-2*D*, cytochrome oxidase reaction, and contrast with normal appearance of untreated living cells in Figure 12-1.

action of chlorpromazine is on oxidative phosphorylation (Abood[1] and Bain[2] have reported uncoupling in mitochondrial preparations), and our morphological examinations with the light microscope seem to implicate the mitochondria as preferential binding sites in these dorsal root neurons. Staining seems to follow the mitochondrial aggregates whatever their position; it follows them as they reorient themselves during neuron maturation. One might expect that the emission spectrum of the chlorpromazine initially bound to mitochondria would be orthochromatic but that after some time, with the production of sulfoxide metabolite, the spectrum would shift. However, when the spectrum obtained with the line-selector instrumentation from three cultures a few minutes after staining is compared with that of another culture incubated for $2\frac{1}{2}$ hours after drug application and then read, they appear essentially similar (Figs. 12-5 and 12-6). The peaks of fluorescence intensities in the cytoplasm of 4 cells used for sampling are at 468 to 478 mμ, with band widths at peak ranging from 0.86 to 4.3 mμ. Many more cells must be measured, however, before these peaks can be regarded as certain. The morphological localization in living and fixed cells is identical upon fluorescence examination also. If these cultures are fixed with formalin and then stained with chlorpromazine, it still binds in the mitochondrial area, which fluoresces brilliantly, as does the myelin (Fig. 12-3*B* and *E*).

It appears clear that the chlorpromazine spectrum which we see is definitive; binding is strong and localization definite in the mitochondrial area of the soma. The pattern is held after fixation, confirming appearances that the drug originally penetrates into the living neuron—is not held back by the capsule of satellite cells, but quickly passes through them. As regards this property of chlorpromazine, there have been several published observations on the action of the drug in altering the permeability of cell membranes so as to cause leakage or to enhance the penetration of other substances. The latest of these, by Nathan and Friedman,[11] which recapitulates, notes the effect of chlorpromazine to increase membrane permeability in *Tetrahymena*. Also pertinent to our data may be reports[12] on phosphate swelling of mitochondria in rat heart and liver. It is possible that the mitochondrial swelling that we observe may be a by-product of chlorpromazine's interference with oxidative phosphorylation.

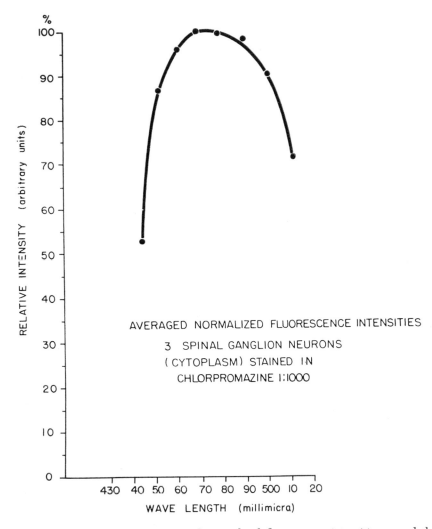

FIG. 12-5. Curve showing averaged normalized fluorescence intensities recorded for the cytoplasm of three living chick neurons by spectroscope, line-selector, oscilloscope assembly. Observations made immediately after administration of chlorpromazine.

233

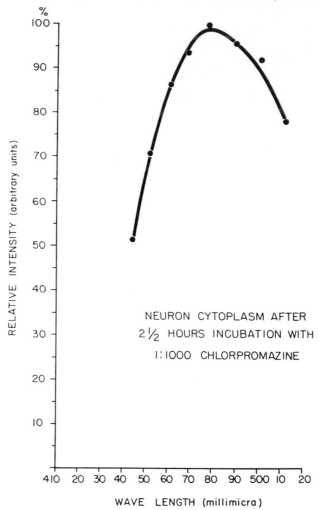

FIG. 12-6. Curve showing fluorescence intensities (cytoplasmic) of single chick neuron after 2½ hours' incubation (in dark) with chlorpromazine.

Acridones*

Here, however, we may have in our material a basic penetration problem. Mayer and Bain[8,9,15] traced a diethyl derivative of a

---

* M-223 (Pfeiffer) 10-(2-diethylaminoethyl)-9 acridone. HCl. M-129 (Pfeiffer) 10-(2-dimethylaminopropyl)-9 acridone. HCl. These were kindly supplied by Dr. Stephen E. Mayer of Emory University, and by the Mallinckrodt Chemical Works, St. Louis, Mo.

convulsant acridone through the CNS and found that it stains selectively the nuclei and nucleoli of certain cell types, such as the granule cells of the cerebellum and the inner nuclear layer of the retina. Neither of the convulsant acridone derivatives (223 and 129) that we have available, in very small quantity, give a sufficiently bright fluorescence at concentration of 5×10^{-6} M with chick ganglion cells for photography in the Reichert fluorescence microscopy array which is adequate for the chlorpromazine photographs (Figs. 12-3 and 12-4). In spindle cells at the periphery of the culture and in an occasional satellite cell, as well as in cultures of ascites cells, there is perceptible but entirely nonnuclear fluorescence. At double this concentration (10^{-5} M) a faint neuronal membrane and neurite fluorescence can sometimes be seen. Nucleoli and mitochondrial areas are then also stained. With the spectroscopic instrumentation a sample curve (Fig. 12-7) for cytoplasm was obtained in M-129.

At this preliminary stage of investigation we can ask several questions, formulating alternatives among which we cannot yet choose: (1) Are we dealing with autofluorescence in damaged cells emanating from breakdown products? The normal neurons and myelin, unexposed to drug, do not fluoresce in our setup. (2) Are the sensory ganglion cells not stainable by these acridones at physiological concentrations? Mayer and Bain[8] used M-129 in their CNS studies which showed high selectivity of cell type. (3) Do the fibrous and cellular capsules of the ganglion cells exclude passage of the drug to the neuron? Other types of observations exist which suggest that there is a protective function for this capsule, whether or not it may be operating in the case of these two acridones. For example, we have found it next to impossible to get penetration of Janus green B into these dorsal root ganglion cells as long as the capsule is intact. Wolf,[17] as well as ourselves, has made a similar observation with acridine orange.

Acridine Orange

Wolf recently published[18] a report on the acridine orange fluorescence and metachromasy of several types of *nonnervous* cells when living, when sustaining reversible photodynamic injury, more severe irreversible injury, and finally death. Dye concentrations in the neighborhood of 10^{-6} gm. per milliliter are not toxic to cells kept

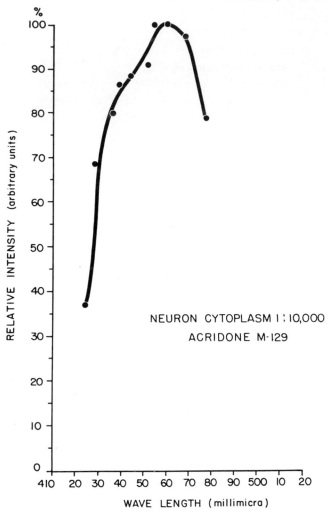

FIG. 12-7. Curve showing fluorescence intensities (cytoplasmic) of single chick neuron immediately after administration of 10-(2-dimethylaminopropyl)-9 acridone. HCl (M-129).

in the dark, but photodynamic injury occurs with exciting radiation, as in chlorpromazine. Apparently only the orthochromatic fluorescence (green), principally localized to nucleus and nucleoli, appears in the uninjured cells; red metachromasy first appears in cytoplasm, deepens with progressive injury, and is once more lost in death. With Bradley,[3] Wolf has advanced a theory based on dye-stacking to account for these changes. He has also applied this acridine orange treatment to cultured dorsal root ganglia and reports that as long as the satellite (or capsular) cells are living there is little coloration of any sort in the neuron.[17] As the capsular cells begin to be injured, there appears a metachromatic (red) staining of a few granules in the mitochondrial region of the neuron; upon progressive injury of the satellite cells, the expected metachromatic staining of neuronal Nissl (RNA) areas appears. In oral discussion he has pointed to an apparent "protective" function for the capsular cells in this situation. Our own observations on cultured spinal ganglion cells parallel Wolf's. It is next to impossible to produce an acridine orange staining of the ganglion cells without first subjecting the surrounding cells to insult, greater or less. Following the time when these supporting cells begin to show injury (i.e., begin to present cytoplasmic metachromasy) from exposure to acridine orange at 10^{-7} M or at five times this concentration, the neuron may begin to show red staining of dispersed granules in the mitochondrial area. If the insult is prolonged or increased, more dye penetrates to the neuron, and the expected metachromatic display of Nissl pattern appears. This can of course be produced directly in our cells, without the intermediate stages, by staining after fixation. It is possible that the isolated bright red granules which appear in the non-Nissl area on early insult *are* mitochondria; selective staining of mitochondria by acridine orange has been observed in certain types of cells.[18] Another possibility is that these granules contain mucopolysaccharide, which stains intensely red with acridine orange. Eventually this problem might be resolved with the use of RNAse, by the electron microscope, or by refinement of spectrometric method.

SUMMARY

Preliminary attempts are described to correlate morphology and spectral analysis in living cultured dorsal root ganglion cells exposed to several fluorochromes at physiological concentrations. Chlorpro-

NOTE (July 1963): Preliminary studies of chlorpromazine-treated cells with the electron microscope (by Dr. Mary B. Bunge) show no deviation from the normal in either mitochondria or myelin at any time. However, after 24 hours the cytoplasm displays a conspicuous accumulation of membrane-bound, lamellated dense bodies, which replace the normal complement of lysosomes, and is presumably derived from them. Possibly these dense bodies represent the brightly fluorescing particles observed during this period with the light microscope.

mazine (7×10^{-5} M) localizes to the mitochondrial area of the neuron soma and to the myelin sheath; it does not bind so permanently to the myelin as to elements of the perikaryon. The drug penetrates readily into the neuron, notwithstanding envelopment of the latter by capsular cells; the Schwannian envelope does not prevent staining of the myelin. The peaks of fluorescence intensities in the cytoplasm of four cells used for sampling are at 468 to 478 mμ.

Two convulsant acridones applied at a concentration of 5×10^{-6} M do not give with living spinal ganglion material the nuclear localization pattern that has been reported for certain cells of the CNS; with one of the acridones a faint cytoplasmic fluorescence can be seen, which in a single cell measurement gave an intensity peak of about 460 mμ.

Acridine orange does not penetrate readily through the capsular investment into the living neuron at concentrations of either 10^{-7} or 5×10^{-7} M, and it at first stains the cytoplasm atypically. Only after fixation or photodynamic injury to the neuron–satellite cell complex does the typical pattern of chromidial metachromasy emerge.

REFERENCES

1. ABOOD, L. G. Effect of chlorpromazine on phosphorylation of brain mitochondria. *Proc. Soc. Exper. Biol. & Med.* 88:688, 1955.

2. BERGER, M. "Effect of Chlorpromazine on Oxidative Phosphorylation of Liver and Brain Mitochondria," in *Progress in Neurobiology*. II. *Ultrastructure and Cellular Chemistry of Neural Tissue,* ed. by Waelsch, H. New York, Hoeber-Harper, 1957, pp. 158–163.

3. BRADLEY, D. F., and WOLF, M. K. Aggregation of dyes bound to polyanions. *Proc. Nat. Acad. Sc.* 45:944, 1959.

4. DEITCH, A. D., and MURRAY, M. R. A comparison of the Nissl substance of living and fixed spinal ganglion cells: I. A phase contrast study. *J. Biophys. & Biochem. Cytol.* 2:433, 1956.

5. LOESER, C. N. "Television Scanning Microspectrophotometry," in *Progress in Neurobiology*. II. *Ultrastructure and Cellular Chemistry of Neural Tissue,* ed. by Waelsch, H. New York, Hoeber-Harper, 1957, pp. 224–242.

6. LOESER, C. N., and BERKLEY, C. Electronic quantitation of light absorption and nuclear fluorescence in living cells. *Science* 119:410, 1954.

7. LOESER, C. N., WEST, S. S., and SCHOENBERG, M. D. Absorption and fluorescence studies on biological systems: Nucleic acid-dye complexes. *Anat. Rec.* 138:163, 1960.

8. MAYER, S. E., and BAIN, J. A. Distribution of a new central convulsant: 10-(2-dimethylaminopropyl)-9 acridone. *J. Pharmacol. & Exper. Therapy 111:* 210, 1954.

9. MAYER, S. E., and BAIN, J. A. Intracellular localization of fluorescent convulsants. *J. Pharmacol. & Exper. Therapy 118:*1, 1956.

10. MURRAY, M. R. "Tissue Culture Studies of Neural Tissue," in *New Research Techniques of Neuroanatomy,* ed. by Windle, W. F. Springfield, Ill., Charles C Thomas, 1957, pp. 40–50.

11. NATHAN, H. A., and FRIEDMAN, W. Chlorpromazine affects permeability of resting cells of *Tetrahymena pyriformis. Science 135:*793, 1962.

12. PACKER, L. Metabolic and structural states of mitochondria: II. Regulation of phosphate. *J. Biol. Chem. 236:*214, 1961.

13. PETERSON, E. R., and MURRAY, M. R. Myelin sheath formation in cultures of avian spinal ganglia. *Am. J. Anat. 96:*319, 1955.

14. PETERSON, E. R., and MURRAY, M. R. Modification of development in isolated dorsal root ganglia by nutritional and physical factors. *Devel. Biol. 2:*461, 1960.

15. PFEIFFER, C. C. "Observations on New CNS Convulsants," in *Neuropharmacology,* ed. by Abramson, H. A., New York, Josiah Macy, Jr., Foundation, 1955, pp. 162–192.

16. WEST, S. S., LOESER, C. N., and SCHOENBERG, M. D. Television spectroscopy of biological fluorescence. *Ire Tr. Med. Electronics Me-7:*138, 1960.

17. WOLF, M. K. Does acridine orange stain Nissl substance metachromatically? *Anat. Rec. 133:*441, 1959. (Abstract. Full paper in preparation.)

18. WOLF, M. K., and ARONSON, S. B. Growth, fluorescence and metachromasy of cells cultured in the presence of acridine orange. *J. Histochem. 9:*22, 1961.

Index

Acetylcholinesterase in cerebral cortex, 102
  in Alzheimer's disease, 102
  in Jakob-Creutzfeldt disease, 108
Acridine orange, in cultured neurons, 235–237
Acridones, in cultured neurons, 234–235
Adenosine triphosphate, and cerebral metabolism in vitro, 64, 66
  glucose and hexokinase as trap for, in cerebral mitochondria, 212–224
Adenylokinase, in layered structures, 186–189
Aldolase, and glycolytic activity of mitochondria, 207, 208
Alzheimer's disease, cerebral cortex microchemistry in, 103–105
  glial metabolic changes in, 29
Ammon's horn, biochemical studies of, 178–190
Anoxia, and cerebral metabolism in vitro, 66–67
Antidromic stimulation of muscle nerves, 2
Aspartic acid, and oxygen consumption of cerebral slices in vitro, 64–66
Astrocytes, cholinesterase in, 20
  incorporation of amino acids into protein, 45
  in incubated cerebral cortex slices, 80–81
  oxygen consumption in, 45

Axoplasm, peripheral flow of, 41

Basement membrane, in incubated cerebral cortex slices, 69, 81
Bergmann fibers, 133–137
Brain injury, glial metabolic changes in, 29

Capillaries, in incubated cerebral cortex slices, 69, 81
Carbonic anhydrase activity, in glial tissues, 23–27
Cerebellum, biochemical studies of, 178–190
  corticocortical connections in, 142–177
  cortical and fastigial stimulation, 148–151, 161, 166
  gross electrodes, 144–151
  localized responses, 146
  long-latency responses, 144, 151
  micropipette electrodes, 151–171
  short-latency responses, 144, 151
  stimulus strength affecting responses, 147
  Purkinje cell branchlets in cortex, 112–141
Cerebral cortex, incubated slices of, 75–97
  astrocytes in, 80–81
  capillary basement membrane in, 69, 81
  fluid spaces in, 87, 91, 94
  luminal fluid in, 87
  mitochondria in, 80

241